Pedagogy and Learning with ICT

D0076323

ICT has been introduced into education over the last 25 years. What have been the main opportunities? What have been the expected and unexpected effects? Has it resulted in improvements in teaching and learning?

Pedagogy and Learning with ICT explores the possibilities for change in education systems arising from young people's enthusiasm for ICT and their ability to rapidly acquire skills in its use through exploratory play. Its focus is not on technology but on ways of transforming the routine practices of schools to make learning more exciting and engaging. The 'art' of innovation involves teachers and teacher educators in the creative, collaborative process of imagining, experimenting with, and evaluating new pedagogies.

The book provides a fascinating, in-depth analysis of the nature of learning, ICT pedagogies and the processes of change for teachers, schools and education systems. Divided into four parts, it covers the key issues relating to the innovation of ICT that have arisen over this period:

- Understanding Innovation – conceptualises human action as 'mediated' by social contexts and physical and mental tools, including ICT, which can have the effect of stimulating change
- Challenges of Change – explores the challenges of change as they are experienced by teachers in schools or universities
- Challenges of Policy and Practice – presents a critical analysis of the impact of policies for ICT in education
- Research Methods for ICT in Education – argues for new approaches to researching and evaluating educational programmes that involve the use of ICT.

Pedagogy and Learning with ICT provides an invaluable overview of the field for all researchers, graduate students, teacher educators, teacher researchers and trainee teachers interested in the possibility that ICT may enable radical changes to the process of learning and the relationships between young people and teachers.

Bridget Somekh is Professor of Educational Research and Director of the Centre for ICT, Pedagogies and Learning at the Education and Social Research Institute, Manchester Metropolitan University, UK.

Pedagogy and Learning with ICT

Researching the art of innovation

Bridget Somekh

Routledge
Taylor & Francis Group

LONDON AND NEW YORK

WITHDRAWN

BOWLING GREEN STATE
UNIVERSITY LIBRARY

First published 2007
by Routledge
2 Park Square, Milton Park, Abingdon, Oxon OX14 4RN

Simultaneously published in the USA and Canada
by Routledge
270 Madison Ave, New York, NY 10016

Routledge is an imprint of the Taylor & Francis Group, an informa business

© 2007 Bridget Somekh

Typeset in Garamond by
HWA Text and Data Management, Tunbridge Wells
Printed and bound in Great Britain by
Antony Rowe Ltd, Chippenham, Wiltshire

All rights reserved. No part of this book may be reprinted or reproduced or
utilised in any form or by any electronic, mechanical, or other means, now
known or hereafter invented, including photocopying and recording, or in
any information storage or retrieval system, without permission in writing
from the publishers.

British Library Cataloguing in Publication Data
A catalogue record for this book is available from the British Library

Library of Congress Cataloging-in-Publication Data
Somekh, Bridget.
   Pedagogy and learning with ICT: researching the art of innovation /
   Bridget Somekh. – 1st ed.
         p.   cm.
   Includes bibliographical references.
   1. Educational technology – Great Britain.   2. Information technology –
   Great Britain.   I. Title.
   LB1028.3.S624 2006
   371.33–dc22   2006039513

ISBN10: 0–415–40983–7 (hbk)
ISBN10: 0–415–40982–9 (pbk)
ISBN10: 0–203–94700–2 (ebk)

ISBN13: 978–0–415–40983–4 (hbk)
ISBN13: 978–0–415–40982–7 (pbk)
ISBN13: 978–0–203–94700–5 (ebk)

To Laurel, Jake, Lucy and Hector
who have shown me what they can do with ICT

Contents

Challenges of Policy and Practice   **89**

  6 New technology and learning: policy and practice in the UK,
     1980–2010   91

  7 Taking the sociological imagination to school: an analysis of the
     (lack of) impact of ICT on education systems   109

PART IV
Research Methods for ICT in Education   **123**

  8 The role of evaluation in ensuring excellence in communications
     and information technology initiatives   125

  9 Methodological issues in identifying and describing the way
     knowledge is constructed with and without ICT   145

 10 Mapping learning potential: students' conceptions of ICT in
     their world   162

     Notes   177
     References   179
     Index   193

Illustrations

Figures

Acknowledgements

I would like to thank all the friends and colleagues who have worked with me on the research projects that I have written about in this book. My especial thanks go to Alan November who in 1985 inspired me with the vision of children's trans-Atlantic email communications, if necessary 'with a balloon and a piece of string'; all my research partners in the Pupil Autonomy in Learning with Microcomputers Project (PALM) and the Initial Teacher Education and New Technology Project (INTENT) where I learnt most about innovation 'from the inside'; Kate Crawford who has been challenging my thinking about digital technologies and knowledge-building platforms since we first worked together in 1989; and my colleagues in the Centre for ICT, Pedagogy and Learning at Manchester Metropolitan University between 2000 and 2006, in particular Diane Mavers who helped me to set up CIPL, Cathy Lewin who taught me quantitative methods and worked with me in editing our book *Research Methods in the Social Sciences*, Andy Convery who has asked sceptical questions about ICT and provided inspirational leadership for action research by staff and students, Derek Woodrow who has contributed breadth of cultural understanding and wisdom from years of experience, and Matthew Pearson who has made possible the innovative action research into ICT-enhanced pedagogy and learning with students and teachers in the Developing Pedagogies with E-Learning Resources Project (PELRS). The ideas contained in this book have been developed through dialogue with these and many other colleagues over the twenty years it has been in the writing. I would also like to thank Judy Findlay, my old friend and colleague from my first teaching post in 1971, who made an important contribution to this book by suggesting a change in the title.

Chapter 4: 'The human interface: hidden issues in computer-mediated communication affecting use in schools' was first published in 1989 in R. Mason and A. Kaye (eds) *Mindweave: Communication, Computers and Distance Education*, Oxford: Pergamon Press. It was reprinted in 1991 in O. Boyd-Barrett and E. Scanlon (eds) *Computers and Learning*, Addison-Wesley in association with the Open University.

Chapter 5: 'Supporting information and communication technology innovations in higher education' by Bridget Somekh was first published in the *Journal for IT in Teacher Education*, 7 (1998), 11–31, and is republished here with kind permission of Taylor and Francis (http://www.tandf.co.uk/journals).

Chapter 6: 'New technology and learning: policy and practice in the UK, 1980–2010' by Bridget Somekh was first published in *Education and Information Technologies*, 5 (1) (2000), 19–38, and is republished here with kind permission of Springer Science and Business Media (http://springerlink.metapress.com/content/1573-7608).

Chapter 7: 'Taking the sociological imagination to school: an analysis of the (lack of) impact of ICT on education systems' by Bridget Somekh was first published in *Technology, Pedagogy and Information*, 13 (2004), 163–80, and is republished here with kind permission of Taylor and Francis (http://www.tandf.co.uk/journals).

Chapter 8: 'The role of evaluation in ensuring excellence in communications and information technology initiatives' by Bridget Somekh was first published in *Education, Communications and Information*, 1 (2001), 75–102, and is republished here with kind permission of Taylor and Francis (http://www.tandf.co.uk/journals).

Chapter 9: 'Methodological issues in identifying and describing the way knowledge is constructed with and without ICT' by Bridget Somekh was first published in the *Journal for IT in Teacher Education*, 10 (2001), 157–78, and is republished here with kind permission of Taylor and Francis (http://www.tandf.co.uk/journals).

Chapter 10: 'Mapping learning potential: students' conceptions of ICT in their world' by Bridget Somekh and Diane Mavers was first published in *Assessment in Education*, 10 (2003), 409–20, and a revised version by Bridget Somekh is published here with kind permission of Taylor and Francis (http://www.tandf.co.uk/journals).

Introduction

Innovation involves learning to do something in a completely different way by developing new practices which are both personal and social – in that they relate our own practice with the practices of others. It is often associated with new technologies which provide tools that make it possible to do things differently. If one is already skilled in doing something in one way it is likely to seem pointless initially to do it in a different way. Hence, the first time a word processor was described to me back in 1983, it sounded like mere duplication of effort for something previously done by using a typewriter to be artificially separated into two steps: the writing process on screen and the printing process on paper (at the time I had basic touch-typing skills). Once I purchased a Word chip for my BBC Acorn computer, however, I found that the time needed to create a document from scratch to the point where it had been refined, polished and printed in type-script was greatly reduced. The first document I wrote with a word processor, in 1984, was a grant proposal to the Arts Council for a Writer in Residence at the school where I was then Head of the English Department. Having left only limited time for the local authority English Advisor and the representative of the regional Arts Association to comment on my draft, the production of the document on a word processor turned out to be crucial to getting the proposal drafted, commented on by others, revised and submitted to the sponsor on time. Learning to work in this new way was stressful and frustrating – and, as I remember, I must have been a difficult student for the friend who had offered to show me how – but even using the word processor with minimal skills the overall time needed to produce the final document was greatly reduced, and perhaps the quality was also improved as the proposal was to be successful. From that time onwards my practices for drafting, re-drafting, polishing and producing a text have gradually been transformed in ways that go well beyond mere efficiency in production. I now spend much less time on advanced planning on paper (although I still begin by jotting down rough ideas in handwriting), and much more time on drafting and re-drafting on screen. I also rarely produce any text entirely individually; almost always my writing process includes a collaborative element, whether jointly authored or subjected to informal peer review. Writing on a word processor which was painful and stressful on that first occasion is now wholly integrated in my working practices. When I was recently required to hand-write a short proposal for funding in ten minutes and hand it in at the end of a meeting I found the experience difficult and stressful.

Key to this personal example of innovation is that I was learning for an immediately useful purpose, that I had introductory one-to-one assistance from someone prepared to answer questions, and that I had my own BBC Acorn computer with a word processor and printer available to use at home as and when needed. Access to ICT, a real purpose, personalised support and no interference from others expecting me to work in a pre-specified way, could be said to be the factors which set me on the path to acquiring both new word processing skills and transformed ways of working. They make a good starting point for understanding what all ICT innovations require to be successful. The move from initial change to transformation of social practices is always unique and unpredictable, involving incorporating a new technology as an extension of the self (McLuhan 1964, p. 7).

The sub-title of this book is 'Researching the Art of Innovation' because my interest is in finding ways of assisting the creative, collaborative process of change that combines imagining, experimenting with, and evaluating new practices. Innovation is always challenging, or even stressful, because it involves disturbing the established routines through which individuals and groups perform and continuously re-affirm their identity. Innovation requires vision, sensitivity, playfulness and energy at grass roots level and changes to structures and regulatory frameworks at the organisational and policy levels. In thinking of innovation in pedagogy and learning in this way I draw on Eisner's (1979, pp. 153–5) development of the concept of 'artistic connoisseurship' as a means of judging the quality of teaching. Through reflection teachers apply the process of artistic connoisseurship to their own practice to judge its worth, and over time deepen their level of understanding of the quality and productive power of their interactions with students. Innovations in pedagogy and learning disturb the continuity of this process, bringing with them, usually from outside, a vision that challenges the teacher to change. Artistic connoisseurship now needs to be applied to the process of innovation itself through seriously engaging with its vision, in a cyclical process of experimenting with the possibilities it offers and seeking evidence to judge the worth of the new practices that are beginning to emerge.

In *researching* this art of innovation with a special focus on the introduction of ICT into education I have found socio-cultural theories particularly powerful, both as a framework for analysis and interpretation, and in designing prototypes of innovative pedagogies and new ways of learning. My early work adopted the methodology of action research and involved the integrated process of action, reflection and knowledge generation, or *praxis* (Noffke 1995, p. 1). When, during 1998–2001, I participated in an ESRC seminar series on socio-cultural research methods[1] I was introduced to new theoretical tools that were highly convergent with my prior experience of action research. By then I had spent more than fifteen years supporting the introduction of computers in education, without seeing any real change in pedagogies or learning, and in activity theory I found a means of understanding why this should be the case in schools, although my experience of changes in my own working practices through the use of ICT had been so different. Initially my understanding of the potential mediating role of ICT 'tools' was rather narrow and mechanistic, but later, as I developed a much broader definition of 'tools' that incorporated everything from physical artefacts to the conceptual understandings and practices of our culture, these theories of mediated activity became increasingly illuminating. Nevertheless, the core insight that there is the potential of expanding human capability through integrating ICT into action and co-creating new ICT-mediated practices has remained central to my thinking.

This book is divided into four parts, of which the first was written last. Part I presents the theoretical and practical understandings arising from my most recent work, while Parts II, III and IV are made up of revised versions of previously published journal articles which I have selected to trace the development of my thinking between 1985 and 2005. There is, of course, no need to read the book in either the order it is presented or the order in which it was written. I like to think of it, however, from my days as a poor viola player who very much enjoyed playing quartets with friends, as being like a musical theme and variations.

Part I, entitled Understanding Innovation, consists of three chapters which are closely inter-connected.

In Chapter 1, I develop a broad socio-cultural framework for researching the process of innovation. It is predicated on two ideas: that the inter-relationships between multiple levels of human activity co-construct change, and that there is an active, interventive role for the researcher in supporting this process. In the final section of the Chapter 1 use the framework to analyse examples of transformed pedagogies and learning in contexts where many levels of the education system work together to support and enable innovation.

In Chapter 2, I use the socio-cultural framework developed in Chapter 1 to piece together knowledge from studies focused on single levels of the system, such as classrooms or schools. Most of the research referred to in this chapter was conducted in England which provides an opportunity of investigating the impact of an education system on ICT innovation. Putting together the knowledge from this wide range of studies makes it possible to observe how policies and regulatory curriculum and assessment structures translate into concrete practices and procedures in schools and classrooms, not always with the expected results.

In Chapter 3, I provide a commentary on the research findings from two research studies into prototype innovative pedagogies which used the socio-cultural framework described in Chapter 1. In the first study the research focuses on analysis of a naturally occurring experiment in innovative pedagogy; in the second the research focuses on designing a prototype and generating knowledge through intervention and praxis.

Part II, entitled Challenges of Change, presents two articles about the change process involved in introducing ICT, written ten years apart, and showing both the continuities and the developments in my thinking. Chapter 4, which was written in the mid-1980s, is very short and focuses on the impact of ICT on personal identity and the rituals of practice. Chapter 5, written ten years later, builds on what I had by then learnt from the work of Fullan and George Herbert Mead about the inter-related process of personal and organisational change. Both chapters contain ideas which are still at the core of my thinking on innovation.

Part III, entitled Challenges of Policy and Practice, contains two articles in which I attempt to take a long view of the development of policy for ICT in education in the UK and its impact on practice in schools. Both of these chapters end with a vision for change which entails closer collaboration between policy-makers, researchers and communities. Hence they point the way to the vision of sharing responsibility for innovation across multiple levels of an education system, which is contained in Part I.

Part IV, entitled Research Methods for ICT in Education, contains three articles that set out my vision for innovative, participatory research methods, intended to prevent the dead-end of researching failed innovations by integrating support and participatory research. Chapter 8 focuses on program evaluation and Chapter 9 on research and knowledge generation. Chapter 10 focuses on the use of concept mapping to research children's understandings of 'computers in my world' with the intention of illustrating the use of innovative research methods to generate knowledge that could not be accessed in any other way.

Part I

Understanding innovation

The three chapters in this section represent my current thinking about the possibilities for transforming schooling with the digital information and communication technologies available in the twenty first century. The emphasis is on pedagogy and learning and how innovation happens in social settings, such as classrooms and schools, that have developed traditions of practice that are ritualistic – in the sense that they perform the identities of participants: how you should behave as a teacher, as a student, as a parent, as a headteacher. Changing these ritual practices is disruptive and evokes strong passions because it is either threatening or inspiring, often depending on the ways that it opens up new spaces of power for some and closes down the existing power bases of others. Students are at the heart of this process, and innovation in schooling is in part determined by the constructions of childhood that are prevalent in the society of which schools are part.

The three chapters are designed to be read together. The socio-cultural theories that enable us to understand innovation are explored in Chapter 1 and illustrated with examples of transformed pedagogy and learning; these are drawn from countries where the education system has enabled the development of a shared vision and its implementation in schools through exploratory research-informed practice. In Chapter 2 I have used socio-cultural theories to draw key understandings from research into the use of ICT mainly in English schools, where the education system since 1988 has adopted a 'carrot and stick' approach to change; this seeks to drive innovation by setting clear targets, inspecting schools' performance and 'naming and shaming' those showing 'serious weaknesses', and encouraging competition between schools on the basis of their students' performance in national tests and examinations (published in comparative league tables). In Chapter 3 I focus on two research studies we have carried out in the Centre for ICT, Pedagogy and Learning at Manchester Metropolitan University, in which we have observed the extent to which transformation in pedagogy and learning is possible in the English education system by researching prototype innovative practices informed by socio-cultural theories of innovation.

These three chapters seek to establish that innovation depends on social processes between inter-related phenomenal levels of the national and educational cultural systems: differences in these cultural contexts shape the possibilities for transforming pedagogy and learning, making ICT powerful as a means of enabling change in some contexts and emasculating its power in others. The transformative power of ICT is illustrated in the changed life styles it has opened up for increasingly large numbers of young people in their out-of-school world, among them my grandchildren, Laurel, Jake, Lucy and Hector, to whom this book is dedicated.

1 Insights from socio-cultural theory

A framework for research and analysis

The aim of policy-makers and teachers is to transform education – that is to make radical improvements to its processes and outcomes – so that more students reach higher levels of achievement. For most the goal is also to make education more personally fulfilling for students, to nurture their creativity, develop their cognitive abilities, and give them purpose and autonomy as life-long learners in a rapidly changing world. Potentially, the change to students' learning processes can be transformative as they find ways of using ICT that both extend their capabilities and fit their preferred style of working; but the process of innovation is rarely sufficiently understood to generate the necessary flexibilities in how adults, and the education system as a whole, expect students to work. For example, the emerging social practice of 'multi-tasking' between several applications running simultaneously on the computer using the 'windows' environment designed for that very purpose, is so radically different from the traditional assumption that learning requires the mind to focus on one thing at a time, that it is routinely discouraged by teachers and equally routinely practised covertly by students using the ALT+TAB window-switching facility.

In this chapter I will draw on theories of innovation derived from action research, socio-cultural psychology, activity theory and complexity science, since these provide theoretical frameworks for researching innovation by intervening in socio-cultural practices in order to change them. This is an approach to research which combines the design of models or prototypes of new ways of working with research into their implementation, using participatory methods which develop practitioners' knowledge so that they are able to make informed choices.

Theories with explanatory power for understanding the process of change

> The cultural practice known as 'education' occurs within and among complex systems that span several phenomenal levels: there are individuals, therefore collectives of individuals (including classrooms, schools etc.), there are communities in which schools exist, and there are larger cultural contexts.
>
> (Sumara and Davis 1997, p. 418)

The difficulty in understanding the process of innovation is that we see it necessarily from our own standpoint. We need to make meaning of the activities we are engaged in, but can only attempt this in terms of our own experiences. We have to imagine the future in terms of the meanings we have constructed to make sense of our own past. But our own agency – that is, our ability to exercise some control of today's activities and play an active part in planning and implementing future activities – is contingent on the socio-cultural context within which we are living and working, across all the 'phenomenal levels' listed above by Sumara and Davis. This difficulty often applies as much to those researching innovations as it does to those participating in them, since researchers tend to specialise in working at specific phenomenal levels, for example on teaching and learning (mainly at the classroom level), school improvement (mainly at the whole-school level) or policy analysis (mainly at the national level). Research which spans all phenomenal levels is necessarily large-scale and unattractive to sponsors because of its cost and supposed lack of focus. In order to understand the innovation of ICT in education, and in particular the mechanisms which enable innovative work with ICT to transform pedagogy and learning, I will draw as much as possible in this chapter on research which focuses on the inter-relationships between local phenomena and the wider socio-cultural context. However, it is possible to create a larger analytic framework using socio-cultural theories which clarify the relationships between levels, and to use this as a lens for understanding the significance of knowledge from a larger range of research studies at different phenomenal levels and I will use the framework in this way in Chapter 2. Inevitably I will also draw in both chapters on my own experience as a researcher and evaluator of innovative ICT programmes, since relationships between phenomena at different levels become clearer when one develops a sustained programme of research made up of a number of projects within the same field but with different specific foci (see Chapters 4–10 of this book).

I want now to describe the analytic framework that I am using to understand innovation. It brings together ideas from a number of writers who adopt different theoretical perspectives which have considerable overlaps between them. All are concerned with understanding the actions of individuals and groups and how these are co-constructed and contextually shaped and mediated, hence they all have direct relevance to understanding change processes. Their points of overlap serve to highlight those features which have the greatest explanatory power, and the variations between the theoretical perspectives create sensitivities to factors which might have been lost by working with only one. This deliberately heterogeneous approach to theory is described more fully in an article written with my colleague, Matthew Pearson (Pearson and Somekh 2006, pp. 528–31). It can be seen as akin to Levi-Strauss's notion of the 'bricoleur' who works with tools that come to hand, bringing them together in ways that are creative rather than following an agreed orthodoxy.

My starting point is action research which integrates research and action in a cyclical process of inquiry, action, reflection and evaluation (Somekh 2006b). Its theoretical origins are in the work of Lewin whose 'force field' theory focused on analysing the relationship between social context and behaviour (Lewin 1951). Cole quotes Lewin's proposition that behaviour at time 't' is a function of the situation at time 't' only, 'hence we must find ways to determine the properties of the lifespace at a given time' (Cole 1996, pp. 222–7). Action research, therefore, focuses on human behaviours in specific contexts and develops understandings of the factors that shape behaviour rather than generalisable truths. It places participants at the heart of any attempt to adopt an innovation within a social situation. By playing an active and leading role in researching their own practice they generate unique 'insider' knowledge which informs the change process. In part this is through making their tacit knowledge of pedagogy and learning explicit (Polanyi 1958), coming to understand other points of view and observing both the intended and unintended consequences of their actions. Through reflection on research data they are able to understand their own interconnectedness with other participants – for example teachers come to understand that their pedagogy is co-constructed with their students and colleagues – and by undertaking a new role as researchers they learn to use knowledge to inform the planning and implementation of action steps, and evaluate their impact. Action research emphasises participation and mutual respect between participants at different levels in an organisation and facilitators or co-researchers from outside the organisation. It shifts the traditional balance of power, enabling participants to develop new kinds of agency by positioning themselves politically and strategically to form new relationships. Through methods such as interviewing and observation (often using audio- or video-recording) action research generates new insights into the relationship between self and others and often reveals the unintended consequences of actions. Through the high degree of reflexivity that this work engenders action research integrates personal learning with the process of changing professional practice. For a fuller statement of eight methodological principles for action research see Somekh (op. cit., pp. 6–8).

The second body of theory I draw upon is complexity theory which is described by Sumara and Davis (1997) specifically in relation to action research. As will be clear from the quotation from their work at the beginning of this section, complexity theory emphasises the 'interrelationship of things'. It draws on a wide range of disciplines, such as physics, biology, economics and psychology, to illustrate how even the most complex systems have a capacity for 'spontaneous self-organisation'. Just as human beings seek to find meanings and relationships between phenomena, as is illustrated by the way that languages are deeply embedded with metaphorical usage of terms, so any system with or without the human mind's capacity for consciousness will respond to additions/events/disruptions by adapting to maintain its own coherence. In this sense complex systems 'embody their histories' (quotations are from Sumara and Davis 1997, pp. 416–17). In a later article, Davis and Sumara (2005) describe how complexivists in recent years have gone beyond using these theories to describe and explain existing systems and increasingly turned their attention to 'the deliberate creation and nurturing of complex systems'. They set out the four 'key conditions' that need to be present in complex systems to enable 'nurturing', hence interventions in an existing system (say a school and its wider context) need to set out purposefully to create these conditions. There must be a number of people involved so that there is opportunity for interaction; there must be 'some level of diversity' of participants and activities so that 'novel responses' are possible; they must have 'a means by which individual agents can affect one another,' and have 'a distributed, decentralised control structure'. These match well with the conditions that are established through engagement in action research which, as described above, encourages collaboration and dialogue among participants, changes in their roles, a shift in the power balances towards more democratic decision-making, increased flexibility of working practices and the development of unique, data-informed, insider knowledge of the patterns of social interaction. Other important concepts from complexity theory are that change in complex systems is not predictable, hence nurturing is a responsive, opportunistic process that cannot be reduced to a set of agreed procedures; and that complex systems are characterised by 'emergent phenomena' which are studied to gain 'enhanced understandings of the common features of complex systems, while preserving the particularities of those systems' (quotations are from Davis and Sumara 2005, p. 457).

In many ways complexity theory is akin to chaos theory. Kompf (2005, pp. 226–7), in an essay review of three books on ICT in education published between 2001 and 2003, describes how processes of globalisation and 'the concomitant alternative ways of knowing provided by ICT' have radically changed the way we judge the validity of knowledge, and 'how it is learned and subsequently reconstructed by learners'. He characterises theories of knowledge and learning as 'a complex adaptive system' drawing on chaos theory rather than complexity theory as a framework for analysis. Taking the human characteristic of searching for meaning as his starting point he sees ICT as having created a large number of perturbations in what was previously an accepted order underpinning social mores and customs. The interconnectedness of the order of things which is illustrated by fractal patterns in mathematics, and the concept originating with Lorenz that tiny movements such as the flap of a butterfly's wing in Brazil can affect the inter-related meteorological patterns of the whole world, leading to changes in the weather in Texas (Wikipedia, accessed 7.9.06), means that the Internet has created an environment of challenge. 'Such challenges have introduced an element of chaos into the intellectual and social order that had previously provided a stable, predictable, and secure environment' (Kompf 2005, p. 277). As described by Kompf, ICT is not an innovation in the sense commonly used by Rogers (2003) and Fullan and Stiegelbauer (1991) of an initiative introduced purposefully into an existing system in order to bring about improvement, but a major perturbation that has destabilised the existing order and led to a large number of unpredictable changes. Kompf warns that while we lag behind in our understanding of 'the full impact of ICT on learning and teaching' the self-organising capacity of an ICT-rich social order may, itself, lead to control over education passing out of the hands of educators 'into the hands of administrators and corporate opportunists' (Kompf 2005, p. 233). This is certainly plausible. While it is true that there have been many initiatives in many countries which have attempted to control and use the power of ICT to develop and improve existing education systems, these have been set in the context of ICT's massive and unpredictable impact on the larger social order, which is increasingly creating a 'backwash' of unexpected challenges for schools. Kompf's description of changes brought about within universities, and society as a whole, by access to the Internet, fits well with McLuhan's conception of 'electric technology' having gone beyond all previous technologies which 'extended our bodies in space' and become an extension of the human mind and consciousness:

> We have extended our central nervous system itself in a global embrace, abolishing both space and time as far as our planet is concerned. Rapidly, we approach the final phase of the extensions of man (sic) – the technological simulation of consciousness, when the creative process of knowing will be collectively and corporately extended to the whole of human society, much as we have already extended our senses and our nerves by the various media.
>
> (McLuhan 1964, p. 3)

New light is shed on these theories from action research, complexity science and chaos theory by a fourth body of theory put forward by Burbules and Smith (2005) in a response to Jim Marshall's reading of Wittgenstein (Smeyers and Marshall 1995) as 'a theorist of sociocultural practices, and practices constituted within systems of discursive power'. They begin by emphasising Wittgenstein's concept that 'human activity is rule-governed' which they see as fundamentally important in understanding education. They list four ways in which he uses this concept to develop specific insights. It is key to understanding 'how young people learn and are initiated into social practices' which Wittgenstein likens to learning the rules of a game, not by memorising them but by 'learning how to go on'. It follows that in human activity the priority should always be to find out '*what* rules are at work and *how* they are being followed' (original emphasis). Further, Wittgenstein's concept of rule-following often involves 'tacit' knowledge rather than knowledge that can be articulated, indeed that this knowledge 'may be beyond the capacities of language to articulate'. It follows that it is crucial to seek to understand the rules that govern human activity through developing knowledge *from the inside*, because it is simply not possible to understand human behaviour by observing it from the outside; and it is, therefore, never possible to generalise from behaviours of people in one setting to predict the behaviours of different people in other settings. The increased interest among policy-makers, influenced by writers such as Hargreaves (1996, p. 2), in seeking evidence of 'what works' through funding quantitative empirical research and systematic reviews of research literature is therefore seen by Burbules and Smith as 'simple-mindedness that flies in the face of the Wittgensteinian notion of rule-governedness and its consequences for achieving a useful knowledge of human affairs'.

As in complexity theory, Wittgenstein's theory shows that social practice is governed by a multiplicity of factors, including unpredictable tacit rules, which mean that controllable features of schooling such as specified teaching methods, tasks, resources and assessment procedures are always insufficient to shape students' behaviours. The example that Burbules and Smith give is of skate-boarding as a social practice which, although dangerous and to outsiders apparently purposeless, can be understood by 'conceiving and framing the social phenomenon in a way that presumes its meaningfulness and coherence to its practitioners'. Thus skate-boarding can be understood as a means of young people exercising power *vis-à-vis* adults and conforming to norms of peer culture (quotations are all from Burbules and Smith

2005, pp. 426–8). Another example from secondary schools in England, noted by Hope, is that the culture of staff surveillance over students' Internet use gave rise to a culture of resistance among students. As a result, they 'played online games, accessed recreational material, downloaded pornographic images, utilised chat-lines and accessed sites that had been labelled as undesirable by staff', following peer-group rules of '"playfulness" that occasionally challenged staff authority' (Hope 2005, p. 367). Another important concept in Wittgenstein's analysis of social practice is seen by Burbules and Smith (op. cit.) to be his understanding of the flexibility of meanings in language. They remind us that this is where Marshall sees Wittgenstein's philosophy coming closest to the ideas of Foucault and the postmodernists. The meanings of words are always contingent upon the rule-governed tacit knowledge of the social group. Through language, therefore, 'the mind is essentially public, not essentially private' (ibid., p. 429) and notions such as *what works* are always used discursively 'as exercises of power' (ibid., p. 427).

I draw also upon a number of writers whose ideas can be loosely grouped as contributing to socio-cultural-historical theories of human activity. Wertsch provides a good starting point when he writes:

> The task of a sociocultural approach is to explicate the relationships between human action, on the one hand, and the cultural, institutional, and historical contexts in which this action occurs, on the other.
>
> (Wertsch 1998, p. 24)

Many overlaps with the theories discussed previously begin to emerge from this quotation. Human action takes place 'in interrelationship with things' and 'embodies the histories' of its cultural and institutional contexts. It is 'adaptive' to these contexts and their normative values and organisational structures. Cultural psychology is primarily focused on the development of mind through social interaction, following the Vygotskian concept of mediation of human actions, which Wertsch clarifies may be both 'external' and 'internal' and 'may be carried out by groups, both small and large or by individuals' (ibid., p. 23). Wertsch proposes that for the purposes of analysis human action cannot be separated from its mediational means – the 'cultural tools' of concepts and artefacts embedded in the history and culture of the group – both being co-constructors of human activity held together in what Wertsch calls 'an irreducible tension' (ibid., p. 25). Since the actions of individuals are always mediated by their interaction with others, the self is not a separate unique identity but a participant in the co-construction of discourses and social practices, essentially public rather than private. Cognition and meaning-making are in this sense 'distributed' (Salomon 1993b). As Pea (1993) puts it, 'the "mind" rarely works alone' and cognition is shared not only in the sense of generating knowledge and ideas through dialogue with others, but also in skilful use of the affordances of available cultural tools. The term 'affordances' is used in a particular way in socio-cultural theory to indicate a tool's latent possibilities for mediating human activity (Pea 1993, p. 51). ICTs and other technologies do not of themselves determine innovation (Fisher 2006): they are dependent on human agents exploring their use, ideally through play, and developing skills in their use together with mental models and imaginative perceptions of their possibilities (Wartofsky 1979, pp. 203–10). Wartofsky sees human perceptions as active representations of the experienced ('on-line') world which underpin the enactment and development of practice, but need to become familiar and extensive before they can be taken 'off-line' and used by the mind for 'the imaginative construction of off-line worlds' (ibid., p. 208). The development of new social practices will therefore be transformative to varying degrees, depending on the affordances of the tool, the skill with which human agents learn to use them and their ability to imagine new possible uses. It is not the Internet itself which has changed knowledge and communication systems, but rather the creativity and skill of human designers and users who explored those affordances, and used their emerging mental models to imagine new possibilities. Perkins' (1993) concept of 'person-plus' distinguishes between effects *with* and *of* information-processing technologies, effects *with* being amplifications of the user's cognitive powers during the use of a technology and effects *of* being cognitive spinoff effects that occur without the technology. We can perhaps see the latter as an indication of the unpredictable 'backwash' effect of technology on social practices described by Kompf.

The term 'activity system' is used by many writers, although not by Wertsch, to denote the inter-relatedness of human activity, both mental (including communicative) and external, and many describe their theoretical base as cultural-historical activity theory (CHAT). Cole and Engeström (1993) trace the origins of activity theory from the work of Vygotsky and his followers and present an expanded triangular model of the mediated nature of activity systems that includes the object of activity, and the tools, rules, divisions of labour and social community that are integral to the activity. Rules are understood to encompass both explicit and tacit assumptions of expected behaviour, and their impact upon the object of activity fits well with Wittgenstein's concept of the rule-governed nature of human activity. (For example, in a classroom if we focus on the questions *what* rules are at work and *how* they are being followed, it is often observable that students and teachers do not share the same object – although they are assumed *from the outside* to do so.) Divisions of labour indicate the roles that individuals are allocated in the community, and therein lies the site of the operation of power, both formally and micropolitically. The community embodies and formalises mediational processes and Cole and Engeström (1993, p. 8) point out that 'when activities become institutionalised, they are rather robust and enduring', for example, as they are encountered in schools 'they appear to reproduce similar actions and outcomes over and over again in a seemingly monotonous and repetitive manner that gives cultural constraints on action a seemingly overpowering quality'. This model of the activity system is described more fully in Chapter 9 of this book where Engeström's diagram of 'the activity triangle' is reproduced. What I want to emphasis here is the complexity, communicative inter-dependence and dynamic nature of the CHAT concept of an activity system. As Langemeyer and Nissen (2005, p. 190) point out, its origins in the work of Vygotsky in the post-revolutionary Soviet Union is sometimes thought to imply a functionalist, collective undercurrent of 'social engineering', particularly as its emphasis on 'the integration of basic theoretical work with empirical-practical engagement' led to it making claims to be a 'science' during the Stalinist and Cold War periods. But this was always a misreading of Vygotsky's original notions of the development of the mind through human interaction, including, for example, the internalisation of previously external speech, and support for an individual's learning potential within their 'zone of proximal development'. In formal school learning he noted that testing the current levels of students' attainment was much less accurate in determining their mental development than testing what they could achieve with 'some slight assistance'. Students whose mental age was assessed as 8 on traditional tests were found to achieve more *differentially* with assistance, in that the extent of the gains ranged between one and four years. It was this range of possibility of achievement that Vygotsky termed the 'zone of proximal development', and he concluded that 'the ease with which [a child] is able to move from independent to assisted problem solving is the best indicator of the dynamic of his (*sic*) development' (Vygotsky 1986, pp. 187–8).

Vygotsky was concerned with the development of an education system in the new Soviet Union and his work was oriented towards establishing and improving formal education. The concept of the development of mind through social interaction and, in particular the notion that students' learning can be accelerated by providing support (or scaffolding, as Bruner termed it) within the zone of proximal development (ZPD), has been used extensively by innovatory programmes in education. Socio-cultural theories of learning have also been used to describe and analyse learning in informal situations and some theorists go as far as to say that all communicative action (sign making) is a form of learning and all learning is transformative: '[Learning] is not ever seen as mere acquisition, as imperfect copying, as deficient imitation, but as always the best possible new making from existing cultural material transformed in line with the sign-maker's interest' (Kress and Mavers 2005, pp. 173–4). Lave (1996) relates the context of human activity specifically to learning which she sees as 'ubiquitous in ongoing activity, though often unrecognised as such' (ibid., p. 5). Like the other authors in the same edited book (Chaiklin and Lave 1996) and Brown *et al.* (1989), she sees learning as 'situated' in contexts which shape its nature. She notes that formal educational contexts, while they intend to support learning, often in fact constrain it through what she terms 'the *sociocultural* production of failure to learn' (ibid., p. 10). This 'learned failure' is itself learning, co-produced by the student (agent) and the mediating cultural context, that prescribes the curriculum and employs practices of pedagogy and assessment designed to sort and categorise students according to their individual performance and allocate or withhold rewards (test scores, certificates, university places and employment).

Langemeyer and Nissen (2005, p. 190) characterise CHAT as 'methodologically, a form of action research' which draws upon psychology for its theoretical foundations but with a strong emphasis on 'employing hermeneutic methodologies – above all the qualitative interview – to elicit participants' subjective perspectives'. Like action research and the kind of 'creative and nurturing' approach to complex systems described by Davis and Sumara, activity theory provides a set of tools for combining analysis with development, integrating research with purposeful action. Langemeyer and Nissen (2005, p. 189) suggest that intervention is an essential element of research within CHAT: 'If thinking is basically a social activity mediated by tools, and research is no exception, the implication is that we always gain understanding through intervention.' Cole (1996, pp. 257–325) describes a process of 'creating model activity systems' such as the Fifth Dimension in which children were given opportunities to undertake informal ICT-enhanced activities as an extension of normal schooling with the aim of 'culturing' or growing their abilities, while at the same time researching the impact of the intervention and the theoretical robustness of the model. Langemeyer and Nisson (op. cit., p. 191) call this process 'design(ing) or engage(ing) in prototypical practice'. This is the approach adopted in the Developing Pedagogies for E-Learning Resources (PELRS) project, see Chapter 3 of this book. Engeström envisages external intervention through knowledge-building workshops as a means of assisting participants in an extended activity system to develop understanding of how it functions and introduce changes to overcome contradictions (Engeström *et al.* 1999). He and Cole suggest that an internal contradiction in the activity system can be a site for regeneration (Cole and Engeström 1993, p. 40). The places where activity systems overlap (for example the home use of ICT and ICT use in school) create 'boundary objects' which can be the sites for knowledge work. What they call 'the activity system in crisis' leads to a challenging of the assumptions and norms of previous practice ('internalization') through a process of 'externalization'. At first this is by means of 'reflective appropriation of advanced models and tools that offer ways out of the internal contradictions', but it is through the development of new practices – through 'discrete individual violations and innovations' – that an activity system can develop self-knowledge and instantiate a process of regeneration:

> As the disruptions and contradictions in the activity become more demanding, internalization increasingly takes the form of self-reflection – and externalization, the search for novel solutions, increases. Externalization reaches its peak when a new model for the activity is designed and implemented. As the new model stabilizes itself, internalization of its inherent ways and means again becomes the dominant form of learning and development.
>
> (Cole and Engeström 1993, pp. 40–1)

Sharing the same socio-cultural roots as CHAT but significant as a body of theory in its own right is the concept of 'communities of practice' developed first by Lave and Wenger (1991) as a means of describing informal, situated learning of apprentices through a process of 'legitimate, peripheral participation' with 'acknowledged adept practitioners' (ibid., p. 110) in the workplace; and later developed as a systematic means of analysing and judging the quality of any organised group activity (Wenger 1998). The term 'community of practice' has proved to have extraordinary discursive power and has been widely taken up as a theory to assist in the improvement of organisational effectiveness. This seems to be because both the words 'practice' and 'community' have a number of different meanings allowing the co-option of the term for many purposes. In the two seminal books cited here, however, the term has a specifically socio-cultural meaning, closely related to activity theory: 'practice' refers to social practices developed through the mediated action of agents (individuals and groups); and 'community' to the rules, divisions of labour, shared objects and embedded values and practices of the group as a whole. Wenger analyses the dimensions of such a community in a tripartite categorisation of its practices as joint enterprises, mutual engagement and shared repertoire. This is neatly summarised in his diagram of the dimensions of practice as the property of a community (see Figure 1.1).

As in the literature about activity systems, Wenger's account of communities of practice is concerned with understanding the boundaries of the community, its boundary objects, brokers and multimembership (ibid., pp. 103–21), its tacit knowledge base ('competence'; ibid., pp. 137–9) and its creative roots in both participative, local knowledge and global knowledge: 'the experience of knowing is no less unique, no less creative, and no less extraordinary for being one of participation' (ibid., p. 142).

Where Wenger's work makes its most original contribution to socio-cultural theory is in his analysis of individual identity and its relationship with community. Socio-cultural understandings of identity support the notion of a confluence of the individual and the group. The connectedness of human activity defines one in terms of the other, and vice versa. As Wenger puts it:

> Building an identity consists of negotiating the meanings of our experience of membership in social communities. The concept of identity serves as a pivot between the social and the individual, so that each can be talked about in terms of the other.
>
> (Wenger 1998, p. 145)

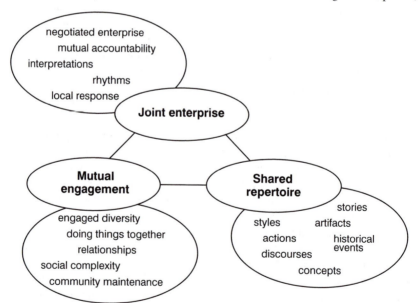

Figure 1.1 Dimensions of practice as the property of a community

Source: Wenger (1998, p. 73).

Wenger presents an analytical framework for understanding this process, identifying five categories of 'identity in practice': (1) identity as *negotiated experience*; (2) identity as *community membership*; (3) identity as *learning trajectory*; (4) identity as *nexus of multimembership*; and (5) identity in *a relation between the local and the global* (Wenger 1998, p. 149, original italics). A key feature of Wenger's framework is the notion that 'identity in practice arises out of an interplay of participation and reification' (op. cit., pp. 153–4), which I understand to mean that members of the community are engaged simultaneously in building, naming and clarifying its identity (reification) and developing and changing that identity through practice (participation). Wenger sees this process as one in which identities have a 'trajectory', because they are 'not an object, but a constant becoming'. He further clarifies that 'the term trajectory suggests not a path that can be foreseen or charted but a continuous motion – one that has a momentum of its own in addition to a field of influences' (op. cit., p. 154). However, identity is shaped not only by participation in a community but also by non-participation and positioning oneself as peripheral and marginal. Individuals move between many groups and cannot participate equally in them all. However, movement between groups is important both for individual identity and group identity. He describes the process of moving between groups as 'the work of reconciliation' (op. cit., p. 160) and emphasises the importance of 'maintaining an identity across boundaries', seeing it as an integral part of being human: 'Membership and the work of reconciliation are intrinsic to the very concept of identity' (op. cit., p. 161).

All these theories combine to provide me with a flexible, inclusive framework for reading and interpreting the research literature on pedagogy and learning with ICT in schools. They provide a lens for seeing how the insights from one study relate to insights from another. In the remainder of this chapter I will discuss some studies of innovatory programmes with ICT which have attempted a broad systemic approach, in several cases by explicitly adopting socio-cultural research methods.

Examples of transformed pedagogies and learning

Two early innovative programmes have combined research with a developmental intervention. Both continued over a long period and have generated longitudinal research on ICT-enhanced learning. The first, the Apple Classroom of Tomorrow Project (ACOT), funded by the Apple Corporation, ran from 1986 to 1998 when Apple sales suffered a temporary downturn and ACOT work was terminated. The second, the Fifth Dimension programme (referred to briefly above) was also established in 1986 and has become a self-sustaining network of projects loosely linked to the Laboratory of Comparative Human Cognition at the University of California at San Diego, where the Director, Michael Cole, still spends most afternoons working with children in one of the local Fifth Dimension locations.

ACOT was set up as a research and development project, initially in two high schools in the USA, where Apple could observe how teachers and students used its products. It was comparatively lavishly funded and the numbers of participant schools increased substantially over its twelve years' duration. Indeed, ACOT was expanding into Europe and had set up ACOT schools in Scotland, Belgium and Sweden immediately prior to its dissolution. Its mission was 'to deepen understanding of how technology can be used as a learning tool' (Fisher *et al*. 1996, p. 1) and its team of researchers was given considerable freedom to work in partnership with teachers and students in ways that prioritised educational gains without the need to deliver commercial gains. There is no doubt, however, that Apple gained a deep understanding of how its products were used in schools and the kinds of products that teachers and students found most compatible with their needs, so that ACOT fulfilled an important purpose as a test bed for technology developers. In this way, ACOT schools were carrying out their work within a larger commercial–educational activity system from which they gained a sense of being part of a powerful community. ACOT methodology placed priority on 'conversations about learning' (ibid., p. 2), running regular summer institutes for participant teachers and involving them in research activities – writing weekly reports and dictating monthly audio-taped diaries. The very substantial quantities of data were stored by the ACOT team in a database and used to produce numerous research summaries, articles, conference presentations and at least one book (Fisher *et al*. 1996). When enthusiasm for ACOT began to take off Apple was unable to sustain the high level of funding to all new schools and 'ACOT's response was to develop a strategy that would capitalise on the expertise of experienced ACOT teachers and embody the lessons about integrating technology into instructions' (David 1996, p. 241). ACOT teachers adopted technology initially as an extension of their existing pedagogical practice but by 1988–9 teaching was becoming more learner-centred and ACOT began focusing staff development sessions on a constructivist conception of learning (Fisher *et al*. 1996, p. 4). The ACOT programme generated a considerable body of knowledge about transformative ICT innovation: in ACOT classrooms there was more collaboration between students; students' enthusiasm for technology did not wane over time and they appeared to become more positive in their attitudes to learning. Teachers reported increased job satisfaction and, as their pedagogy changed, so too did their relationships with students; they engaged in more interdisciplinary work with other teachers, including team teaching. As students increasingly worked in new ways it was apparent that they were learning things which were not captured in standardised tests and ACOT became involved in developing alternative assessment procedures (ibid., p. 5). However, although ACOT students generally performed well on standardised tests, assessment was the area where teachers continued to have 'serious concerns' and to 'struggle' (Sandholtz and Ringstaff 1996, p. 288).

The Fifth Dimension programme, described by Cole as 'a specially constructed computer-mediated activity' (Cole 1996, p. 288), has now been in existence for 20 years and has spawned a network of sites across the USA. It provides a model of an intervention in children's mental development in which university faculty, undergraduate and post-graduate students, adopt the dual role of researchers and helpers (Wizard's Assistants) to the children in solving problems which they might not otherwise be able to solve without adult help. This is a process specifically designed to support learning within 'the zone of proximal development'. The Fifth Dimension was established in 1986 in a library, a boys and girls club and a childcare centre to test whether work of this kind could be sustainable. It quickly demonstrated, as socio-cultural theory including the work of Lewin upon whom Cole draws (see above) predicts, that 'same task, different setting', generates considerable differences in practices (ibid., p. 305). Its culture of voluntarism and inclusiveness (with frequent changes of adult helpers) proved incompatible with formal settings and within the first couple of years it developed to become a model in which the researchers took responsibility for organising teaching as well as research in 'a unique combination of education and play'. Students in the Fifth Dimension move their 'cruddy creature' (personal identifier) into a maze that is 'usually constructed of cardboard' with 21 'rooms' where they find tasks – usually but not always computer-based – and progress according to rules (contained in the Fifth Dimension Constitution) which ensure that they move up to higher levels and are always suitably challenged. The Fifth Dimension was 'a gift' from the wizard with whom the children can communicate electronically by asking questions, requesting help or making complaints. The wizard, who is described by Cole as sometimes 'changing gender mid-sentence' is 'as a rule helpful, but It is often flaky In fulfilling responsibilities, and It has a terrible sense of humor' (ibid., p. 293). The participation of adults and children in this fantasy scenario, which encourages questions about the wizard's origins, gender, temperament and so forth, creates new kinds of relationships and radically shifts the balance of power among the participants. The children are aware that the apparent games environment actually involves considerable reading and focused attention if they are to progress through the maze. Nevertheless, they continue to participate on an entirely voluntary, although irregular, basis.

More recently, examples of transformed pedagogy and learning in schools in Finland and Norway have been noted by a number of writers. Finland has adopted, at a national level, a model of innovation which involves the entire learning system and all its stakeholders, including government departments and commercial organisations, and this has been powerful in transforming education as well as the economy. As the report of a workshop on The Future of ICT in the Knowledge Society, sponsored by the European Commission, expresses it:

> ICT-enabled learning is more likely to be successful if it is accompanied by social and institutional change in educational settings. Social innovation and social engineering is what seems to distinguish the Finnish model of innovation from other countries where technology is at the centre.
>
> (Punie *et al.* 2006, p. 37)

Although the term 'social engineering', used in this quotation, is often seen to suggest a top-down, autocratic approach, the Finnish model has in fact been strongly influenced by socio-cultural theory through the work of Engeström and others at the University of Helsinki and is strongly consultative and participatory. Law *et al.* (2005) draw on case studies of innovative pedagogical practices with technology from 28 countries in the SITES M2 study sponsored by the IAEEA (International Association for the Evaluation of Educational Achievement). They note that Finnish schools demonstrated high levels of collaboration and team work, and had high levels of 'connectedness of the classroom' to other schools or external bodies. They related this to the high level of support that Finnish schools received from both the National Board of Education and local municipalities, as well as to the fact that case study schools were selected because they demonstrated innovative pedagogies with ICT, thereby showing the top priority given to pedagogic innovation in the Finnish education system. This finding is supported by an article reporting on a case study of a Finnish school (Ilomaki *et al.* 2004) from a second major international study of ICT pedagogies sponsored by the OECD (see Venezky 2004). Länsimäki school, which caters for lower secondary age students in an area with socio-ecomonic status somewhat lower than elsewhere in the local municipality, was involved in two innovative ICT projects between 1994 and 2000: the Laptop project and the European CL-Net project for advancing computer-supported collaborative learning. Data from these two projects were available to complement interviews carried out in 2003 for the OECD study, providing the opportunity for a longitudinal analysis of the school's development of ICT-enhanced pedagogies. By 2001 a number of changes in pedagogical practice were observable by comparison with the base-line study in 1994. Student-centred learning had become the leading approach. In classroom observations, ICT was seen to be used 'naturally' by students without specific instructions. Students worked autonomously and industriously and this was related to the fact that 'process-oriented and project-oriented activities directed students' motivation to questions and problems that interested them' (ibid., p. 61). In activity theory terms their 'object' was learning and in Wittgenstein's terms their rule-governed activity was in harmony with the school's aims. Teachers worked as a community under the leadership of two 'key persons': the ICT teacher who provided both technical and pedagogical support and the principal of the school. Both the externally-funded projects involved working in partnership with a university-based team of researchers, and five or six teachers, including the key leaders, 'developed a new kind of professionalism' (ibid., p. 63), participating in networks of colleagues from other schools, writing articles about their project work and seeing the work in their school as informed by theories of pedagogy from the (phenomenal) level of research and policy. In interviews in 2003 teachers reported that they had regularly engaged in reflective practice, had received active support for development work from the universities and the local municipality, and felt themselves to be working in a transformed community, described by Ilomaki *et al.* as 'a pedagogically-directed teacher community' (ibid., p. 65). It is significant that no conflict is reported in this study between the new process-oriented and project-oriented activities of the students and assessment practices. In many studies, adopting innovative pedagogies with ICT alongside preparing students for tests and examinations is highly problematic (e.g. see ACOT above) yet Finnish students have performed well in several international comparative tests (Law *et al.* 2005, p. 177).

In Norway, Erstad (2005) reports that that there have been sustained government programmes promoting the use of ICT in education since 1995 and 'digital literacy' has recently been adopted as one of the five 'core competency areas' of the national curriculum. Norway is a country with a long tradition of project-based learning and these existing pedagogical practices have made it easier for schools to integrate ICTs as tools for students to use in open-ended tasks. An extended case study of the transformation of pedagogical practices in the Godøy island school is given by Krumsvik (2006). As part of the national PILOT project looking at how teachers adopted ICT over time and the impact it had on school structures, the principal invited Krumsvik to work with the school over an extended period and he decided to make it the focus of his doctoral studies. Adopting an action research approach and using socio-cultural activity theory to inform the design of the study, Krumsvik worked closely with the teachers and describes how the action research process developed:

> Through contradictions and discussions in the school on questions of technology-use, the school experienced a process of small cycle forward movements, but also minor setbacks in this change-process.
>
> (Ibid., p. 142)

A major transformation in the school's working practices and organisation resulted. In conversation with me when I visited the school in summer 2006, the principal placed great emphasis on the frequent and lengthy discussions involving the whole staff in planning and evaluating each stage of the development. The first major innovation was the development by the teachers, with some funded assistance, of a subject-portal (Themeweb) containing a large amount of curriculum materials. Then, as students began to use this resource, the teachers decided that they needed to reorganise the school day so that Themeweb could become a major part of the curriculum. They introduced 'study time every day' (90 minutes) in which students could carry out independent work using their teacher and other students as an additional resource. Classrooms were reorganised to create carrels (with hinged side panels) for independent study, areas with a more formal layout of desks and chairs where teachers could work with groups, and larger spaces where painting, construction of models and group activities could take place. Krumsvik reports that this led to considerable changes in the relationships between students and teachers, and also involved parents in discussions of the purposes and processes of schooling. The presentation and consumption of knowledge changed as students were able to access information from the Internet. Gradually, the school developed its own new understanding of 'digital epistemology' and this led to the development of a new assessment framework. They were fortunate that they were able to get permission from the local Directory of Education to develop a written ICT-based examination in English for 10th grade based on their framework and students took this instead of the traditional examination. The external examiner expressed some anxiety about the difficulties of distinguishing what material had been accessed electronically and what was the students' own work, because cross-checking proved very time-consuming, but he was able to clarify some points through oral examination (Krumsvik 2006, p. 172).

The transformation of pedagogy and organisational structures and the process of knowledge acquisition and assessment at Godøy school provides a good example of what can be achieved by a community of teachers, led by a visionary principal, supported by a university-based researcher knowledgeable about the socio-cultural processes of innovation, and able to get support from a national project (PILOT) and the regional Directorate of Education. Many stakeholders from different phenomenal levels worked together over a long period of time and new social practices were able to develop through exploratory use of ICT tools and cycles of planning, action and evaluation. There remains, however, the problem of how to use such cases successfully as models for other schools to build on, 'as well as scaling up of such activities to involve more teachers, students and schools' (Erstad 2005, p. 242).

Erstad (op. cit., p. 239) produces an interesting typology of 'trajectories of innovation related to mechanisms of learning', in which he distinguishes between 'traditional classroom use of ICT', 'flexible use of ICT in schools' and 'ICT use representing new learning arenas'. He concludes that project-based work with ICT, which he classes as flexible use, does not necessarily lead to 'knowledge production and inquiry, based on students ideas' but may, rather, be merely 'production and inquiry based', changing the students' activities and improving their motivation but not changing the nature of their learning or their knowledge-building capacity (ibid., p. 241). Yet, drawing on the ideas of Kompf (op. cit.) discussed earlier in this chapter and Lankshear (2003), as well as observing our own work as researchers teachers and Internet-users, it is clear that how knowledge is constructed, stored, reported, accessed and used changes radically through using it as a mediating tool in social practices. It may be that the nature of the activity is of little consequence: as McLuhan (op. cit.) said, 'the medium is the message'.

It is useful to draw further here on Wittgenstein's analysis of social practice that includes language as a cultural construction with the implication that the meanings of words are determined by the rule-governed behaviours of the social group (see Burbules and Smith discussed earlier). This applies, of course, to all knowledge discursively constructed with cultural signs (words, images etc). Lankshear *et al.* (2000, p. 21) call Wittgenstein's concept of the development of knowledge through a tacit process of 'learning how to go on', a 'performance epistemology' that 'conceives of knowing as making, doing and acting'. This would suggest that changes in activity noted by Erstad in ICT-enhanced project-based learning are a form of tacit knowledge building and contribute to the gradual change in the students' practices of coming to know over a period of time. Further evidence for this is provided by Hinostroza *et al.* (2002) writing about the Chilean national *Enlaces* (links) programme which has formed an important strand of the national programme of educational reform since the early 1990s. By 2005, 88 per cent of primary schools and 85 per cent of secondary schools were participants in *Enlaces* and equipped with computers, local networks, educational and productivity software, and free and unlimited access to web-based educational content relevant to the Chilean curriculum. In a country whose population is spread over a long, thin territory consisting of many hundreds of miles of mountains and coastland, ICT provides an extraordinary new resource for learning. This is another large-scale initiative that draws together stakeholders from many phenomenal levels to support the process of innovation. *Enlaces* has established close links with researchers at the University of Bristol's Graduate School of Education and has used socio-cultural theory to inform the development of the initiative and its support mechanisms. On-going technical and pedagogical support is delivered locally to each school through a partnership of the Education Ministry with 24 universities, hence schools are part of a networked community. When participating in the SITES M2 international programme, case study schools were selected using a local definition of innovative pedagogical practice as well as the SITES M2 criteria required of all countries (Law *et al.* 2005, p. 178). Local criteria included collaborative cross-curricula work using ICT, flexible lesson planning, increased student participation and control over their own learning, a focus for teachers on the process of learning rather than its products, and pedagogical 'planning in such a way that there is a correspondence between the goals, the evaluation and the "success" criteria' (Hinostroza *et al.* 2002, p. 461). Students' activities included data collection, information processing and product development, as well as the use of email and video-conferencing to communicate with other schools. Teachers noticed that changes in their pedagogy led to them adopting new roles, particularly in 'scaffolding' students' learning through assisting individuals and groups and in producing 'activity guides' to provide structure for exploratory projects. They reported that the student's role had also changed to 'learning on his/her own' (ibid., p. 467). Teachers and students reported that this approach had an impact on learning achievements and student motivation. Although the case studies did not provide evidence of measurable gains on traditional tests (a criterion of SITES M2 which did not fit well with local Chilean criteria) students provided many examples of becoming fascinated by learning things directly relevant to their local community and their own lives and gaining new understanding of the interdisciplinary nature of knowledge. Hinostroza *et al.* record in the conclusions section of their article that these new kinds of knowledge are not captured in current test regimes and indicate that new forms of assessment need to be developed:

> These projects did not provide evidence of having impact on students' learning achievement as defined in the national curriculum and measured by the national students' assessment tests. However, they show that students participating in these projects could learn other content, had the opportunity to develop abilities defined as cross-curricula and practised ICT related skills. The challenge now is to deepen the identification and definition of these impacts and opportunities, and eventually include them as part of the national assessment tests.
>
> (Ibid., p. 468, my italics)

Finally I want to draw on an example from Australia which takes the relationship between ICTs and knowledge as its starting point. Bigum (2002) places knowledge creation at the heart of his innovatory programme, Knowledge Producing Schools (KPS). The emphasis here is on schools developing new ways for students to use CCTs (Computers and Communication Technologies) that would make radical changes in the school's relationships with the local community. By this means, students' experience of CCT use outside school could become an important resource for the school. In an earlier study (Lankshear and Bigum 1999), Bigum had noted that teachers who lacked experience of using CCTs for their own purposes could do little more than attempt to make them fit into existing pedagogical practices, that schools also lacked knowledge to provide teachers with the right kind of support, and that as a result students experienced extreme discontinuities in their use of CCTs at school. In developing the vision for KPS Bigum wanted to get away from this process of 'domestication' of CCTs by schools, in their effort to make them 'conform to the requirements of the curriculum and the classroom' (Bigum 2002, pp. 132–3). His starting point was the realisation that constraining the use of CCTs to existing curricula and pedagogies was inappropriate at a time when social practices outside schools, in particular practices relating to knowledge and learning, were shifting radically and unpredictably as a result of their mediation by CCTs. In KPS he envisioned, and went on to implement, a way of using CCTs that would allow the school to build new relationships with their local communities. It could be said that KPS envisages that, rather than CCTs being made to fit in with existing pedagogical practices in the school, these pedagogical practices will be radically changed to fit in with the CCT-enhanced social practices being developed in the larger community – exactly the reverse of the phenomenon of 'domestication':

> [KPS] reads the external world as much changed because of the deployment of CCTs. It sees these changes in terms of changed relationships which flow from additional modes of communication. It acknowledges that schools need to examine new kinds of relationships with the world outside.
>
> (Bigum 2002, p. 137)

KPS is based on the concept of the school developing uses of CCTs, such as digital video and still images, to carry out inquiries in either the school or the local area. Students are given the opportunity to work collaboratively, assisted by their teachers, to 'produce knowledge products that are directed at audiences beyond the school' (ibid., p. 138). Bigum records that in a small primary school that purchased two or three cameras per class, and installed 'a small central facility that allows easy editing of video and still images', all students very soon used this equipment 'in a routine way' to do their work. They started with projects such as 'producing a PowerPoint-based CD to offer advice to students about bullying' and went on to carry out work explicitly for an external audience, such as preparing and presenting three workshops, including one on how to make claymation movies, to a group of visiting principals interested in the way the school was using CCTs.

In Chapter 2, when I discuss research focused more specifically on single phenomenal levels, I will look in more detail at students' use of ICTs in the home. In concluding this chapter I want simply to emphasise that students are part of the larger society whose social practices are changing radically as individuals, families and communities, including technology developers and researchers, become increasingly skilled, and often increasingly inventive, in using ICTs. Schools, too, are part of the larger society, but they are resilient organisational structures, resistant to change (Bidwell 2001); and, to capitalise on the affordances of ICTs and develop new social practices to transform pedagogies and learning, they need to be supported by a range of inter-related strategies that mediate socio-cultural change at multiple phenomenal levels.

ICT-enhanced education systems: policy-makers' visions and tensions

Between 1999 and 2004 three extensive international research projects investigated the relationships between ICT and student learning within education systems: the SITES M2 study carried out by the International Institute for Educational Planning on behalf of UNESCO (Pelgrum and Law 2003); the OECD/CERI's ICT and Quality of Learning study (Venezky 2004); and the EU-sponsored THINK and NOW studies of Technology in Education (focusing on policy and practice respectively) carried out for the European SchoolNet (Scrimshaw 2002; Wood 2002, 2003). In the previous section, case studies from the first two of these were discussed as examples of transformed pedagogies and learning in Finland, Norway and Chile. The broad socio-cultural framework I am using to understand innovation suggests that these examples of successful innovatory practice in classrooms will have been enabled by changes in regulatory structures at the policy level. So, in this final section I want to place these examples in the context of the analysis of visions and tensions relating to national policies for ICT in education contained in the *Think Report*, and end with some recommendations for governments taken from the conclusions of the UNESCO research.

The *Think Report* (Wood 2002) was developed from a series of in-depth interviews with key members of educational ministries and agencies from six European countries: Denmark, France, Holland, Portugal, Sweden and the UK. From these, Wood developed four scenarios for change which provided contrasting visions of the future development of education and the role to be played within education by ICT. A later report, *Think Again* (Wood 2003), incorporates the responses from a second round of in-depth interviews, but for my purposes here the scenarios in their original form, together with eight 'axes of tension' identified from the original interviews, provides a useful framework of 'ideal types' stripped of some of the clutter of minutiae from the evidence without losing the complexity of the issues. The scenarios can be summarised as:

- Scenario 1, in which ICT is fitted to the existing regulatory frameworks of curriculum and assessment and used to augment and strengthen centralised control.
- Scenario 2, in which policy-makers acknowledge that the impact of ICT is complex and uncertain, and relax state controls to enable 'a research and development role for teachers and schools'.
- Scenario 3, in which schools use ICT to re-focus the curriculum on learning how to learn and responsible citizenship, and become 'key nodes in new communities'.
- Scenario 4, in which failures in policy (in)actions undermine attempts to innovate with ICT, and there is 'melt down'.

(See the slightly more detailed summary in Wood 2003, p. 2.)

While it is easy to see in scenario 1 how the 'rather robust and enduring' nature of institutionalised social practices, noted by Cole and Engeström (op. cit.), serve to prevent the mediating impact of ICT from being available to students and teachers, scenarios 2 and 3 are more subtle and less well differentiated, though scenario 2 focuses more strongly on changes in the role of the teacher and scenario 3 more on changes in the role of the student. Scenario 4 is perhaps best seen as echoing Voogt and Pelgrum's (2005) reminder to policy-makers that they have a responsibility to reform structures without which change at the classroom level will be impossible.

Wood's eight axes of tension relate strongly to the evidence that has already emerged from other studies discussed in this chapter. First, innovation with ICT is 'stifled' by failure to reform curriculum; second, innovation with ICT is inhibited without the support of the whole community; third, innovation fails because assessment tools and practices 'do not support the achievement of new objectives'. Hence, the examples of transformed pedagogies and learning come from schools that see themselves as part of the larger community (e.g. researchers, policy-makers, local education officers or the community locally) and have freedom to teach a student-centred curriculum, but in almost all cases they experience tensions between new ways of teaching with ICT and their national assessment regimes. Wood's fourth axis of tension, that innovative uses of ICT will increase the gap between high and low school achievement, emerges in a rather different form in the example studies: these are all well-equipped schools that focus on enabling students to use ICT to learn in new ways, but by their very success they demonstrate what is lost for students whose schools do not have these levels of ICT. Wood points next to tensions surrounding the roles of teachers and learners, the extent to which they are encouraged to be autonomous and given freedom, or at the other extreme expected to conform to a prescriptive curriculum and teaching methods: teachers can be expected to perform as technicians or respected as professionals; students can be cast in the role of consumers or respected as 'an asset to the local and wider communities'. When the curriculum and assessment methods are not obtrusive 'learners and schools become "time rich"' (Wood, op. cit., p. 10) and are able to contribute actively to the community as in the case of Bigum's Knowledge Producing Schools. The seventh axis of tension that emerged from Wood's interviews with policy-makers was their sense that 'the burden of maintaining high quality of ICT provision exceeds available public funding' and this will remain a key concern for all countries that constrains the possibilities for innovation. His eighth axis of tension involves the difficult choices that have to be made in relation to students' use of the Internet, between protecting them from perceived dangers of pornography and paedophiles and giving them free access to 'the information society'. It is particularly interesting that in Wood's scenario 3, where students are given more autonomy and schools work closely with parents and the local community, the focus shifts away from protection (and censorship) to seeing these issues as part of 'the moral, legal and economic dimensions of ICT [that] will be an integral part of the intellectual concerns of learners, schools and the local community' (ibid., p. 12).

Voogt and Pelgrum (2005) provide evidence from the SITES M2 case studies that ICT can be used transformatively if curriculum specifications and assessment procedures are changed to allow innovative pedagogies to develop. Positive outcomes of using ICT shown by the case studies include: for students, increased motivation and self-esteem, easy and rapid acquisition of ICT skills through using them to fulfil a need, improved collaborative skills and the ability to take greater responsibility for their own learning; and for teachers the development of new pedagogical skills and ICT skills (ibid., pp. 171–2). Undertaking case studies was a new departure for IEEP, which has a long tradition of carrying out comparative international studies on the basis of standardised tests, and the intention was to collect objective data on learning gains for students in case study schools, in addition to qualitative data. Such data were generally only available, however, as measurements of traditional learning gains, and case study schools and their researchers were clear that the experience of using ICT had brought about new kinds of learning that were not captured by these tests. There were also very few studies which demonstrated the use of ICT for new approaches to assessment, suggesting that teachers and schools had very little freedom of manoeuvre in all matters relating to assessment (Voogt and Pelgrum 2005, pp. 171–2). Voogt and Pelgrum conclude their article by pointing directly to the constraints placed on teachers' ability to take advantage of the mediating power of ICT, to change curriculum and pedagogy, by the national curriculum and examination requirements of their countries. This has obvious and serious implications for governments, they say:

> If it is indeed true that countries around the world have to move to drastic curricular changes, then governments should provide more room for such change, which implies that curriculum and examination requirements need to be reviewed and probably adapted.
>
> (Voogt and Pelgrum 2005, pp. 173–4)

2 Inside innovation

Learning from research into pedagogy and learning with ICT

In this chapter I want to explore the process of innovation as it is experienced at the different levels in the education system. I will draw on the framework of analysis developed in Chapter 1, but whereas there I used it to comment on innovative ICT activities involving schools working with the support of researchers, communities and national governments, and transforming pedagogy and learning with a considerable degree of success, here I will use it to piece together knowledge from studies focusing mainly on single phenomenal levels. The framework, which draws on a range of theories with considerable overlaps, embodies an expectation that attempts to innovate within complex systems, at one level only, are likely to be impeded by constraints resulting from lack of change at other levels. The main focus of the chapter, however, will be on gathering insights from a range of studies on how to overcome barriers, or at the very least on seeking to understand their historical–cultural nature and refuting over-simplistic interpretations that sometimes allocate blame for failure inappropriately.

Understanding the imagination gap that leads to technical breakdowns

A factor which adds to the difficulty of interpreting research outcomes is the nature of ICT as *an innovation in progress* in which, at the same time that schools and teachers are attempting to integrate its use, the technology itself is constantly changing and developing. This makes considerable demands on technicians involved in procurement and systems management, as well as teachers, so that despite large expenditure by governments researchers frequently find that teachers' attempts at innovative practice are impeded by technical breakdown. Writers such as Cuban *et al.* (2001) rightly point to the devastating impact of systems defects on teachers' confidence and motivation to use technology, but seem to assume too readily that these failures are endemic to technology rather than being effects of mismatches in assumptions and differences in vision between administrator-managers, technicians and teachers. This is a process which I will call the 'imagination gap' and seek to understand in terms of competing interest groups within organisations, in particular differences between technician-users and teacher-users, bearing in mind that the former are constantly under stress attempting to keep up with technological change and keep systems up and running.

Recently my colleague, Matthew Pearson, was helping five-year-old children and their teacher to make videos with digi-blue cameras. The teacher organised the children in teams of producer, cameraman and presenter and they embarked on designing and making an instructional video for other children on how to make a paper windmill. The children produced all the necessary bits of the paper windmill, planned the sequence of activities to be filmed and shot several 'takes' of all the sequences. They were very engaged in what they were doing and by midday were ready to begin work on editing. With difficulty they were persuaded to take a break and eat their school dinner. At this point it became essential to transfer the digi-blue films which were currently on a stand-alone PC in the classroom to the school network which had sufficient memory and the necessary software for editing, but this could not be done because the software had been designed to allow the transfer to a single machine only. Once the transfer of files was complete, the software erased the video files from the camera which meant sharing them across a number of machines was not possible. By working throughout the lunch break, Matthew was able to work out a method of transferring the files onto the network and provide a 'mirror' of the original file structure downloaded to the single machine so that pupils could work on clips taken from one camera on a number of machines and save their edited versions back on to the network. Without this intervention, the teacher's planned lesson would have been seriously compromised at lunchtime and only one group at a time would have been able to edit the video shot in the morning session.

This is a fairly typical example of the kind of practical problem that frequently occurs when children are carrying out flexible and creative tasks with ICT. Although apparently all the facilities needed to make the video films were available, the technology infrastructure had been set up without envisaging that teachers and children would need to transfer digi-blu files from the stand-alone PC to the network. There was an 'imagination gap' between the technical experts who set up the system and those who would *learn over time how to use it* to transform pedagogy and learning. Teachers, who make innovative use of ICT for teaching and learning, moving beyond uses which merely 'fit in' with their existing practice, are of necessity depending on the way the technology has been installed. However, the presumption that ICT will fit into existing practice is usually embedded in the minds of technicians who procure and install ICT systems, and they tend to assume a simple transmission model of pedagogy. As a result there are frequent examples of this imagination gap built into the installation and operation of ICT systems. From the point of view of individual teachers the problems resulting from inflexibilities in infrastructure are compounded by issues relating to power and social status within the organisation.

This is why strong leadership, which provides formal support structures and informal encouragement and championing, is a crucial factor in the success of ICT innovations. In organisations without strong leadership the main barriers to innovation may be the gate-keepers of technology rather than technology itself. This often arises not from ill-will, but from a desire to keep things simple and ensure that the system is easy to maintain. The job of technical experts procuring and installing new ICT systems in educational settings is very demanding, partly because of the high costs of equipment. Often they do not have control over budgets and decisions are made by senior managers or administrators, on the basis of their advice, within the existing financial constraints. What teachers and children will need the system to deliver is impossible to predict in advance, but will emerge over time as they develop new pedagogical practices mediated by ICT. The affordances are latent until ICT becomes, in McLuhan's (1964, p. 3) terms, an extension of the teacher's and students' body and mind. Therefore, the more flexible the system that technical experts are able to install, the more affordances the system will offer users. Because we know from Wartofsky's work (op. cit.) that it is impossible to imagine how ICT might be used if you have little or no user experience, the opportunity to learn from those with experience is invaluable. Technical experts and school principals could almost always procure and install systems that are better value for money if they visited schools already engaged in innovative pedagogy with ICT before taking any decisions.

The changing nature of knowledge and implications for the curriculum

The curriculum has traditionally embodied knowledge that is not absolutely current. If a curriculum is locally determined it can be frequently refreshed, but by its very nature a national curriculum, such as the one introduced in England after the Education Reform Act of 1988, is established on a relatively long-term basis and difficult to change. One of the affordances of the Internet is that it makes current knowledge available to schools in a more fluid, less packaged form. Knowledge is emergent and contestable, part of the on-going project of humankind to establish and codify what is known; but whereas in the past this process of knowledge creation was separated from knowledge consumption by academic reviewers and publishers, and quality control systems were in place to sort and select knowledge claims so that students and the general public were presented with a relatively orderly body of truths, now it is open to public scrutiny directly through the Internet or indirectly through the mediation of newspapers and broadcast radio and television (Lankshear 2003). Every teenager who logs on to MSN is offered an up-to-date news service as well as facilities for communicating with friends. Through the Internet, educational institutions have lost one of their traditional functions as the source of knowledge and the guardian of its quality. What has traditionally counted as knowledge – books, academic journals, research reports – is now available on the Internet alongside a huge quantity of other kinds of material, so that the overlaps between knowledge and information, evidence and hearsay, are blurring. Indeed, it is often said today that it matters little whether what is reported in the media about a politician or celebratory is true, because once it has widely circulated it enters the public's imagination and becomes accepted as part of the story. Although this kind of gossip has always been part of human communities, its public nature on the Internet makes its impact different.

In addition to making the provisional and contestable nature of knowledge more visible, ICT has fundamentally changed the way it is represented, with 'a shift from the verbal to the visual in textual production' (Snyder 2001). Mutimedia representations are much more accessible to learners than linear verbal texts. The power of the image and its subtlety as a form of communication (Barthes 1983, pp. 194–210) is often compelling and the greatly increased use of still and moving images is a shaping dynamic of changes in communication and knowledge transfer. What were previously discrete media – film, radio, television, music production, can now be merged in the one-stop shop of the Internet. Snyder (ibid., pp. 51–3) calls this blurring of multimodal communication and representation 'hybrid vigour' and describes experimental hypermediacy – 'Televised news programmes feature multiple video streams, split-screen displays, composites of graphics and text' – which were novel in 2001 but are now commonplace.

These changes in the nature of knowledge have a number of implications for the curriculum and pedagogy. Andrews (2000) provides a striking example of how two emails he received enabled his children in England to track the travel time of migratory birds between New Hampshire and Ottawa, and how they were then able to use the Internet to answer a question in the second email on whether the idea that geese transported humming birds on their backs was true or a legend. It took them just 90 seconds to find the answer. He argues that in the context of these new information and communication technologies the conceptualisation of learning in the National Curriculum – 'finding things out, developing ideas and making things happen, exchanging and sharing information, and reviewing/modifying/evaluating work as it progresses' – is 'laudable, but somewhat static'. He argues for a more dynamic conceptualisation of learning with 'four main characteristics: community, dialogue, transformation and framing' (ibid., p. 5). The first three of these suggest a more learner-led curriculum, akin to the project-based learning typical of Norwegian schools, or the shifts in curriculum in the Chilean Enlaces project towards more local knowledge related to children's interests. The fourth refers to 'the act of *framing*' (original italics) by which the subject, the classroom and the school locate the process of knowledge acquisition and transfer. The wide range of multimedia resources available through the Internet, and the shifting status of traditional resources such as libraries, disturb learners' and teachers' established ways of framing knowledge and learning. Understandings of literacy have shifted, for example, as a result of the great increase in resources incorporating still and moving images.

McCormick and Scrimshaw (2001) extend this line of analysis by exploring how one of the impacts of ICT is to change the nature of teachers' knowledge. They use a model developed by Banks *et al.* (1999) which distinguishes between subject knowledge, school knowledge and pedagogical knowledge and relates all three to the teacher's personal constructs. ICT, they suggest, is likely to be either threatening or stimulating to the teacher's personal identity and this will be a factor in the level of change they embrace when using ICT in teaching. Even at the lowest level of improving efficiency with ICT, in which 'ICT replaces some conventional resource, but the other elements in the situation remain largely unchanged', they note that 'there can be unexpected effects', which is of course to be expected from a complexity theory perspective (McCormick and Scrimshaw 2001, p. 45); at the second level the Internet extends the reach of the classroom, drawing upon rich resources available on the Internet, such as the Sutton Hoo burial site; at the third level not just the knowledge content but the whole conception of the subject may be transformed, challenging teachers' understandings of the nature of knowledge and demanding considerable personal change as their relationship with students changes from knowledgeable authority to co-learner and adviser (ibid., pp. 48–9).

Learning in the context of the information society

The changes in the way that knowledge is produced and communicated have dramatically shifted the social role of the learner. Drawing on the ideas of Vygotsky (1986) it is clear that learning is a product of inter-relationships between learners and adults using cultural tools (both cognitive tools and artefacts), a form of apprenticeship which Polanyi described as the 'passionate participation' of an individual's mental powers in the active process of coming to know, through dialogue with adults and ideas. By changing the nature of the tools – for example by giving learners access to the Internet and Google – what is learnt changes. As Saljo (1999, p. 147) defines it, 'learning is not only inside the person, but in his or her ability to use a particular set of tools in productive ways and for particular purposes'.

In school the teacher's challenge is to motivate students to focus their activity on learning curriculum knowledge, an effort which is fraught with difficulty in direct relation to the extent that the curriculum is mandatory and not subject to negotiation. We learn most creatively when in the state of total engagement and accelerated mental processing which Csikszentmihalyi (1996) calls 'flow', but it might be a near impossible task for a teacher to orchestrate the activity so that learners experience 'flow' even occasionally in a traditional classroom. However, the introduction of ICT tools, providing learners with new possibilities for autonomy in their choice of learning activities, a hugely increased range of resources, and opportunities to place the products of their learning in a public forum such as a website or blog, can transform some of the characteristics of classrooms. Roschelle *et al.* (2005), in their introduction to a special issue of the *Journal for Computer Assisted Learning*, review how wireless and mobile technologies merged education with students' social life as they developed new routines for managing learning over time. These are fundamental rather than superficial changes in the learning process if we conceive of learning as productive tool use (Saljo, op. cit.), or in term's of Wittgenstein's performance epistemology as 'making, doing and acting' (Lankshear *et al.* 2000, p. 21).

In the early days of computer use in English schools, ten years or so before schools were to be connected to the Internet via broadband, Underwood and Underwood (1990) focused on how children's minds could be extended with computer-based learning. They identified two kinds of activity which could serve this purpose: the first equipped children with 'a toolkit of basic mental skills', by means of drill and practice software, to help establish 'automatised sub skills' and give opportunities for extended practice to build up proficiency; the second involved 'the application of those skills in generalised problem-solving'. In the latter category they included learning to program in Logo which had been promoted by Papert (1980) as a means of giving children control over mini-environments and allowing them to develop higher-order cognitive processes through engaged creativity. These ideas of the 1980s and 1990s are even more applicable with the kinds of ICT tools available in the twenty-first century. Claxton, although he makes no mention of ICT, urges that learning in the twenty-first century should no longer focus on the acquisition of discrete bodies of knowledge, but be a process of cultivating 'the transferable capabilities and dispositions of effective, real-life lifelong learning' (Claxton 2002, p. 32).

I am not meaning to imply, however, that ICT's only value for learning is as a generic set of tools to develop thinking skills and problem-solving abilities. ICT has many affordances which can be taken up and used pedagogically to transform students' learning. Ideally, teachers and students should have the kind of ubiquitous access to Internet-connected ICTs to enable their use flexibly within a range of different pedagogical practices. They can be used for students' exploratory use of the Internet, or for a range of production activities using generic tools for word processing, image manipulation, calculation, knowledge management and presentation. Through interactive whiteboard technology, they provide an excellent means for teachers to enliven formal expositions, including demonstrations of practical procedures such as measurement, and explanations of complex concepts in mathematics and science which require students to visualise possible concrete enactments arising from abstract concepts such as the theory of calculus in mathematics. They also have numerous uses for group activity, for example in the course of conducting scientific experiments, or using computer simulations for investigations (Somekh *et al.*, in preparation). ICT use in classrooms should encompass a range of pedagogies rather than only one, but until all students have their own portable 'digital learning companions' and access to the Internet wirelessly, as and when needed, its use for learning is inevitably constrained.

There has been much less interest in schools in England than in higher education in the development of on-line teaching although the UK government, the BBC, many local education authorities and some schools provide on-line resources to support students' learning. Video-conferencing to provide teaching at a distance in specialist subjects has proved valuable in rural areas such as north-west Scotland or outback Australia. Davis and Niederhauser (2005) report on two case studies of virtual schooling, one an ambitious attempt to use two-way interactive video to provide 'live' synchronous teaching on two campuses in the USA, the other a school 'replacement' model that provided interactive teaching to children in remote areas in Australia with some synchronous but mainly asynchronous communication. A more radical approach, described by Selinger (2004) is a global ICT-based curriculum developed by Cisco to teach Internet technology skills and prepare students for industry certification. The curriculum was designed and is continuously refreshed by Cisco in the USA and taught by local providers in educational institutions in over 150 countries, world wide. Since this course has not been developed to fit into the regulatory practices for curriculum and assessment in any country it provides an example of what can be achieved when teachers have the opportunity to introduce innovative ICT pedagogies with the support of a high status international sponsor. Selinger bases her evaluation on web-based questionnaires, face-to-face interviews with students and instructors and lesson observations in eleven countries (ibid., p. 229) in EMEA (Europe, the Middle East and Africa). Analysis of the data is informed by a review of the literature on differences in national culture and their impact on pedagogic practices. Selinger suggests that an area of particular relevance to the design of e-learning materials is the extent to which national culture privileges 'high or low uncertainty avoidance'. For example, countries which have uncertainty avoidance (UA) cultures prefer teaching resources which are simple, provide limited choices and give priority to clear navigation schemes and help systems, whereas those which have low UA cultures 'prefer complexity with maximal content and choices'. The evaluation showed that the course was popular in all countries, but that the way in which teachers used the e-learning materials differed markedly. This was partly related to language (the materials are all in English) and partly to ease and speed of access to the Internet both in the educational institution and students' homes. However, it was also related to cultural assumptions about the teacher's role and authority, the students' autonomy, and established practices in the use of paper-based resources. Overall, it provides a clear example of the kind of 'take-over' of education by commercial companies envisaged by Kompf (op. cit.) (see Chapter 1), but it is significant that the focus of the course is on technical knowledge directly related to working in the technology industry and therefore relatively lightly inscribed with national cultural traditions.

Towards the transformation of learning with ICT

Between 1984 and 1990, while carrying out action research into computer use in my own classroom and later with teachers in the Pupil Autonomy in Learning with Microcomputers project, I became excited by the way in which ICT could change the nature of relationships between teachers and their students. Two changes appeared obvious: first the students' attention was to varying extents, depending on the activity, shifted away from me, their teacher, to the computer screen; and second, interactive computer-based resources could take over some of the teacher's traditional function of maintaining students' levels of motivation for task-completion. The metaphor that best represented this for me was that of a circus performer keeping a line of plates on sticks spinning by running from one to another and giving each in turn a small spin: teachers did not need to worry about keeping students using computers 'on task'. There were some obvious implications of these changes. First, it was necessary to explore how teachers could best support this intense student–computer interaction – to determine the critical features of teacher behaviour that would maximise the value of this new tool; and second, it was crucial to examine what exactly was the nature of computer-based tasks – to ask what (if anything) was being learnt rather than assuming that high levels of motivation necessarily equated to intended learning (Davis *et al.* 1997). Quality in learning, with or without ICT, depends on the nature of the task (activity) and its goal (object). High motivation is an important element of the activity because it can be assumed that the student is focused on completing the computer-based task, but if the task is low level and mundane or, following Wittgenstein's concept of the fluidity of discursive, rule-governed behaviour (Burbules and Smith 2005), if the student's object shifts to speed in task completion rather than learning something *by means of* task completion, *what* is learnt may not constitute quality. Kozma (1991) provided an early analysis of the particular features of information systems that could support learning: their speed in processing, their ability to proceduralise information ('operating on symbols according to specific rules'), their ability to transform information from one symbol system to another (by changing the form of representation), and their ability to assist novices in building and manipulating mental models 'so that they are more like those of experts'. From Kozma's work I came to understand that an important contribution made by some ICT-enabled tasks is in supporting the learner's ability to understand 'decontextualised' concepts in which coming to know is largely an abstract rather than a practical process.

Ridgway and McCusker (2003) adopt a Vygotskian theory of learning and suggest that in a society that is experiencing radical change as a result of ICT, there is a need to 'map a new cognitive agenda', since cognitive abilities valued by one culture may be 'rendered redundant by a new technology'. They turn Kozma's features of ICT around and see them as essential components of a new kind of curriculum focused on: 'the promotion of meta-knowledge; using new representations and symbol systems; and modelling complex processes and problems' (ibid., p. 312). Their research consists in designing software that supports the development of problem-solving skills. These tasks are intended to assess students' learning, as a means of promoting their cognitive abilities; they are intended to be used in assessment *for* learning rather than summative testing. Their software is designed to extend the cognitive abilities of students by letting them manipulate complex data sets that would be very difficult to work with on paper. For example, they can use a dynamic model (represented on screen with icons and clickable buttons) to explore the implications of manipulating a number of variables relating to cost, weather, distance and time of year before taking a decision on purchasing a holiday.

> This allows students to be set tasks in realistic contexts, using realistic data to address real problems of considerable complexity, using resources and methods that are familiar to professionals working in the relevant field.
>
> (Ridgway and McCusker 2003, p. 327)

The implication of the kind of ICT-based tasks designed by Ridgway and McCusker is that students engage in a different kind of task. This is what Perkins (1993, p. 89) calls an 'effect *with* ICT' in which the user's cognitive powers are amplified by the use of technology. These kinds of effects are contentious in traditional education systems. They can be seen as giving students assistance which is somehow 'unfair' or may prevent them from developing skills needed to complete the task unaided. In England we have seen moves at various times to ban calculators from classrooms and it is still assumed at all levels in our education system that students should not have access to the Internet during examinations. However, Pea sees this as one of the 'trade offs' that are necessary in using ICT tools within an activity system characterised by 'distributed intelligence'. ICT tools can take over part of the cognitive load, in what Perkins calls 'person plus', and this challenges us to re-assess the value of what has traditionally been taught and consider making radical changes. When ICT tools are available, 'more universal access among learners to participation in complex thought and activities may be gained at the expense of low-level understanding' (Pea 1993, p. 74). As Ridgway and McCusker remind us, across all areas of activity human beings now use ICT tools routinely, so designing an education system that includes their use by students is increasingly important. Furthermore, the practices of disciplinary knowledge are changing to incorporate ICT tools that provide new kinds of affordances that extend the mind as well as the body, in McLuhan's sense (op. cit.). Algebra provides an elegant and time-efficient set of tools for solving mathematical problems that would otherwise involve extensive, time-consuming calculations, but the number-crunching facilities of computers have changed the nature of mathematicians' needs. This, in turn, has implications for the kind of mathematical skills that should be part of a twenty-first century curriculum. It is no longer necessary to teach algebra as an essential computational tool, but teaching algebra may remain important in giving students higher-level mathematical understandings. As Ruthven (2002) points out, in the 'instrumentation' of mathematics it is important not merely to teach students new routine procedures which incorporate ICT into mathematical problem solving, but to use ICT to assist the development of their cognitive structures. Classroom practices and use of the available tools are an integral part of developing these structures: 'If tasks are strongly compartmentalised, techniques highly prescribed, and discourses severely restricted, then the mathematical senses and cognitive schemes that students develop will be correspondingly fragmented and inflexible' (ibid., p. 281). But instrumentation of mathematical activities in classrooms should both aid efficiency and assist the development of higher-level mental functions because, as Ruthven says, 'it is widely agreed that teaching and learning should aim to build the coordinated mathematical senses and cognitive structures which constitute the two faces of conceptual understanding' (ibid., p. 281).

Understanding constraints to innovative pedagogies with ICT and seeking ways to overcome them

Turning now to case studies of innovative practice, it seems clear that transformation of pedagogies and learning is constrained in the English education system in a way that it is not in countries like Finland and Norway from which examples were drawn in Chapter 1. Harris (2002) provides an evaluative account of the SITES M2 case studies in England and it is noticeable that in the primary schools the focus is on innovative projects carried out with a selection of students rather than on the work of the schools as a whole, and in two of the three secondary schools it is in relation to enhancing performance in national tests and examinations. In the three primary schools the initiatives are innovative and valuable but they are *de facto* 'add-ons' to the rest of the work of the schools concerned. In one primary school all 46 students aged 10–11 in one class were provided with a desktop PC and Internet access; in another, 25 students were paired with adult volunteers in a nearby mobile phone factory with whom they communicated by email; in the third, 44 11 year olds used an Internet-based resource for collaborative problem-solving in groups of four to seven. The first and the third of these cases involved substantial changes in pedagogy with more open-ended, student-centred assignments and less directive teaching; the second provided rewarding enrichment activities, but students were selected from more than one class because they were seen to need additional support in developing communication skills and it appears that there was little or no impact on pedagogy. In one of the secondary schools 97 students were volunteers who enrolled in a two-year on-line course leading to formal accreditation in ICT at age 16. A pass in this course 'counted' as equivalent to four General Certificate of Secondary Education (GCSE) passes at grades A*–C (the recognised benchmark), making it highly attractive to students with the result that, despite being designed for students who would be unlikely to achieve five passes at GCSE, most of the students who enrolled were of above average ability. This course was widely taken up by many schools over the ensuing five years, illustrating that in an education system driven by high-stakes assessment the most effective mechanism for introducing an innovative course is to tie it to a new examination. Similarly, another secondary school introduced a new ICT system for collecting data about students' performance in formal tests and using this to set individual targets for approximately 2,000 students. Here the motivation was again linked to success in examinations: teachers were able to target support more quickly on students who were underachieving, and students were aware that their performance was being more closely monitored by teachers. The emphasis was on improving the efficiency of the existing system rather than making changes to pedagogy. In the third secondary school students in two upper ability classes were offered the opportunity of spending 20 minutes each week for 10 weeks, in optional lunchtime sessions, participating in video-conferencing sessions with a French school in order to improve oral skills in each other's languages. Although valuable, this is also clearly an add-on to existing practice that had no impact on pedagogy. The selection of these three cases from secondary schools as representative of the best available in England clearly illustrates the high level of constraint that the curriculum and assessment systems place on innovative ICT-enhanced teaching and learning in secondary schools. The constraints are much less for primary schools and evidence from other research carried out in England strongly suggests that innovative uses of ICT to support teaching across the curriculum are much more common in primary than in secondary schools.

Loveless (2003) provides a further account of innovative work with ICT in primary classrooms in England, looking specifically at the supportive context provided by 'creative subjects'. Her focus is on creativity in learning in primary schools in art, drama, music, design and technology, with some discussion of writing in English and she suggests that these subjects provide more space for creativity because, with the exception of writing, they are not subject to the same 'high stakes' testing regimes. Loveless illustrates how government has funded a major report on creativity (NAACE 1999) and put in place resources to support creativity through the provision of on-line resources, including resources from BBC Education. In her article she maps creative opportunities onto the elements of the national curriculum for ICT showing that opportunities are there, within the overall framework. She cites Kimbell's (2000) crisis warning about lack of opportunities in practice for creativity in primary – let alone secondary – schools, but attempts to remain optimistic, referring to these anxieties as 'the grit in the oyster' which 'provokes the action and engagement to "create spaces"' for creativity. She ends her article by presenting the vision statement for 'Creating Spaces', a new network of educational professionals dedicated to using ICT to develop children's creativity, encompassing teachers, journalists, software developers, artists and researchers.

There is no formal role in England for universities to support teachers and schools in the development of ICT-enhanced teaching and learning as there is in countries such as Chile and Finland. However, it is important to note the contribution of Mercer (1995) and Wegerif and Dawes (2004) in working with teachers to develop new pedagogical practices that enable ICT to support the development of children's talk. In early research, such as my own PALM project, it was noticeable that in classrooms children often worked with the computer in groups (as a result of shortage of computers) and that they appeared to be working together and highly engaged. This led to an expectation that the computer might encourage more focused talk in groups than would normally happen without a teacher present. The Spoken Language and New Technology project (SLANT) explored this phenomenon and found, however, that children's talk around the computer was neither collaborative nor supportive of cognitive development. For example, the child holding the mouse tended to dominate access to the screen and others gave mainly 'yes' or 'no' responses; those with computers at home became impatient with those who lacked keyboard skills; and the main focus of conversation was on mechanisms for turn taking (Wegerif and Dawes 2004, p. 10). These disappointing findings led to the development of 'talk lessons' in which children were given specific training in how to ask questions of one another and how to back up their replies with reasons. Mercer and colleagues went on to develop 'ground rules for exploratory talk' based on a set of clear principles drawn from linguistic and socio-cultural theory. These encourage children explicitly to share information, provide reasons for their views, accept challenges and discuss alternatives before reaching a decision (Wegerif and Dawes 2004, p. 23). The successful implementation of these methods to transform the quality of children's talk in English, maths and science lessons provides an excellent example of how radical pedagogical change is possible, even within classrooms constrained by a prescribed curriculum and a tight assessment framework, if there is support from university-based researchers funded by a nationally recognised charitable foundation (that is, support from higher phenomenal levels). This research into innovative practice is tightly focused, however, on the conduct of children's talk, either with or without an ICT-stimulus, without any need for radical changes in the overall organisation of the classroom or the shape of the school day. It enhances rather than disrupts preparation for national tests. Teaching children to conduct group work within the ground rules ensures that the contribution of ICT to the children's cognitive development is maximised through dialogue, and with this proceduralised exploratory talk in place ICT interactive resources are very effective in sustaining focused 'on task' group work.

The evidence from both Loveless (op. cit.) and Wegerif and Dawes (op. cit.) suggests that drawing schools and teachers into collaboration with researchers and the wider community has an important impact in encouraging as much innovation with

ICT as possible within the constraints of the English education system. In Chapter 3, I will discuss how far it is possible to develop innovative pedagogies with ICT in our current education system, focusing on our own research in the evaluation of the GridClub children's website and the Pedagogies with E-Learning Resources project.

Informal learning with ICTs in the home

Socio-cultural theory suggests that the context in which cultural tools are used shapes their transformative possibilities: in other words, the affordances of information and communication technologies lead to radical changes in human activities in some contexts, but this effect varies between contexts and in some is very greatly reduced. One of the best examples demonstrating this is the stark difference between young people's experiences of using ICT at school and at home. Homes are all different, of course, but for many young people a computer with a broadband Internet connection is readily accessible at home to use for extended periods, without undue restrictions on what they use it for. They may have to negotiate to take turns with their siblings, and parents may impose some rules about the length of time they spend, the extent to which they use the computer for playing games and, if connection to the Internet is by an expensive dial-up service, the time spent on-line. However, by comparison, at school there are always many more restrictions: typically, students have access to computers for limited periods of time, for purposes specified by the teacher, access to the Internet may be restricted by filters, and because a large number of people are likely to be on the system at the same time the speed of Internet connection will often be slow.

Computers came into young people's homes very rapidly. My colleague, Cathy Lewin (2004) reports from the ImpaCT2 evaluation carried out for the UK government that, during the year 2000 to 2001, from a sample of 2,100 the proportion of students between 10 and 16 who reported having a computer at home rose from 81 per cent to 90 per cent, with some skewing towards higher percentages among older students. During the same period Internet access at home among this sample rose from 59 per cent to 73 per cent. Since 2001 there has been widespread provision of broadband to homes throughout England, replacing slower dial-up services and young people's personal ownership of a computer or laptop is increasing. A pattern that emerges clearly from research is that young people spend much more time using ICT at home than at school. For example, Lewin reports on students' logs of their use of ICT that a sub-sample of 280 primary school students reported spending on average one hour a week using a computer at school and three hours at home. The 115 secondary students who kept logs reported on average 2.5 hours a week using a computer at school and 10 hours at home, of which 3.5 hours of home time was spent on school-related activities. Word processing and accessing the Internet were the most frequent home uses of ICT for school work. For leisure, the Internet, CD-ROMs, email and chat were the most popular and, interestingly, not word processing. Lewin reports that of 227 respondents to a questionnaire about use of the Internet, 81 per cent said they spent more time on the Internet at home than at school. In the logs and in hand-drawn concept maps of 'computers in my world' young people in the same study reported extremely varied uses of ICT at home, including in many cases pursuing specialist interests to find information, downloading music and images, or producing and printing their own material.

A key difference between using ICT at home and at school is between informal and formal learning, hence we should not be surprised to find a replication of Lave's (1996) finding that learning in informal settings is ubiquitous and continuous whereas 'it often seems nearly impossible to learn in settings dedicated to education' (ibid., p. 9). What is at stake then becomes the nature and quality of the learning in informal settings. In the various research studies, ICT is observed entering homes and becoming embedded in family life, at first with some uncertainty about its purposes. Downes (2002), reporting on a study carried out with 500 children in Australia between 1995 and 1998, said that they thought of the computer as either a toy or a 'playable tool' – saying things like, 'I played typing stories' and 'I played the encyclopaedia'. From their descriptions it was clear that they used the computer for 'exploratory learning and "learning by doing", demonstrating the co-agency of the relationship between computer and child' (ibid., pp. 30–1). Similarly, in the ImpaCT2 evaluation we found that students habitually referred to their computer use at home as 'playing games' and reserved the word 'learning' only for activities that they engaged in at school: when they were asked to list their ICT activities at home it was clear that 'games' was a generic term used for a wide range of activities and categorised in this way because the computer was perceived as a site for leisure and autonomy. Facer *et al.* (2003), reporting on research between 1998 and 2000, describe how adults construct the family computer variably through discourses of entertainment, education and work, which parallel the fluidity of their constructions of childhood. Facer *et al.* provide photographs showing the various locations in which computers are positioned in the homes they visited, suggesting that 'ownership' varies: sometimes the computer is perceived as a shared resource for all the family and sometimes as more personally owned by a child, a sibling or a parent. They suggest that key features of ICT, such as the volume and speed of information and varied forms of interactivity, create a 'life on the screen' which is 'powerfully engaging' but that these features are not apparent from young people's accounts of using ICT at school. The problem they suggest is that 'at present, in school, computers are seen primarily as a *resource* for learning rather than a *context* for learning' (ibid., p. 232). At school, computer use is planned to support more rapid and more effective acquisition of a prescribed curriculum, whereas it is clear from the way that it is used at home that the computer's appeal to young people is that it accords them the same status as adults and gives them access to choices. The Internet allows them to take control, provides direct links with popular culture through accessing music and images, and keeps them in contact with their friends through messaging services and chat rooms. Since Downes (op. cit.) and Facer *et al.* (op. cit.) completed their studies most young people in England have acquired MP3 players and mobile phones and are able to access the Internet away from home. The technologies are merging: phones are turning into digital cameras and becoming Internet-enabled, MP3 players are extending to store and play back video films as well as music.

This mismatch between ICT use at home and at school is a cause for concern, mainly because it indicates the extent of the lost potential for ICT to transform schooling. A closer examination also reveals that there are aspects of ICT use that home does not provide, and moreover that ICT use at home is strongly differentiated between homes, not so much through what is traditionally called 'the digital divide' (access or non-access to a computer and the Internet) as through the family's cultural ambience or 'habitus' (Bourdieu 1977, pp. 183–5). Angus *et al.* (2004) describe the wide variation in computer and Internet use by four families, three of which were recipients of a special offer that aimed to 'make technology affordable for all Australians' and one which had already had a home computer and Internet access for some time. Differences in the patterns of family life and inequalities of aspirations quickly led to different patterns of computer use, with the least-advantaged family making much less use of the educational advantages offered by the Internet. This was compounded by a lack of empathy among teachers for the children from the most disadvantaged home, manifested for example in their failure to recognise and value the ICT skills of the family's teenage boy. The mother in this family used ICT to enhance her social life through participation in chat rooms, but this did not add to the family's cultural capital in any way. In another of our own studies (Lewin *et al.* 2003) we found, similarly, that the real digital divide was not between those with and without access to ICT at home, but related to the purposes for which home computers were used: only the students from advantaged homes used ICT for school-related work, either of their own volition or because their parents suggested it. Had teachers requested that ICT should be used for homework many others would have had the facilities to do so, but teachers operated a *de facto* policy of not setting ICT-related activities for homework for reasons of equity. This differential between kinds of use, rather than merely access to, ICT has been called by Natriello (2001) the 'second digital divide'.

The implications of all this research are clear: schools need to find ways of using ICT that give young people the transformed learning opportunities that some are already experiencing with ICT at home. This would involve giving students more time for extended engagement with ICT and encouraging them to use it to extend their creativity and productivity and take greater responsibility for their learning. At present the support for ICT use in the home is very unequal. There are also areas of ICT use, such as work with spreadsheets and calculations, that are virtually absent from patterns of ICT use even in homes with high cultural capital (Facer *et al.* 2003, pp. 235–6). It is clear from these research studies that there is a vital role for schools to play in helping children to acquire new digital literacies: skills in searching for, and selecting, websites, identifying their provenance, discriminating between their qualities and using them appropriately to produce new knowledge representations. November (2001) urges the importance of teaching essential digital literacies without which students using the Internet are open to misinformation and deception. Kerawalla and Crook (2002) in a study which shows strongly differentiated patterns of ICT use in homes and a prevalence for games playing, even in homes where parents have purchased the computer and software with specific educational purposes, recommend that schools should 'respect and locate within the classroom children's spontaneous achievements on home computers' and 'incorporate ICT more prominently into the school–family dialogue'. It may be that the potential for ICT to transform pedagogies and learning in schools will come only when all students have continuous access to small, robust Internet-linked laptops but together these research studies provide the explanatory evidence needed to develop and implement prototypes of innovative practice such as that described in Chapter 3.

The potential of assessment as a lever for pedagogical innovation with ICT

Despite the complexity of pedagogical practice, and indeed as a result of its inter-dependence with the regulatory frameworks of the national community, there is very strong evidence that innovations in pedagogy can be introduced rapidly if they are tied to changes in what is assessed. When I became a teacher in England in the 1970s it was a time of considerable curriculum reform. The Schools Council, a body that brought together teachers' unions, policy-makers and representatives of local education authorities and universities, had a responsibility for reforming schools. New curricula were developed by university researchers, working closely with teachers, with funding from either the Schools Council (e.g. the History Project and the Humanities Curriculum Project) or charitable foundations (e.g. the Nuffield Science Projects, and the Ford Teaching Project) and were grounded in state-of-the art disciplinary knowledge and theories of child development and learning. An example from the USA was Bruner's Man a Course of Study (MACOS) curriculum in which elementary children were given artefacts, texts and films from the social and life sciences to investigate in order to 'discover' what it means to be human (e.g. documentary films about the kinship patterns of baboons; and the way of life of the Netsilik Eskimos). These new curricula incorporated innovatory pedagogical practices since curriculum was understood to be enacted in the process of teaching (Stenhouse 1975). There was a recognition that what was learnt by students might not be the same as what the teacher intended to teach, and the new curricula were linked to forms of assessment which would allow teaching to be more closely aligned with students' social and cognitive needs. In England, to enable these reforms to be introduced, examination boards (at the time all linked with major universities) developed new syllabuses especially to assess the intended curriculum outcomes. For example, the Cambridge Board introduced the 'Plain Texts' English Literature syllabus which permitted students to bring unmarked copies of the texts they had studied into the examination room, thereby shifting the balance of the focus of what was assessed to critical response and interpretation rather than factual recall and the ability to quote from memory.

This strong link between what is assessed and the process of educational innovation is in line with the broad socio-cultural framework developed in Chapter 1. Human activity is object-oriented and performed in inter-relationship with others; so it is a necessary condition for changes in educational practice that educational purposes should be renewed in line with values recognised and formally sanctioned by all the phenomenal levels of the community. In education systems where public examinations play an important role in rewarding the achievements of students and teachers, changes in what they set out to assess provide a publicly recognised organising framework for innovation. Without fundamental changes to the aims, purposes and practices of assessment, pedagogic innovations are likely to be very seriously constrained. There is considerable evidence from research that this is the case for the innovation of ICT in education in England.

At the heart of policies for ICT in education in England there is a confusion of purposes. Interestingly, this can be seen to mirror the shifts in discourses surrounding computers in the home outlined in the previous section – is the computer there to assist children's learning, to develop their ICT skills in preparation for work, or as a 'playable tool'? McFarlane (2001) lists three discourses surrounding ICT in UK policy documents that assume, without relationship to one another, that it is: a set of skills or competences; a vehicle for teaching and learning; or an agent of transformative change. She points out that each has significant implications for assessing and accrediting learning outcomes. Moreover, as the national curriculum gives priority to the first of these, the teacher training national curriculum to the second, and policy documents emanating from the government to the third, it is clear that teachers and schools are placed in an impossible position in trying to respond to all three. In a brief review of research she identifies that the educational gains attributed to ICT are largely in terms of learning processes such as problem-solving capability and critical thinking skills, which 'are surely desirable outcomes of the compulsory education phase' but are not captured in regimes of assessment focused on measuring the acquisition of subject knowledge. Impacts of ICT use are, therefore, 'indirect rather than direct effects on learning as measured through test performances'. The implication of McFarlane's argument is that ICT is changing the nature and quality of students' learning but that this is not currently being measured; and that teachers, as a result, may be discouraged from using ICT as a vehicle for teaching and learning across the curriculum since its use does not lead to rewards for students in terms of improved test scores. This effect is exacerbated by the status of ICT skills as a separately assessed national curriculum subject.

There is a small amount of evidence of the impact of ICT on students' learning as measured by traditional methods, but this appears to be predominantly linked to students' use from home of websites that contain materials closely tailored to improving test scores. The ImpaCT2 evaluation (Harrison *et al.* 2002) showed small but statistically significant gains in Science GCSE examinations for 16-year-olds and in national tests for English at age 11 and science at age 13, as well as positive indications which were not statistically significant in one or two other subjects at all three levels. However, as students reported relatively low levels of use of ICT in lessons (e.g. 30 per cent of 16 year olds reported using it in English lessons in 'some weeks'), it seems that these gains were the result of using ICT at home, including websites that provided self-assessment tests to help with revision. In Scotland, Livingston and Condie (2004) report positively on the evaluation of the SCHOLAR support materials for students preparing for Higher and Advanced Higher examinations at 16 and 17. SCHOLAR was a collaborative project between Heriot-Watt university and schools and FE colleges, with the aim of improving students' attainment and encouraging greater take-up of university places. SCHOLAR materials included printed text booklets, interactive on-line materials, assessment materials, revision materials and an on-line discussion forum/noticeboard (the latter was hardly used). An analysis of examination results showed a degree of superior performance for students in the study sample. Students were very positive about the facilities with more than 50 per cent reporting using *the on-line materials* at least 3–4 times per month. However, the majority of students' use of SCHOLAR was at home, which was probably the reason for teachers underestimating the extent of their use. Writing from the point of view of an examination board, Raikes and Harding (2003) make it clear that the need to ensure there is no discontinuity between years, so that standards can be compared, makes radical changes in assessment impossible. They discuss possibilities for computerising traditional examinations and propose the need for a transitional period when paper-based and computerised versions of traditional tests would be offered alongside one another. They are enthusiastic about the efficiency gains likely to result from computer-based tests, marking and record-keeping, but clearly regard transformation of the system to assess new kinds of knowledge and learning as something beyond the scope of the current system.

McCormick (2004) takes McFarlane's article as a starting point for exploring the relationship between assessment and ICT, although his focus is on formative assessment, as part of the teaching and learning process, rather than on formal assessment of learning gains in national tests and examinations. His article provides insights into current practices and the impetus towards innovation in the two separate educational fields of ICT and assessment. He shows that most of the work that has looked at ways of using ICT for assessment 'ignores developments in the field of assessment, particularly with regard to … what has now become known as the field of "assessment for learning"' (ibid., p. 117). Equally, those developing innovatory practices in this form of assessment have paid little attention to the facilities that ICT offers to support this, for example through the development of digital portfolios. Researchers in the two fields have tended to work discretely and there has also been very little sharing of evidence between developing ICT practices at HE/FE and school levels.

McCormick's article is useful in identifying many of the tensions that teachers face in using ICT within the current regulatory frameworks for curriculum and assessment: for example, using ICT for an hour a week in a specialist suite makes it impossible to embed ICT in subject teaching; and teaching students with access to the Internet, where they have easy access to cutting and pasting material, raises questions about 'the nature of evidence of learning' that teachers should look for and reward. McCormick ends by discussing possibilities for identifying and assessing 'new outcomes' which result from students using ICT. These may be in relation to students' using multimedia authoring tools 'to allow them to externalise their thinking and to express their ideas through this media in ways that are not evident through conventional tests' (ibid., p. 130). New understandings of learning as more distributed between collaborating partners and resulting from activities in which ICT tools act as extensions of learners and co-construct learners' agency (Salomon 1993a), and major changes in the development and representation of knowledge, such as those discussed earlier in this chapter, pose difficult challenges for assessment. For example, if electronic communications and Internet use are an integral part of the learner's practices, how can it make sense to assess their performance without allowing them access to these tools? I would argue, rather, that students should be assessed on what they can achieve when *working in new ways they have developed to make use of the affordances of these tools* that have the potential to transform learning.

Research into the possibilities of pedagogic change with ICT in English schools

In this section I will explore the evidence of pedagogical change with ICT from studies of schools and classrooms in England, and the extent to which this is enabled or constrained by national frameworks for the assessment of students' learning. I will argue that innovations in pedagogy do not lie within the teacher's gift, or even within the school's gift, because they always have implications for how students, teachers and the school are recognised and valued by the community, locally and nationally. At the level of the classroom, pedagogy is extremely complex. A key factor is the range of pedagogies made possible by working with ICT, including the kind of close work in supporting students' conceptual development in the ZPD described by Ridgway and McCusker (op. cit.). Alexander's comparative study of culture and pedagogy in five countries makes a useful starting point. He provides a review of theories and comes to the conclusion that it is not possible to understand teaching as either an art, or a science or a craft, but only as a combination of all three together with the values and beliefs of teachers:

> The position from which I approached this project was that in transaction the act of teaching has elements of both art and craft, but not of laboratory or experimental sciences; but that in conception and planning teaching draws on general principles and laws, some of which have been validated by disciplined scientific enquiry (the art or craft of the science). However, it also draws on the cumulative and collective craft knowledge of teachers in general (the art or craft of the craft); and on the personal experience, theories and beliefs of the individual teacher.
>
> (Alexander 2000, p. 275)

Webb and Cox (2004, pp. 238–9) provide a framework for analysing pedagogic practices relating to ICT use and an extensive review of research mainly carried out in England. They take Shulman's (1987) model of pedagogic reasoning as their starting point and add to it 'knowledge of affordances of ICT and decisions about their use'. Although they include 'students' knowledge, beliefs and values' in the model the underlying assumption of their analysis is that pedagogy is a rational process whereby teachers decide on the resources they need and 'build these into lesson plans'. They describe the affordances of ICT as additional to the other affordances of the classroom, including the teacher and students. The teacher's role is to provide an ICT affordance, prompt students to use it fully and explain and demonstrate it. This model places responsibility for pedagogic change firmly in the hands of individual teachers, rather than seeing teachers' pedagogic practice as a function of the education system that regulates the purposes of schooling and the organisational structures and reward systems within which teachers and students co-construct classroom activities. On the other hand, it is also a model which predicts little fundamental changes in pedagogy as a result of introducing ICT, because it assumes that ICT is an additional resource, of the same nature as other resources, rather than a tool with transformative possibilities. Their review of research on pedagogies with ICT largely confirms this position as they find little evidence of transformation in students' learning. Like many other writers, Webb and Cox (2004, p. 278) conclude their review by calling for more teacher professional development because ICT is 'making the role of the teacher much more complex'.

Watson (2001) adopts a larger frame for her analysis of the innovation of ICT in education in England. She contrasts what is happening in classrooms with the ubiquitous use of technology in the business world and seeks to understand the disappointingly low level of its uptake by teachers. Like McFarlane (op. cit.) she identifies the root of the problem in confusions at the policy level. The difference between teaching people *with* computers and teaching people *about* computers has become blurred at the policy level, with the result that the use of ICT as a resource for learning has been reduced at the level of the school to a focus on teaching ICT skills and competencies. She likens this to students being taught the component parts of a car 'but never actually take[ing] a vehicle onto the road for the purpose of travelling from A to B'. She also points to the logistical problems teachers face in booking and teaching in specialist ICT rooms and the way in which this separation of ICT resources from the classroom creates for teachers a sense of professional separation in the ICT room from their primary object of teaching a subject. Watson draws on a UNESCO report (Moran 1999) on 'seven knowledges necessary for education for the future' to suggest that current policies for ICT in education in England are backward-looking and failing to meet the current and future needs of students. Rather than calling for more professional development for teachers, she concludes by calling for 'an intervention of educational philosophy and debate' to which teachers would contribute because they are 'both well suited and informed'. ICT should be used to service new educational goals negotiated between policy-makers and teachers, rather than being expected to provide a catalyst for change without any theoretical foundation to the direction of change that is needed.

The framework of analysis I am adopting, described in Chapter 1, gives priority to understanding pedagogic practice in relation to the education system as a whole. A small number of studies published between 2001 and 2005 present evidence of ICT use in classrooms and indications of the factors that support or constrain change. Higgins (2001) focuses on using ICT to teach for understanding, adopting Dewey's definition of understanding as 'meaning making'. Focusing specifically on the use of ICT to teach mathematics, he emphasises the importance of the mediating role teachers need to play in making connections between the software and other mathematical activities. However, at the start of the article he notes that almost all ICT use in primary schools is for discrete skills teaching and he ends by saying that the challenge for research is to support teachers in playing this active, mediating role when using ICT 'in the range of social and curriculum contexts in schools'. A new context which has become commonly available in English schools since 2004–05 is the interactive whiteboard which directly supports teachers in whole-class teaching. Several studies report on the rapidity with which it has been taken up and integrated with classroom practice (Kennewell and Morgan 2003; Cox *et al.* 2004; Miller 2004; Hall and Higgins 2005; Higgins *et al.* 2005). Whereas teaching the current national curriculum and preparing students for national tests does not provide a clear rationale for teachers to involve students in using ICT individually to support their learning, an interactive whiteboard that is used by the teacher as a presentational tool perfectly fits their needs in delivering the whole-class teaching required by the mandated numeracy and literacy strategies (Somekh *et al.*, in preparation).

Hennessy *et al.* (2005) report on research undertaken in partnership with 15 secondary school teachers, using socio-cultural theory to inform the analysis. They focused on the need for teachers to adopt the role of facilitators or mediators of learning and work collaboratively with students. The research set out to 'compare the rhetoric of transformation with classroom reality' in secondary subject teaching (ibid., p. 269), focusing specifically on the teacher's role in selecting ICT resources and framing these 'to exploit ICT in structuring, sequencing, monitoring and assessing learning with ICT' (ibid., p. 270). In phase 1 the teachers undertook small-scale, classroom-based, exploratory projects and in phase 2 these were used for cross-case analysis to draw out learning from across the sites. The research found that teachers integrated ICT resources with established classroom cultures wherever possible, gave priority to pre-structuring tasks, and planned particularly carefully for students' Internet research, often by pre-selecting websites and placing time limits on students' searching activities. They were concerned to avoid diluting the focus on subject content and ensure that time spent on computers was limited so that the benefits of interactive whole-class teaching were retained. However, the use of ICT shifted classroom organisation towards more small-group work, encouraged teachers to devise pedagogic strategies for facilitating and mediating students learning, and increased students' responsibility for their own learning. They conclude by saying that if ICT is to be integrated into subject teaching there is a need for involving teachers in discussions about pedagogy, something which they describe as 'an unusual step' (ibid., p. 288). In a second article drawing on the same data, Ruthven *et al.* (2005) focus on how Internet resources were incorporated into classroom practice. They report that in all 15 case studies using the Internet for subject-teaching required relocating the class to a specialist room, which disrupted normal routines as well as requiring special planning. There were also significant technical problems that disrupted lessons. The research showed that Internet use led to 'modifications to the texture of classroom teaching and learning' rather than radical change. Given the logistical difficulties experienced in giving students access to the Internet and the short time frames in which they had to work, this finding is unsurprising.

In the InterActive research project, into the use of ICT within subject teaching in secondary schools, special emphasis was placed on integrating ICT within subject cultures (Sutherland 2004). A team of 59 teachers worked with researchers and teacher educators in Subject Design Initiatives to plan and evaluate focused studies carried out within classrooms. The examples of studies presented by Sutherland *et al.* (ibid.) show that they are largely teacher directed and make use of ICT tools to carry out work very similar to what might otherwise have been done. ICT is seen as providing a new analytic lens 'for enhanced theorising of teaching and learning, whether or not ICT is being used in the learning process' (ibid., p. 9). Sutherland emphasises 'that learning within a subject discipline means learning about the discourses, practices and tools which relate to the particular subject world' and uncovers some problems that arose: for example, sometimes removal into a specialist ICT room shifted the teacher's discourse away from the subject towards ICT specifically, so that unintentionally the lesson had lost its subject focus; and in another article from the same research (John and Sutherland 2005) there were two examples of lessons where the games genre of the software re-focused the students' attention on completing the work rapidly rather than thinking through the conceptual issues it was intended to teach. While it is clear that ICT tools can never be neutral and transparent, but will always have an impact in shaping the learning of the subject, it should not be forgotten that this is also true of learning in classrooms without ICT tools. School physics and school English are not the same as physics and English in a university, or again as physics in an industrial company or English in the life of a poet or novelist. The introduction of ICT into subject teaching will certainly disturb established school knowledge of that subject, but now that ICT is ubiquitous in constructions of disciplinary knowledge outside school we cannot assume that this will have negative consequences. Indeed, as McCormick and Scrimshaw (op. cit.) suggest, the developing nature of teacher's knowledge is an essential feature of pedagogic innovation.

Conclusions

The theoretical framework for understanding the process of innovation, developed in Chapter 1, has provided an extremely useful lens through which to explore the recent research into pedagogy and learning with ICT in the UK. Most of the studies I have looked at in this chapter focus on one phenomenal level (either home, or classroom, or school or policy development), yet they all show that attempts to use ICT in ways that transform pedagogy and learning are strongly constrained by factors beyond participants' control: for example, teachers have to work within curriculum and assessment regulatory structures mandated by central government. The research literature shows, however, many indications of the potential of ICT to give learners: an extraordinary degree of control over accessing and handling information; tools to support them in constructing knowledge; and radically new ways of producing and publishing their own work. The strongest evidence comes from looking at what students are doing with ICT at home; and it is simply not sensible or practical to continue to allow students' use of ICT to be so utterly different in these two settings. Schools need to be remodelled to take on some of the advantages of homes as contexts for learning with ICT; and the means of doing this need to be developed at the policy level.

3   Engaging with innovation

Learning from intervention

The framework for researching innovation developed in Chapter 1 presumes an active, interventive role for the researcher. Innovation does not simply happen as a result of new policies; it involves people at all levels of human activity in experimentation, boundary crossing, collaborative negotiation and strategic opportunism. Researchers can play a crucial part. Social structures have in-built mechanisms that ensure their reproduction (Schön 1971) and at a time when technology is creating radical changes in many aspects of our lives, often in ways that seem beyond our control, it is important to design and explore divergent models of social practice integrated with research. The model is one of praxis – the integration of action with knowledge generation through a cyclical process of experimentation, evaluation and refinement of new practices. In this chapter, I describe how I have used the framework to design research into prototypes of innovative practice. The importance of this approach in ensuring quality in research into innovation is theoretically justified in Somekh and Saunders (2007).

The evaluation of GridClub[1]

The evaluation of the GridClub educational website for 7–11-year-old children, which we carried out during 2001–3 with funding from the Department for Education and Skills, provided us with a policy-driven prototype of innovative practice. GridClub took its name from the National Grid for Learning initiative which spearheaded the introduction of the Internet into English schools. It was established by a partnership of Channel Four Television (4Learning), Oracle Corporation and Intuitive Media, on behalf of the UK Government, with the aim of extending children's learning opportunities beyond the school day as part of the national drive to raise standards. GridClub[2] contained a portal with an extensive suite of resources, and 'edutainment' games covering all the areas of the National Curriculum; and a password-protected 'clubs' site, within Oracle's well-established *Think* learning environment, where children could contribute articles and respond to activities, as well as sending e-mails and 'stickies'. Key features of GridClub were its design and 'branding' with a Meccano-like surround and brightly coloured images to make it attractive to young children; and its status as a 'safe site' for children, protected by means of schools taking responsibility for authenticating individual children's identity before they could become a member and be given a password.

GridClub was designed to provide a form of supported, curriculum-led but informal learning for children. The support took two forms. One was through the design of the games, reference materials and activities provided and the other was through children's participation in a series of clubs, with adult 'mediation'.

Knowing from experience that we were unlikely to be able to gather sufficient data by on-line questionnaires, and wanting in any case to be able to talk to children and their parents rather than relying on written responses, the evaluation design included six 'key informant' schools. These were not intended as sites for case study but locations where we could talk to children and their teachers and, if possible, their parents. However, it soon became clear that the local, physical contexts of use were having a major impact in mediating the affordances of the virtual environment, so in some senses we were unavoidably looking at six individual 'cases' with some further variations between homes. The impact of classroom contexts was stronger than might have been expected because the security procedures placed teachers in the position of gatekeepers to GridClub. Initial habits of use were, therefore, established when passwords were issued and the site demonstrated, either in ICT lessons in the school's computer suite or in computer club at dinner time or after school.

Researching children's 'informal' learning with GridClub offered us a rare opportunity, within government sponsored research, to define learning broadly rather than seeking to measure impact in terms of students' attainment in national tests. Data collection was focused on key indicators of learning identified in the research literature: interviews with children to elicit stories of 'flow' experiences (of intensive engagement) while using GridClub (Csikszentmihalyi 1996); analysis of children's contributions to the 'clubs' area of GridClub, and interviews with teachers and parents to identify constructions of childhood (being or becoming) (James and Prout 1997); and concept maps of 'being in GridClub', similar to those used in the ImpaCT2 evaluation (see Chapter 10) to identify the nature of children's participation in a community of practice while using GridClub (Lave and Wenger 1991).

'Flow' as an indicator of children's learning

We interviewed children, looking for evidence of the mental state of 'flow' and the GridClub activities that triggered it. Could they remember experiencing 'flow'? and what exactly were they doing at the time? Almost all the children knew what we meant when we described 'flow' and were able to give examples:

'I was at home and I was on Zooglebust. You get different scores to go to places like Italy... You have to go through a maze to get somewhere... It's like I'm playing as a Roman. I'm at home and I have all these things around me and I've got a computer in front of me but I felt like I was somewhere else.'

'It's like having your head in the computer and your eyes and nose and mouth, but your hands are outside doing things.'

Many told stories about failing to hear an adult ask them to log off GridClub because they were so absorbed. Another common story was about forgetting to stop at an agreed time. The level of engagement was confirmed by repeated accounts of children missing their favourite television programmes because they forgot the time.

The stories fell into two kinds, depending on whether GridClub was being used at home or at school. At school, children said they frequently were interrupted in a flow experience because time had run out. Sometimes this happened at home, because parents wanted them to stop for a meal, or to go to bed. The more common experience at home, however, was of spending much longer on GridClub than intended and being surprised to find out that they had missed doing something else they had planned. These stories involved spending anything from 15 minutes to an hour longer than intended on GridClub.

Children said it was annoying to be interrupted and told to stop when they were experiencing flow (in one case it was 'embarrassing because everyone else had left the room'). One parent confirmed that her daughter was, 'annoyed If she gets stopped on the computer, when she feels that the flow's broken'. Another parent said, 'They don't care you know that they've got something else to do. They go on there and they lose themselves.'

Children reported experiencing 'flow' when playing all kinds of computer games, including those on GridClub. This evidence was reinforced by many accounts of 'flow' occurring in association with features common to computer games: trying to complete a task and get to the next level, competing against the clock, solving a problem, answering 'lots of questions' to get a high score. 'Flow' also occurred in relation to a different kind of experience, associated with the 'Clubs' site within *Think*, in which children appeared to be engaging in higher-level tasks such as finding things out, working on a personal website or contributing to debates ('I was so involved in making a debate that I was like, "Uoho!" when I was told to stop.').

The differences between the 'flow' stories at home and at school are more significant than they at first seem. 'Flow' as described by Csikszentmihalyi (op. cit.) is a feature of high-level, creative engagement and most adults' accounts of 'flow' include spending more time than intended and experiencing a high degree of satisfaction and accomplishment when a task is completed. 'Flow' interrupted is not likely to be beneficial; hence the short time spans for using GridClub at school would appear to undermine learning significantly.

'Being and becoming' as indicators of learning

We defined the difference between 'being' and 'becoming' mainly in terms of children's level of independence and their resulting enhanced self-esteem. This was a feature of how the learning environment – and the adults who mediated it – constructed childhood itself. GridClub offered an environment in which children were empowered to create their own web pages, communicate by email and 'live talk' with other children, and enter competitions to win certificates and sometimes prizes. However, the extent to which they were able to take advantage of these affordances varied significantly according to the nature of their relationship with the adults who provided the framing context for their GridClub use. This varied widely between schools and presumably also between homes, although without visiting homes this was more difficult to establish.

At school, the rules that governed use of GridClub varied. In one school, children became frequent users of GridClub, participating fully in the virtual environment, and this transferred easily into logging on from home. The positive impact that participation in GridClub and interaction with an on-line mentor could have on children's construction of identity and sense of agency is illustrated in this exchange between child and researcher:

IMOGEN: With stickies,[3] if you manage to do it right, you can put pictures on or moving words that go through the screen, then disappear, and then they come back on again, and then they disappear, and then they come back on again. And I sent a note to [a moderator] asking how she done it and she replied something like, 'Hi Imogen! If you click on this icon (and it's got that underlined) then you can do what you want to do and you can put pictures and smiley words on,' and so I clicked on it and then you get all these instructions. You can print out the page so you know how to do it or you can put it all in a blue print or whatever that's called and then you click on 'Copy' and then you go to your sticky and then you click on um 'Paste' and then you have, or whatever way it is, 'Paste' then 'Copy', and then …

EVALUATOR: But why is it important to have an image and moving words?

IMOGEN: Because it makes it fun. Your friends think oh this is good, maybe I could try and copy it, and at the same time you're learning how to do things on the computer.

In another school children aged between 8 and 9 said they were unable to reply to emails received within the Clubs environment because 'we have to do it to people in the room … we're not allowed to send any to other people yet'. An 8-year-old pupil in this group, who had become an experienced user of email at home, was instructed by the teacher to send an email to everyone in the class and later reprimanded when the teacher noticed that he was composing an email to go to someone else.

This was only a temporary rule for the younger children, as could be seen by a 10-year-old child in the same school who spoke of sending something to his email address at home because 'I can't save it at school'. Nevertheless, this example too suggested a constraining environment where the importance of children being able to save their work did not appear to have been considered. In this school children also showed they were very conscious of the dangers of email and didn't appear to distinguish between using email within the GridClub environment or outside, seeming generally timid about communicating. This was surprising given the emphasis on safety that is part of GridClub's marketing.

In a third school, the computer facilities were more extensive and children were able to spend time in 'computer club' much more frequently than in the second school. (All children had a chance of attending every day, whereas in the second school only one group had been selected to attend the computer club during the lunch hour, which took place just one day a week and was sometimes cancelled.) The nature of use was generally very different in this third school. This was partly, of course, a result of the much better access to facilities, but the teachers' expectations of the children's independence and their enthusiasm for giving them freedom to explore GridClub were also very significant factors.

The visual and auditory nature of the site was generally novel and motivating. Feedback was often immediate and children in the schools where GridClub use was well established worked hard for rewards such as certificates. In those schools, children who had created their own websites within the password-protected Club site used them to project their chosen identity, with a clear link to high self-esteem. In one school the ICT coordinator provided the children with many of the features of a learning organisation by the way that he mediated their use of GridClub. It was clear that GridClub motivated them, provided authentic feedback and meaningful rewards; and that through its use the children were able to build a positive identity. The GridClub environment gave this teacher a tool which helped him to break down some of the constraints of the formal education system and construct childhood as 'being' rather than 'becoming'. The teacher's educational philosophy and constructions of childhood enabled him to use the affordances of GridClub to develop radically new pedagogical practices. The provenance of transformation cannot be disaggregated between agent and tool.

An exceptional chance for an exceptional child

The GridClub environment provided very different communities of practice depending on the community of practice that existed in the physical location of use. Intended in its original conception as a website for children to use at home, we observed a shift towards GridClub being seen more and more as a computer club activity at school. The relationship between the children and the teacher (always the ICT co-ordinator in our 'Key Informant' schools) was often, therefore, a decisive factor. However, GridClub remained a resource available to children who had good access to the Internet at home and an encouraging parent. Jacob's story provides an interesting example.

Jacob, aged 8, was one of only three children in his school who had found out how to send 'stickies' by exploring the 'clubs' site at home. He ticked the highest box on the questionnaire saying that he had sent 'between 51 and 100 stickies'. In the group interview he was careful at first not to claim to be more proficient than the other children, saying that he had trouble through forgetting his password, but towards the end of the interview his enthusiasm and pride burst out:

> Bridget, do you know when I go on GridClub, I go onto these things and I have a whole bunch of emails and I send about 15 stickies and that's each time I go on there. (You do? You didn't tell me that.) I do send stickies, but not often, because I've stopped going on there because I find my hands hurt when I keep on sending them. (Do they?) Sometimes it gets irritating. (What gets irritating?)

Going on the Internet, going onto GridClub and then you don't go in places that you're doing it for and then you realise you've got about 20 emails.

This testimony is extraordinary not merely because it confirms that Jacob has mastered the GridClub environment way beyond the capabilities of either his classmates or the older children in the school, but because it shows that he has begun to experience all the familiar problems of frequent users – how to cope with the work when you get too many emails, and how to avoid getting distracted into doing something other than you intended when you go on-line.

Jacob's mind map of 'being in GridClub' focused predominantly on positive identity, shown by the large image of himself with arms raised in the air and the words 'happy', 'joyful', 'cool' and 'fun' surrounding the computer (Figure 3.1). In his presentation to the class, he explained one of the links, 'a bit unhappy', as being about forgetting his password. He also associates having fun in GridClub with learning, shown particularly in the image on the left-hand side which he explained as 'This is the brain where the imagination is growing bigger,' and which he has placed just above an image of himself about to climb a tree because 'tree climbing is fun and enjoyable'. The link with GridClub, he explained, was because 'GridClub has got games on'.

The exceptional experience that GridClub offered Jacob was also very much appreciated by his mother who saw it as an extension of his learning at school:

They are doing work at school and he comes home and he carries it on and he picks up from it. I can see the difference in terms of his writing for example and how he constructs sentences you know, and stuff like that. ... He's created in the last couple of days – and I think this comes about from him getting comfortable

Figure 3.1 Jacob's mind map of 'Being in GridClub'

using the computer – even though we've always had one, he's never been on it as much before – and now he's creating certificates and letters in terms of this club and that club. … I have seen him doing that and it's fantastic.

Jacob's success was very much his own, by her account. Happy to take the role of a novice observer she provided one of the ideal kinds of adult mediation:

I don't actually stand over him and watch as he opens it up and stuff. I'll observe as he's doing stuff and I'll say 'Oh what are you doing?' that kind of thing. I take an interest, but he's quite good at it, he's better than me.

Jacob's account of his use of GridClub shows an 8-year-old child's lack of awareness of the significance of his achievements. His motivation is largely pure enjoyment, but he is undoubtedly pleased that someone has come along to ask him about this activity in which he knows he excels because he is constantly in demand by other children asking him to help them.

The Developing Pedagogies for E-learning Resources project – PELRS[4]

Developing Pedagogies for E-learning Resources (PELRS) was a research and development project exploring ways of transforming teaching and learning through innovative uses of ICT (www.pelrs.org.uk). It was funded by the General Teaching Council for England and Manchester Metropolitan University (2003–6). PELRS was a collaborative project in which teachers and pupils worked with the university-based researchers as equal partners focused on the question: 'Could we organise teaching and learning in radically different ways now we have the Internet, Internet-look-alike CD/DVD materials, digital imaging, video and other new technologies?'

In designing PELRS we were able to draw on what we had learnt from the GridClub evaluation. The physical location in which students accessed digital resources strongly mediated the quality of their learning experiences. Relationships between adults and students that constructed childhood as inexpert, not-yet-fully being and needing adult regulation created learned dependency and made students fearful of exploring ICT environments; whereas pedagogies that embodied constructions of childhood as fully being, and were open to negotiating rules and activities, enabled students to take control of ICT environments with enjoyment and develop confidence in their own agency.

Designing a prototype – strategies for both stimulating and nurturing change

PELRS was designed as a prototype of new practices in which teachers were invited to participate on the basis that the project would begin by brainstorming how things might be done differently, rather than 'starting where teachers are at'. Our intention was to circumvent the interlocking habits and assumptions of existing practices whereby schools and classrooms, constrained by the regulatory structures of the larger education system of which they are part, retain the stability and coherence of the system by either blocking change or subverting it to fit in with what is perceived as feasible and practical. In the first two years we worked with four case study schools,[5] selected for their commitment to innovative uses of ICT and located in catchment areas with socio-economic backgrounds varying from impoverished to average (all also had slightly better than average levels of ICT equipment for English schools at that time). PELRS aimed to explore the possibilities for transforming students' learning through their use of ICT. It set out to develop, implement and evaluate innovative pedagogies with ICTs in teaching curriculum subjects, not the teaching of ICT skills. In the third year, 2005–6, the project widened to include a dozen new schools that tested the usability of the pedagogic strategies and planning frameworks and further refined them in the light of their own school contexts.[6] Although the small scale of funding limited what was possible, work in the third year of PELRS provided evidence that its approach can be 'scaled up'.

PELRS started with a provisional working model of the conditions that students need to meet before they can be said to be experiencing transformative learning:

- Learning creatively (exploring, producing, designing, experimenting)
- Learning as active citizenship (taking decisions, solving problems, making choices)
- Engaging intellectually with powerful ideas (using thinking skills, grappling with ideas/concepts)
- Reflecting on their own learning (learning how to learn through meta-cognition).

This working model was refined through action research over the first two years to develop a theory of transformative learning mediated by context that builds on a broad range of socio-cultural theories (Pearson and Somekh 2006). This embodies the premise that the provenance of transformative learning cannot be disaggregated between agent and context (the latter embedding the affordances of its cultural tools).

PELRS developed strategies for teaching and classroom organisation that built opportunistically on spaces for change that existed in the education system. For example, previous research (see Chapter 2) had shown that young people were strongly motivated by using computers and the Internet and many had acquired considerable skills in their use through exploratory and creative uses of ICT at home, so PELRS invited students who were already skilled in using ICT to join the research team focusing on the question: 'How could we make the experience of ICT in school more like what we are doing with ICT at home?' We also took opportunities whenever possible to adopt the rhetoric of new policy initiatives that closely related to PELRS' aims of transforming pedagogy and learning, such as the encouragement for teachers to give children a 'voice' contained in 'Excellence and enjoyment: A strategy for primary schools' (DfES 2003). This and other new policies that challenged the established regime of levels of attainment and national tests (that prescribed a linear path for learning) were difficult for teachers to implement alongside continuing requirements of OFSTED and the QCA guidelines. Yet teachers were attracted to these new policies which offered more creative ways of working and PELRS offered strategies for taking them up and external support, both in terms of working collaboratively with university researchers and the formal authority that came from working with a project sponsored by the General Teaching Council. PELRS also avoided asking teachers to work in ways which conflicted with their contractual responsibilities within the education system, so for example teachers in the project designed their lessons around the learning process aims of creativity, autonomy, engagement and metacognition *in conjunction with* the mandatory aims of the national curriculum. These strategies which can be compared to the 'nurturing of complex systems' advocated by Davis and Sumara (2005) (see Chapter 1) enabled us to work with a wide range of teachers and students, including the 14–16 age range in secondary schools working for public examinations.

The design of PELRS built directly on activity theory by seeking to change the traditional division of labour between teachers and students, the expected behaviours governed by formal and informal classroom rules, the culture of classroom learning and the level of commitment to a negotiated object. These included:

- Developing a framework for transformed pedagogies (see below), which represented socio-cultural theories diagrammatically, so they were easily accessible and of immediate practical use.
- Changing the patterns of teaching so that learning events began with a plenary session in which teachers outlined the learning goals (from the national curriculum) and students planned how they would like to work. In particular, they could decide on their learning activities and choose resources to help them from books and e-learning materials, including the Internet.

The PELRS 'generic pedagogic framework' (see Figure 3.2) represents ICT as the third point of the teacher–pupil relationship, mediating the activities of the negotiated learning focus. The learning focus placed at the centre of the diagram is the object of pedagogic practice, which embraces the whole vision of transformative learning for the students, but is concretised in each learning event in terms of national curriculum outcomes and the PELRS 'transformative learning outcomes' of creativity, active citizenship, cognitive engagement and metacognition. The latter are represented at the top right corner of the diagram and the arrow empty of shading that leads to them is intended to indicate that in a three-dimensional representation they should diffuse through the whole activity rather than being merely endpoints. The diagram indicates that with the help of ICT pupils have more opportunities for choice, learning through exploratory play and deeper engagement with their work; and teachers can more easily negotiate new roles for themselves and become co-learners with pupils. The learning focus (or 'event') is not limited in its location to school, but extends into home and on-line environments. The context of learning is also seen to be shaped by pupils' families and peers, and by the other adults who work alongside teachers.

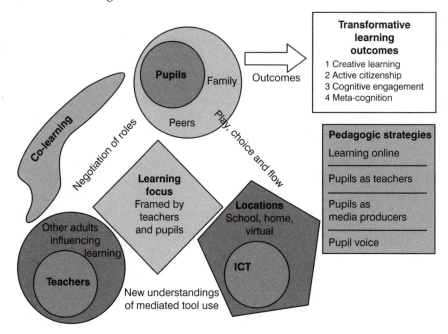

Figure 3.2 Generic pedagogic framework

During the first six months, the research team developed four themed pedagogic strategies which changed the traditional roles of 'teachers' and 'learners':

- pupils as teachers
- pupils as media producers
- pupil voice
- learning on-line.

The generic framework was customised as a tool for planning learning events in the four pedagogic strategies. Teachers found these 'themed' frameworks a creative tool for planning a new kind of student-led learning. In all four strategies, the focus was on transforming pupils' learning experiences to become as creative, active, engaged and metacognitive as possible.

Prototype practices: towards the transformation of pedagogy and learning

Data were collected in PELRS classrooms during the first two years by means of digital video-recordings. These were made by my colleague, Matthew Pearson, with a hand-held camera, in the role of participant observer. As far as possible there was equality of status between teachers and university researchers and children were listened to and treated with respect (as 'being' rather than 'becoming'; James and

Prout 1997) and this translated into frequent and informal access for the researcher to classrooms and easy relationships with students who referred to him always as 'Matthew'. Frequently he talked to the students while filming them to get their explanations of what they were doing now, what had led up to it and how they were planning to go on. The camera sometimes moved to students to take on the filming role. The whole class had a sense of being involved in the research and those who had officially taken on researcher roles spent periods of time of up to an hour with Matthew, away from the classroom, to look at selected extracts of the videos and give comments and interpretations which were tape-recorded. Teachers also spent time with Matthew observing the same selections from the video data as the students so that interpretations of teachers, students and university-based researchers could be compared to deepen and illuminate interpretation. Case studies of PELRS classroom activities are available on the website in multimodal form of text, still images and video clips (access is password protected because of the images of children they contain).

All four pedagogic strategies ('pupils as teachers' etc.) drew on the same generic framework and the customised versions of the diagrams acted mainly to identify a specific vision, almost to give the innovative work a 'brand' which signalled to pupils and other staff that the traditional rules of the classrooms had been set aside. A pattern that quickly emerged from the negotiated plenary session at the beginning of learning events was the organisation of the students into self-selected groups working on 'finding things out' and creating a presentation to show to the rest of the class. Although this was not suggested by Matthew, it fitted the PELRS emphasis on co-learning and maximised possibilities for students to give each other mutual support. In terms of the underpinning theory this could be seen as enabling distributed cognition and providing a social context that maximised the possibilities for supporting students' learning in their zone of proximal development. Usually each group took responsibility for researching one strand of the topic and presenting it to the whole class in the final stages of the 'learning event'. Using the PELRS pedagogic framework, rather than the QCA guidance for lesson planning, teachers planned PELRS work to take place over several lessons or during an extended period when the normal timetable had been suspended, and this entailed moving away from the pattern of teaching lessons as discrete blocks which presented students with the learning outcomes at the beginning and reviewed what had been learnt at the end. This was one small way in which PELRS allowed the object (in activity theory terms) to become more flexible and gave students space for beginning to take some responsibility for their own learning.

The videodata revealed that students engaged in this new style of working with high levels of motivation. An early finding in an inner city school in an area of social deprivation was that the teacher's discourse shifted almost completely away from administrative and behavioural matters; the vast majority of the teacher's talk was now about the curriculum topic. The reason was easy to deduce from observing the high level of the students' engagement with their work. Student researchers reviewing the videos commented on this with surprise: 'Look at John, he's really working, that's amazing, he usually spends most of the time messing about.' This increased level of motivation meant that teachers did not need to fill their usual authority role. The videos also showed examples of students approaching teachers and asking questions about information they had found on the Internet, again a shift from normal patterns of classroom behaviour in which student-initiated speech exchanges were rare. This seemed to indicate the kind of shift in the division of labour that we were seeking.

As students took on more responsibility for their own learning the role of the teacher shifted. In a first school using the 'pupils as media producers' strategy, 6-year-old pupils used 'digital blue' video cameras to produce a video on how to make a model windmill. The teacher negotiated with them to work in groups of three, alternating the roles of 'presenter', 'director' and 'cameraman' during the filming work which took a whole morning. The afternoon was given over to editing the video clips into a finished 'film' of between 2 and 3 minutes, complete with textual labels to contextualise the moving images. The curriculum focus was learning how to communicate instructions clearly and the 'pupils as media producers' discourse was picked up by the teacher who built on her previous familiarity with the roles involved in film production. Much of the teaching intervention during this project consisted of encouraging and supporting the children in using the appropriate forms of instructional language during the filming of the videos, and then during the editing stage of the process, helping them to find out how to add textual labels to the moving images in order to reinforce these linguistic skills.

The 'pupils as teachers' strategy provided a strong discursive re-positioning of the division of classroom labour. The traditional teacher's role is more pro-active than the student's which explains why many teachers have noticed the power of having to teach something as a means of increasing the depth of one's prior knowledge. Preparing to teach is a powerful incentive for deep learning. PELRS transferred this active role to students, giving them responsibility for learning in order to teach their peers, hence increasing their motivation and the effectiveness of their learning. In the case of using ICT the 'pupils as teachers' strategy also freed teachers from having to demonstrate that they knew more than their students. This was enormously helpful on two counts when using ICT: first, it meant that teachers did not need to feel anxiety about any lack of expertise with ICT on their own part, but instead could celebrate pupils' ICT skills and accept and value their varying levels of expertise; second, it opened up the classroom to knowledge and information which the teacher had not pre-selected. In one secondary classroom, the use of the PELRS 'pupils as media producers' strategy enabled a radical shift in pupils' engagement with a project in Media Studies involving the development and marketing of a new product. Whereas in previous years pupils had used paper-based tools to design advertisements for the new product, PELRS pupils chose to work in the computer suite using a graphics package which allowed them to produce 'professional' quality images and logos. The teacher had not felt confident to do this before because of her own perceived lack of technical skills but, adopting the PELRS approach, those pupils who possessed skills with the software worked as group leaders demonstrating how to use the software through their own work and then supporting their peers in developing skills themselves. Another example comes from a primary classroom where pupils used wirelessly connected laptops to search the Internet and find information to contribute to building knowledge about the germination and growth of plants. One group found information about plants that live in very arid, sandy areas of the world and called the teacher over to discuss what they had discovered: their new role as selectors of knowledge gave them a reason to initiate a discussion; and the teacher, who had previously known almost nothing about this kind of plant, shifted role to knowledgeable co-learner, able to share the pupils' intellectual engagement, support their thinking skills, and advise on the various websites they had accessed and their likely reliability.

Giving pupils choice over the resources they used for learning, rather than the teacher pre-specifying the resources they *should* use in the manner specified in the recommended style of lesson planning, re-oriented them towards the object of the classroom activity. There was a shift in the ownership of knowledge although teachers continued to scaffold students' learning by providing a wide range of possible resources and planning the task so that it encouraged creativity and diversity of responses. For example, in a primary school a whole day was devoted to an exploratory project on Victorian people. The teachers provided names of people, chosen to represent a diverse and interesting cross-section of Victorian life, and they gave the pupils a list of things to find out about them. The pupils had access to the Internet as well as all the other ICT and traditional resources in the room for a day. They were given freedom to report back to the whole class in any way they liked. PERLS teachers encouraged pupils to think creatively about how they could provide evidence of meeting the learning outcomes and there was a conscious move away from a homogeneous approach to ICT resource selection which could result in all pupils in a class producing identical or near-identical products. Giving pupils choices created greater diversity of learning between small groups and enabled more productive knowledge-building when the groups presented their work to each other. For example, in another school the teacher used the 'pupils as teachers strategy' as a means of encouraging pupils to learn scientific concepts about the reproduction of plants. Pupils used the Internet as well as traditional resources to collect information and some groups decided to make PowerPoint presentations to teach other pupils what they had learnt. However not all groups wanted to use PowerPoint, and some groups developed some paper-based resources such as informational posters and one group produced a role play which was captured on digital video. This more active role as knowledge producers raised the level of motivation and it seems, also, of intellectual engagement, since several months later the teacher checked for knowledge retention and found they were able to recall the concepts and the correct scientific terminology and use them with confidence.

In PELRS classrooms there was always a tendency for innovative pedagogies to be 'recaptured' by traditional pedagogies through pupils – or teachers – incorporating behaviours from established routines of practice. The video-data and the teachers' and students' interpretations of that data in discussion enabled us to continuously research the effectiveness of the prototype practices in transforming learning and consciously adapt them where necessary. For example, in a primary school in an area of social deprivation, where the pupils' engagement with the task and success in learning were transformed by the process of finding information and preparing to teach their peers, their actual presentations to the whole class were disrupted by the inattention of their peers. All the groups were keen to give their own presentations but were so used to paying attention *only* to a teacher that they switched off their attention when the teacher stood behind them at the back of the room. In a second iteration of this learning event with another class the teacher made the shift in the pupils' role more explicit, talking to them in advance about what would happen during the presentations, how she and they together would learn from other pupils and the importance of paying attention to each other after they had all worked so hard. With this more careful preparation for the role shift the second class paid good attention to each others' presentations. It also led to the pupils thinking more carefully about their role as teachers and the need to hold their peers' attention. One group suggested that they should produce worksheets for the others to complete as a means of keeping their attention, which can be construed as a creative adaptation of the existing classroom affordance of testing coupled with a more conscious alignment of the pupils with the teacher's traditional role. What is certain is that the pupils began to empathise more with the teacher in her task of holding the group's attention. An example of how innovative pedagogies can be slightly changed in ways that shift the students' learning outcomes was the adaptation of the 'pupils as teachers' strategy to the teaching of younger pupils rather than the teaching of peers and the teacher. This approach initially seemed to be completely in line with PELRS vision, but in practice what was learned by the pupils was much more the social skills of communicating with younger children and, rather than deepening their own understanding of what they were teaching, they were engaged mainly in revision of concepts they found relatively simple because they themselves had learnt them two or three years previously.

An important element of PELRS innovative pedagogy was the very frequent use of digital video and digital 'still' cameras as both a resource for pupils' learning and a means of collecting classroom data. It is increasingly the case that pupils come to school with knowledge and skills in shooting and editing video and this can provide an ideal way of motivating learners (Pearson 2005). During the PELRS project pupils became used to watching themselves engaging in classroom activities and this led to spontaneous comments on themselves and others, both as learners and as presenters. One group of nine pupils who made a digital video about their work for presentation to a GTC conference took a large number of 'takes' of each of the planned sequences, demonstrating a high level of concern to produce the highest possible quality of presentation. The editing work was done by one of the pupils in the group with minimal intervention from his teacher who was confident that this pupil could produce a polished end-product suitable to be shown to an external audience. To the great amusement of the conference audience when the video was shown, he added at the end a compilation of the 'out takes', which served to illustrate the group's process of self-evaluation as well as expressing their desire to be 'cool' by producing something a bit different and more fun than a straight presentation. This metacognitive element of the PELRS vision was therefore more or less a by-product of the digital imaging work that most pupils found very engaging and enjoyable, and which had very diverse applications within learning events for all ages.

The PELRS prototype practices demonstrated that the broad socio-cultural framework set out in the opening chapter of this book can provide both theoretical power and practical effectiveness in designing and implementing innovation. By changing the learning context in the classroom – changing the roles and rules and community assumptions – PELRS was able to move some way towards transforming pedagogies and learning in the current English education system. However, PELRS also revealed with great clarity the immovable barriers which prevent ICT from being used in ways that transform learning.

One of these barriers was the organisation of the school day into short time-frames which made it impossible to give pupils control over ICT resources and allow them to use the exploratory power of the Internet . This was particularly difficult in secondary schools where the constant movement of students between rooms meant that continuity of access to ICT equipment was also impossible. All innovative work in secondary schools, and much of the innovative work in primary schools, took place in special 'off-timetable' learning events.

During the first two years access to the Internet was often far from ideal. Aggressive Internet filters, set 'high' with inflexible, technical systems for blocking websites whose URLs were not recognised, sometimes made it impossible for pupils to use the Internet to access anything other than sites pre-determined by the teacher. Considerable work was then needed by the teacher to re-set the system to accept URLs of her choice in advance of the class, where this was possible, but often teachers were not given sufficient technical 'privileges' even to add their own list of URLs to those which the system 'allowed'. These problems were exacerbated by anxieties in English society, often given prominence by the media in news stories, about dangers of pupils being exposed to paedophiles or pornography on the Internet. By Year 3 most schools had more sophisticated filtering systems that allowed more sensitive discrimination between sites so that these major barriers were greatly reduced, but there is still a tension for schools in reaching a compromise between protecting pupils or engaging them in dialogue about these issues and educating them to take responsible decisions.

Innovative uses of ICT also challenge the existing ICT infrastructures which have inevitably been set up to support traditional uses. PELRS showed that, despite teachers' growing technical competence, this new style of work threw up problems which could only be overcome with expert help. As we describe it in the PELRS Summary of Research Findings:

> Many PELRS activities place demands on a school infrastructure which are not normally made by traditional learning activities. For instance multiple groups may be working with still or video images and require access to editing software and the necessary network resources to move this data around. Teachers have been creative in seeking solutions to these challenges but many also report that they need more help in solving these particular issues and in some cases a fundamental rethink of the way the school approaches its network may be needed.
>
> PELRS style work requires that pupils have control over their data and are able to save, open and access files on a long term basis. Some schools, through the provision of network space, have gone a long way to making this a reality

and giving pupils the resources needed to direct and control their independent work using ICT. In other schools, the network is limiting rather than extending the pupils' potential and this issue needs to be addressed at a school level by the relevant managers and leaders.

(GTC 2006, p. 4)

An important focus of our attention in the third year was how to scale up these prototype pedagogic practices to other schools. What was needed was a simple mechanism for putting the key elements of PELRS in place in schools which would have very little external support. Schools that joined PELRS in the third year had all responded to information about the project and an invitation to attend a workshop event at which a teacher-researcher joined Matthew and myself in presenting the PELRS vision and examples of work carried out in the first two years. The new schools were, therefore, self-selected volunteers for whom PELRS offered an opportunity to build on existing innovative work and make use of the 'permission' to make radical changes that came from being part of a project funded by the GTC. To enable them to undertake PELRS work with a much lower level of external support from Matthew, we developed a PELRS Planning Tool which acted as a kind of check-list to ensure that all the key elements of the PELRS pedagogy were included in the planning of the learning event: What national curriculum content would be taught? How many sessions would be devoted to the learning event? Which of the four pedagogic strategies would be used? How would the plenary at the beginning be organised to give the pupils choice of ICT resources? What ICT tools would be available to the pupils? Would there be any scope for them working outside class time, for example at home? How would the pupils collaborate and be able to 'influence the direction of the learning event'? The PELRS pedagogic framework diagram was also given with the Planning Tool as an aide-memoire to the introduction to PELRS work that they had been given by Matthew.

The Planning Tool worked well as a mechanism for ensuring a considerable degree of success in 'scaling up' PELRS to a larger number of schools. Schools were able to access examples of other schools' work from the PELRS website and were also supported by occasional visits from Matthew. The quality and depth of work in Year 3 was testimony to both the teachers' hard work and the good fit between the project's vision and teachers' deep-rooted desire to give their pupils the freedom to learn creatively and productively. Many older teachers told us they felt that PELRS released them to return to the innovative pedagogies they had used early in their career before the introduction of the national curriculum. Yet PELRS pedagogies were never merely a return to open-ended, unplanned project work, but remained focused on both the quality and the 'curriculum coverage' of pupils' learning. Occasional visits from Matthew remained crucially important to scaling up, however, in line with Coburn's analysis of the need to move beyond simplistic models of replication when it comes to scaling up reforms that are designed to have transformative impact (Coburn 2003).

Part II

Challenges of change

My fascination for the last 25 years has been with how change happens, its impact on myself and other human beings and the organisations within which we work, and the social mechanisms which either block or support it. This second section of the book contains two articles, published nine years apart in 1989 and 1998, between them containing many of the ideas about change that have shaped my subsequent work. The first was written to a tight word limit for publication in an edited book of papers presented at a conference and is a distillation of the findings from my first funded research project. What it contains is largely empirically derived and my line of argument is not set in the context of the contemporary research literature on change. The second was written as an invited presentation to an audience of peers in higher education as part of the consultation into the potential of ICT for Higher Education led by Niki Davis on behalf of the Dearing Review for the Higher Education Council (NCIHE 1997). Its purpose is to explore how the research literature on change could inform policy and practice for ICT use in Higher Education.

A story from the summer of 1985 may serve to illustrate both the excitement and the frustrations for me of being involved in the early years of 'micro-computers' in education. As a local English teacher I was a member of the organising committee of the Cambridge Children's Poetry Festival (an off-shoot of the main Festival) and at a gathering one evening found myself talking to one of our invited guests. He 'never had been able to understand poetry', he told me, and 'couldn't see why people needed to write things in such an obscure way'. I responded as one would expect of an English teacher, arguing for the power of poetic language and its positive impact on children's imagination and creativity. The conversation continued for several minutes and I became aware of being bored by reiterating old arguments rehearsed many times before ... and then suddenly realised that I had not actually had this conversation for several months. A year previously I had come out of the classroom and joined the Cambridgeshire support team for computers in education, which involved me in providing professional development courses for teachers introducing computers into their classrooms. The conversation I had been having frequently in the months leading up to the Poetry Festival was actually about computers not poetry – trying to respond to people who told me they 'couldn't understand computers', and 'could never see the point in using them' – for writing or anything else – when pens, paper and a slide rule were easier, quicker and more intuitive to use. I realised that poetry and computers, despite their obvious differences, were perceived as alien culturally to many people's perceptions of their own identity and sense of meaning in being in the world. It is this cultural impact on an individual's identity, together with the challenges of ICT for organisational structures, which is what most fascinates me about the process of technology innovation. Computers arouse strong passions because they challenge the ritual practices of our daily lives.

4 The human interface

Hidden issues in computer-mediated
communication affecting use in
schools[1]

Looking back ...

*During 1985–7, twenty 'Brits' and twenty Americans carried out collaborative research
into the use of computers in education as part of the UK/USA Microelectronics Seminar
(1985–7) of the National Union of Teachers (UK) and the National Educational
Association (USA). I was twinned with Alan November, then the Computer Coordinator
for Wellesley School District in Massachusetts, and our research was into the use of
electronic mail to give a 'real audience' for children's writing. Those who have come across
Alan's book,* Empowering Students with Technology, *written ten years later (November
2001), or heard him present at conferences in the USA or the UK, will understand why
this early partnership was highly formative in my own development. Small-scale funding
from BT, secured with the assistance of the NUT, was used (by bending the rules) to pay
for telephone lines, TTNS (The Times Network for Schools) email software, and expenses
to hold teachers' meetings. The findings reported in this paper encapsulate what we learnt
from research into development work that was extremely novel for the teachers involved. It
threw up all the major issues that I now know to be typical of technology innovations. In
the intervening years I have been engaged in elaborating what I learnt then rather than
disproving it in any way. At the same time as carrying out this research I was working on
the Support for Innovation Project (see the introduction to this section) and beginning to
read the research literature. While helpful, this often ignored the psychological processes of
identity construction that are always central to technology innovation. It was clear that
to understand the process of introducing computers into education a wider analysis was
needed, drawing on theories from both sociological and psychological research. Although
this chapter stands as a historical record, it still has many resonances today.*

The experience so far gained of computer-mediated communication (CMC), at least
in Britain, suggests that one of the main problems lies in getting people to use it. This
chapter is about that part of CMC which constitutes the relationship of people to the
machine. The term 'human interface' is used as a metaphor for that relationship, a
metaphor which suggests a techno-human hybrid, because that is how many people
feel about CMC. The chapter reflects on this human interface as I have observed it,
drawing on my research with the UK/USA Communications Project during 1986–7
and my continuing experience of using CMC in the course of my work (for a full

account of the former see Somekh and Groundwater-Smith 1988). The purpose of the paper is to open up discussion about how people approach CMC in order to capitalise more fully on the opportunities it provides for human communication.

The key factor in establishing an individual as a user of CMC seems to be the social context which surrounds its use. The social context is considered here under two headings: (i) the individual and (ii) the institutional, with particular emphasis in the case of the latter, on British schools.

CMC and the individual

CMC is a tool for people to use. Just like the telephone, CMC can bring people closer together. Yet, the majority don't see it like that before they use it. For many, using a computer itself does not fit their self-image; for others who are computer users the notion of communicating via a computer seems to be perverse, since communication is about human relationships in which they can see no place for a machine.

Much of human behaviour is ritualistic. We sleep on the same side of the bed, dry our bodies bit by bit in the same order after taking a bath or shower. Rituals simplify life so that departing from them takes thought and reduces time for other things. More fundamentally, though, these rituals are closely bound to our personal self-image; they symbolise the way we present ourselves to ourselves and the world. It is not just convenient to have our desk arranged in a particular way, it also indicates our acceptance or rejection of order, and some undercurrents of attitude to our work. Those few people who refuse to own cars or television sets are making proud statements about themselves and their attitude to life. So too are those who reject the very notion of using CMC. It would cut across the familiar rituals of their daily life on two counts: first it would be more time consuming (yes, it would at first) and less familiar than the telephone or letters; secondly it would cut across their self-image as non-technology people – they would not feel good about using it. What becomes crucial is that their concept of themselves as non-technology people prevents them trying out CMC; whereas only through use can they establish new rituals which make CMC integral to the social context (as has happened with radio and television).

For some whose self-image is strongly non-technological the barrier can be broken down. If the terminal literally becomes 'part of the furniture' on someone's desk it loses its cold technological aura. Then, going on-line is endowed with feelings much like those we experience when lifting mail from the doormat or pigeon-hole. Once over the initial barrier, with the system beginning to feel familiar, it is possible for individuals to reach a decision about the usefulness or otherwise of CMC. Until that time any rational decision may be impossible.

There is some confirmation of the importance of this human interface in acting as a barrier to use of CMC in the difference between the ways in which email and fax have been adopted. It seems that, almost accidentally, different patterns of use make fax fit more easily than email into existing behaviour rituals. A fax machine is often dealt with by a specialist operator, and becomes a magic device for transporting pieces of paper produced in the normal way. Email and computer conferencing by contrast are not normally filtered through operators – they demand an intimate 'hands on' relationship with the machine so that side-stepping the human interface is not possible.

In order to establish the use of CMC we need, therefore, to provide access to on-line facilities on every desk to create an environment in which individuals can adapt the machine easily to their own self-image and personal rituals. This goes further than the usual notion of 'user friendliness' and involves looking at the machine in the context of the whole personal work space. Far from reaching this ideal CMC, as it now operates in Britain, almost perversely caters to the prejudices of the non-technology self-image. We still have to key in a twenty-digit series of code in order to use JANET internationally; and we generally use systems which are command rather than menu driven, in small print, without colour, and without the support of a good on-line HELP service.

CMC in the context of British schools

When introducing CMC to a school, there is a further series of institutional assumptions and expectations which strongly affect its use.

The siting of CMC equipment

Apart from the obvious and important consideration of ease of access, there seem to be two main factors about CMC which strongly affect the siting of equipment: the link with the telephone and the high prestige value of computer hardware.

Telephones are strongly linked to emotions in British schools. They tend to be in short supply, and access to a telephone is a status symbol for teachers, as well as considerably easing their administrative tasks. Telephone bills are relatively high and difficult to justify as value for money, so telephones represent one of the items of expenditure which it is felt can and must be controlled. Siting a telephone line in a classroom, and/or giving students access to it, is therefore contrary to accepted institutional norms. Computer hardware is expensive and has high prestige value in terms of the school's public relations with parents, local industry and the community. In this context, security considerations and the perceived opportunities to enhance prestige can play a large part in deciding where to site CMC equipment.

Issues of autonomy and control

The need for teachers to establish control over their students is embedded in the culture of British schools, particularly in the secondary age range. This, together with attitudes to the use of telephones, may account for the assumption made by many teachers that they should retain responsibility for the use of CMC – by spooling their students' word-processed files, transmitting them to other schools and downloading in-coming files. This results in a considerable extra work-load for teachers which can only be handled out of school hours. In consequence, it results in major blocks in the chain of communications and loss of the vital spontaneity offered by CMC. It seems that initially teachers want to use CMC in privacy after school, so that they do not risk loss of authority and control by exposing their lack of expertise in front of students. However, a significant factor may be the ritualistic quality of their pattern of control. Once having done the 'work' by writing the word processed files, the students 'give it in' and the teachers have the responsibility of sending it off as part of the usual 'marking' procedures. Thus new technology is simply being fitted into existing rituals of behaviour in which the teachers habitually assume a controlling role through the setting and marking of work.

Assumptions about the nature of email communications

Email can be used in two different ways:

* for short on-line messages
* for the exchange of lengthier word-processed pieces.

These two types of use have considerable bearing on the nature of the communications and, although there are variations of the first pattern with software capable of downloading mail and transmitting mail in batches, these two types of communication remain quite distinct from each other. Short on-line messages tend to be written without formal patterns of addressing or signing off, without careful attention to spelling or punctuation and with an immediacy and informality half-way between a memo and a phone conversation; whereas word-processed pieces are no different from any other form of writing and adopt style and form appropriate to their purpose and audience in the normal way.

Within schools the assumption tends to be that communications will always be of word-processed files. Partly, this is because of the nexus of control and cost implications outlined above, but another significant factor may be institutional attitudes to students' work.

Writing is the main constituent of a student's classroom activity in Britain. Despite the importance of reading, listening and talking there is overwhelming evidence (see for example Bullock 1975) that students spend an inordinate proportion of their time on writing. There is an assumption that a carefully constructed piece of prose is of more 'worth' for assessment purposes than a memo, a jotting, or a short message. Consequently, teachers can see a piece of word-processed writing sent electronically as purposeful and therefore part of the curriculum. They may feel much more uncomfortable about letting a student loose to write brief notes and 'chat' on-line.

Communicating within the curriculum – issues of classroom interaction

In using email to communicate between classrooms a strong influence seems to be the nature of internal classroom interactions. Despite many ideas for joint projects, the most successful communications are often pen-pal letters, 'relay stories' (in which one group begins a story, the next continues it, and so on), and communications with an 'outside adult', perhaps taking a mystery role of some kind. In each of these examples there is little in-built conflict of purpose. Writing pen-pal letters leaves students at both ends entirely free to write as they wish. The task becomes one of interesting the unknown partner (which is not an easy one, but the parameters of pen-pal letters are familiar and students know exactly what is expected). Similarly, continuing the writing of a story begun by someone else is relatively straightforward – there may be problems of unmatched interest, but with sufficient ingenuity even an entirely unpalatable plot and characters can be subverted to a new purpose. Similarly, too, one outside adult is likely to be very responsive to students' interests.

Other tasks prove much more problematic. The stated curricula of different schools do not match, making it hard to carry out joint work on the same curriculum content. Even at the simplest level a recurring problem is delay or straight failure to reply. I have written elsewhere (Somekh and Groundwater-Smith 1988) of my realisation that classrooms are not structured around the notion of communicating interactively with others. They are closed boxes from which information can be published or into which information can be drawn, but they are not able to interact spontaneously with other closed boxes. CMC between two classrooms is a complex business – in effect team teaching at a distance – and requires extensive and detailed planning between the teachers concerned.

I should like here to elaborate on this a little. Within a typical classroom the teacher will nominally control the curriculum and activities by selecting the topics for study, planning the activities, giving out the books and resources, setting the tasks and assessing the work done. However, in reality a great deal of negotiation goes on between the teacher and students as to the level of noise, the time spent on task, and even the nature of classroom tasks and activities. The work of Doyle (1979) and others has shown that students engage in an exchange of grades for compliance in which they negotiate the level of difficulty of each task. Within this context, only the most careful planning of collaborative CMC can involve the students in both classes so that there is a real commonality of priorities for the teachers concerned. Even quite careful planning is likely to fall by the wayside if an uninvolved class doesn't like the look of the communications when they arrive. No teacher can put a responsibility to other students and another teacher in a remote classroom before the interests of those for whom s/he has a specific responsibility. It will never be worth risking violation of the fragile balance of the negotiated curriculum.

Collaborating at a distance – the human end of the human interface

In the end, even when individuals and schools come to terms with CMC and use it successfully, there remains a remoteness which makes collaboration difficult. If there is a shared purpose, as with colleagues working for the same company or on the same research project, or between a student working at a distance and his/her tutor, CMC will be an excellent addition to other available means of communication. Conversely, when there is no shared purpose at all there may be a sense of adventure in ranging across the mailboxes and making unexpected friends – lets see who's out there to 'chat' to (a kind of 'ham radio' phenomenon). For those like teachers and their students whose purposes are neither urgent nor serendipitous there is the very human problem of depending heavily on other people. On reflecting why it is that I have sometimes been so badly let down by others over CMC links between schools, I realise that it is not an uncommon experience except in that the consequences have been more serious because my reliance has been greater than normal! It is human to promise, with good intentions, to do something and sometimes to fail. With the colleagues we work with from day to day we know them well enough to gauge their dependability and will pick up the job for ourselves when we judge it will not be done after all in any other way. At a distance we do not have the same personal knowledge of colleagues and cannot gauge when our priority is slipping beneath the weight of another's work load. It has nothing to do with technology, only a human failing masquerading as part of the human interface.

Conclusion

Establishing the use of CMC is a complex process involving changes to the personal and social context of daily life. For many there is a barrier to the use of CMC in their self-image as non-technology people. Within schools, there are further institutional assumptions and rituals of behaviour which create an extra layer of complexity. Following the government initiatives which have introduced CMC equipment into British schools there are considerable opportunities to enhance learning, and it is hoped that this paper may give some insights which will enable teachers to overcome problems and capitalise on these opportunities.

5 Supporting information and communication technology innovations in higher education

Looking back ...

In 1996 I was invited to give a presentation on supporting ICT innovations in Higher Education at a consultation seminar to inform an inquiry into the future of HE in the UK. ITATL, the IT Assisted Teaching and Learning in Higher Education Project was led by Niki Davis of the University of Exeter, to advise the committee chaired by Sir Ron Dearing, whose report Higher Education in the Learning Society *was published in 1997. I drew on my experience of working with teacher educators during 1990–2 to introduce ICT into initial teacher training, and subsequently (1992–4) as an evaluator of a project developing computer-based courseware in Management Accountancy within the Teaching and Learning Technology Programme. This was a time for major change in higher education. I got involved with the Computers in Teaching Initiative Support Service (CTISS) which was a leader in providing professional development for HE teachers using technology and in 1993 joined the newly-established Association for Learning and Teaching. Presenting at the seminar gave me the opportunity of discussing my ideas with participants who were all experienced HE teachers and researchers and the article was revised for publication in the light of their feedback. I was also able to include in the published version a brief review of the major recommendations of the Dearing Report which was published in 1997.*

The changes introduced into higher education following Dearing included much greater emphasis on teaching, which in the days before 'mass' higher education had been assumed to be an unproblematic transfer of knowledge from expert to acolyte. ICT – called by Dearing C&IT – was seen by policy-makers as a means of streamlining teaching in HE and above all making it more cost-efficient. Since writing this article there have been many changes in support structures for development in HE. The Institute for Learning and Teaching in Higher Education (ILTHE) was established in 1998 and set up training courses for teaching in HE and the Learning and Teaching Support Network of 24 subject centres. Accreditation and membership of the ILTHE became a requirement for HE teachers. In 2002 the Teaching Quality Enhancement Committee (TQEC) was established and in May 2004, following publication of the Government's white paper The Future of Higher Education, *ILTHE and TQEC were amalgamated into the Higher Education Academy whose mission is focused on all aspects of policy and practice to improve 'the student learning experience' in HE.*

Preparing this chapter for publication I am struck by how many of the issues remain the same, although the kinds of technology now commonly available for teaching and learning in HE have become more sophisticated. There has been an encouraging trajectory of forward development, but stress levels remain high, and it's probably true to say that the vast majority of teachers in HE still do not make regular use of ICT in their teaching.

We can learn from research that generates theories that have explanatory power. This kind of research is seldom able to produce categorical answers to problems but it provides a depth of understanding that enables us to make decisions and take action on the basis of intelligent judgements. Most of the research on innovation, whether or not it relates specifically to ICT, has been neglected by those who took the key decisions about introducing ICT into higher education in the UK, and the inevitable consequence has been the repetition of a large number of problems and failures that could have been predicted and, with care, at least partly avoided. Before turning to the literature, there are some obvious lessons to be learnt from recent experience. First, that innovation takes time: the most successful kind of ICT use in HE institutions today is electronic mail and it was available in many universities for over a decade before it came into widespread use. Second, that innovations are always most successful when they have an obvious, practical value: in the case of electronic mail enabling effective communication within one's own organisation or to anywhere in the world at very low cost. Third, that technology innovation involves winning people over to change the way they do things and this means supporting them to try things out and talk through their ideas to enable their professional development. Fourth, that, despite the crucial importance of professional development, the top priority must be access to the technology itself. It is these last two factors that delayed the widespread use of electronic mail for ten years: in many HE institutions the facilities for email were not available, and in those where they were there was insufficient will and/or resources to enable individuals to explore its use and understand its value (and it was not very user-friendly in the days when international links could only be established if you could find a 'gateway' – i.e. a computer on the UK network that had established a protocol for the connection with that particular country).

Innovation is complex and challenging within large organisations such as universities that are part of a mass system of higher education. What interests me is how we get leverage on the organisations where we work. Can we acquire power to act if we understand more about the complexity of innovation and our own role within it? How can we act strategically? How can we think our way creatively around problems and take action which will make innovation move forward? I believe that a lot depends upon us all seeing ourselves as 'change agents' rather than merely 'users' and, finding ways to make a conscious contribution to change both in our own teaching and in the organisation as a whole.

Between 1982 and 1998 there was major investment in promoting the use of ICT in HE through initiatives such as the Computers in Teaching Initiative (CTI) and the Teaching and Learning Technology Project (TLTP). Although both had a measure of success this money could have been spent more effectively if policy-makers had been guided in their decisions by what was already well known from research about effective innovation. The evaluation of TLTP, conducted by Coopers & Lybrand, the Tavistock Institute and the London Institute of Education, was saying nothing new (Fullan 1982; Kemmis 1987; Davis 1997; Laurillard 1993; Somekh 1993) when it found that:

> ... existing products need to be embedded into teaching and leaning structures for students. This requires the addressing of issues such as cultural change within departments, time for academics to work CBL into their teaching curricula, staff development and training and even a fundamental change in the role of teachers in some higher education institutions.
>
> (Coopers and Lybrand *et al*. 1996)

Providing money for the development of courseware was not sufficient. The 'soft' factors that are essential for effective innovation also needed to be dealt with at a fundamental level.

The context of the ICT innovation – the move to 'mass' higher education in the UK

Higher education in the UK is going through a maelstrom of change and this in turn is putting pressure on those who work in the system. In market terms, these are pressures to improve productivity. Widening access means that the character and needs of the student population are changing; there are increased numbers without any additional resources, leading to larger classes and increased assessment loads; there is pressure to provide more vocational courses that equip future employees with a wider, less 'academic', range of knowledge and skills. In short, HE is subject to economic imperatives defined by government and employers. Of course, it is essential to have a system that provides value for money. The UK cannot afford to develop mass higher education without reducing the unit of cost per student. But huge increases in student numbers are not easy to manage and all kinds of other linked changes are causing new problems; for example, semesterisation has doubled the assessment load in many universities by dividing the academic year into two separately-assessed parts; and modularisation which has done away with coherent course groups, has made it more difficult to establish any depth of rapport between teacher and students, or between student and student. These things make up a higher education system which is stressful for those who work in it, and it is important to remember that this is the context in which ICT is being introduced.

The dream of policy-makers and politicians is that ICT is the answer to the problem of how to create a mass higher education system that is affordable within the national budget. The hope is that ICT will deliver more cost effective teaching and learning. As a result, the introduction of ICT into higher education has been strongly politicised. There have been huge expectations without full realisation of the difficulties that are an inevitable part of any technological innovation in education. An example of this political euphoria was the announcement in 1996 that £33 million had been awarded, by the millennium fund, to establish a multi-site University of the Highlands and Islands using ICT as a main medium of teaching. This was a visionary idea, aimed at providing higher education in their home location to students in extreme rural areas, widely separated from their teachers by moors, mountains and lochs. It was a visionary idea, but it also involved enormous complexity in establishing both the ICT networking and the changes in work practices essential for collaboration and sharing between many, many individuals in a large number of institutions.

To understand the impact upon staff of these changes in the context of higher education, it is useful to look at some of the typologies of institutional management developed by researchers. For instance, as you read you may like to consider whether you are working in a bureaucratic or a collegial institution (Hoyle 1989). To decide on the answer you would need to consider factors such as the extent to which your institution is one in which decisions are made by a small management team and implemented by passing requirements down to more junior colleagues through a line management hierarchy. Or the extent to which it is one in which decisions are made by committees that share power democratically among colleagues, through a process whereby colleagues meet in a forum for open and free debate and, through negotiation, reach a democratic decision. Of course, few if any will recognise the latter as being the way that their institution works. The so-called collegial organisational type is more likely to be one of 'restricted collegiality' (Bush 1995) where certain professors exercise enormous power in these apparently democratic committee fora and lobbying prior to the meeting is crucially important. In relation to the focus of this article, the key point is that the impact on individuals of externally imposed change is mediated by institutional culture. The experience of the ICT innovation differs widely between one institution and another. One factor in this is that differing values of institutions create different kinds of power structures. For example, the ICT innovation creates career opportunities for the 'early adopters', but these opportunities tend to be much greater in bureaucratic organisations, with line management structures, in which promotion is largely on the basis of administrative responsibility; and much more restricted in the old traditional universities where promotion is on the basis of excellence in research and scholarship.

Overlaying these traditional – and still prevalent – organisational types in higher education, the political debate within the last 20 years has moved higher education institutions more towards being kinds of enterprises. Both ideologically and in practical terms there are many forces impelling universities towards an enterprise culture. Some are recruiting students from all over the world, and staff may be spending their time crossing the globe to teach part-time masters degree courses in different countries. Some are recruiting many more mature students, often part time, and working closely with local business and industry. These changes in our system of higher education are important and exciting, but they imply a change in the culture. In particular, they do not fit easily with the pseudo-democracy of patronage and restricted collegiality. There is a need for more rapid procedures for decision-making and for systems that can support the quick action stream of the entrepreneur. In this new type of business-style organisation McNay (1995) distinguishes between two categories – the more solid 'corporation' and the more flexible 'enterprise'.

In trying to promote innovation it is important to be able to analyse this process of culture change in the organisations where we work. It helps us understand the fury that individuals often experience when they find themselves pushed by the imperatives of a different value system from the one that has underpinned their work over many years. A particularly useful analytical tool is provided by Morgan (1986), who has created a typology of organisations in terms of metaphors. Some organisations, for example, are more like a human body, others are more like a computer. How does each function? In each, the various bits of the organisation will relate to each other in very different ways. As with all typologies, the fit between an ideal type and an actual organisation is never exact, but once the appropriate metaphor is identified it is possible to analyse the organisation in considerable depth by exploring the ways in which it does or does not fit the type. This kind of analysis can have considerable explanatory power.

The key driver of organisational culture is its underpinning system of values, so that a change in culture equates with a change in values. In October 1996 a confidential report from the Higher Education Quality Council, leaked to the *Times Higher Education Supplement*, revealed a crisis among academics about the values of the system they were working within. According to the *THES*, the report said that research had found 'a considerable confusion over the nature and significance of UK first degrees'. Most academics consulted by HEQC 'seemed unclear whether a graduate today should be expected to possess the same general characteristics, specialist subject knowledge, or capacity for future development as 15 years ago'. The report concluded that there was a need for institutions to be more explicit about what achievements are being judged, the distinctive character of particular degrees, and what is the minimum satisfactory level of performance or 'threshold' standard. This crisis of confidence is an important part of the context for the ICT innovation in higher education. The uncertainty is by no means all bad. It provides an opportunity for (and is symptomatic of) redefining the nature of knowledge and breaking down the isolation of the traditional 'ivory tower' style university. Within the redefined university it is possible to give credit towards a degree not just for demonstrating conceptual 'academic' knowledge, but also for experiential knowledge acquired in the workplace, for example for the generic competencies that are an essential characteristic of expertise in management (Klemp 1977; Ebbutt 1996). As a tool for teaching and learning, ICT has the potential to support the acquisition of these new kinds of knowledge. Within the redefined university, the introduction of ICT contributes to this process of redefining the nature of knowledge and radically changing the style of teaching.

The process of innovation

There is general agreement in the research literature that innovation always takes time. Early studies reviewed by Mort (1964) showed that the likely time-span between 'the insight into a need' and 'diffusion of the adaptation' was around 100 years. House

(1974) uses the metaphor of a frozen lake to describe the inertia of the American schools system prior to 1974. The thrust of his analysis is, therefore, an explanation of the reasons why innovation is difficult and rare:

> There is an implicit order in American society basic to all else. The schools do not exist freely outside that order; they are an integral part of it. Education can deviate only in the direction and to the extent that society allows.
>
> (House 1974, p. 5)

However, there is also agreement that the process of change has been more rapid in recent years. According to both House (op. cit.) and Schön (1971) the progress of any one innovation is interdependent with the extent to which the social system as a whole is static or in flux. In the previous section I have suggested that the confusion over the purpose and underpinning values of higher education creates a context favourable to innovation. This is supported by Schön's holistic theory of organisations as interlocking, open systems:

> Social and technological systems interlock. An apparently innocuous change in technology may emerge as a serious threat to an organization because it would force it to transform its theory and structure. Technological, theoretical and social systems exist as aspects of one another; change in one provokes change in the others. And change in organizations has its impact on the person, because beliefs, values and the sense of self have their being in social systems.
>
> (Schön 1971, p. 12)

Schön's attack on bureaucracy, and on the processes of 'dynamic conservatism' (ibid., pp. 46–8) which make social systems 'self-reinforcing', reads like a rationale for the radical iconoclasm of British government policy under Thatcherism in the 1980s. Indeed it is certain that the ideas he presented in his Reith lectures on the BBC, and later published in *Beyond the Stable State*, raised considerable interest and led to wide-ranging debate.

There is also general agreement in the research literature that innovation goes through stages. According to Fullan's classic study (1982, p. 6) there are four stages:

- First the approach when the innovation becomes known to potential participants leading to a period of negotiation during which they decide whether or not to become involved.
- Then a period of adoption in which participants begin to use the new resources (a computer, for example) and make a preliminary assessment of the opportunities they offer.
- Next the implementation stage, when the innovation is put into practice: at this stage, the innovation inevitably goes through a process of adaptation which may or may not subvert its original purpose.
- Finally, if the innovation has not been rejected during any of the previous stages, comes the stage of continuation or institutionalisation, in which the innovation

becomes fully integrated with the routines of practice and achieves permanency, insofar as that is ever possible.

Fullan's research shows that many innovations fail to reach the stage of institutionalisation, and many are only partially implemented or are largely subverted to better suit the values and practices of those required to implement them. There is a pattern of passive resistance and incremental withering of the initiative. Fullan's main concern is therefore to look at the features which support innovation and enable it to overcome these barriers. For each stage he identifies likely problems and suggests strategies for tackling them drawn from research evidence. He stresses the importance of the roles of all the different players and identifies the following characteristic features of successful innovation: staff development and participation, good relationships between teachers, support from the head, a clear time-line, good communications and an internal (or local) consultant to support teachers.

In an evaluation carried out for the Scottish Office (Somekh *et al.* 1996b) we drew upon various theorists to suggest an alternative six-stage model:

- Orientation is the stage when participants seek out information about the innovation.
- Preparation comes next when participants are getting ready to begin.
- Routine is the first stage of implementation when participants establish low-level, routine use.
- Refinement is the stage when participants seek to refine and improve their use of the innovation.
- Integration is the stage when participants take steps to integrate their use of the innovation fully into their practice.
- Creative Integration is the stage when participants seek more effective ways of using the innovation, going beyond what has been achieved by others.

This is a useful model when analysing the experience of individuals, particularly in explaining why an innovation can 'get stuck' at the stage of low-level routine use; in terms of using ICT for teaching and learning in higher education, this is minimalist use without achieving any change in the nature of teaching and learning. To go beyond this stage participants need to do a lot of creative work refining their use, thinking it through, changing it, integrating it much more seriously with what they were doing before. What makes this stage both fascinating and difficult is that integration should change both sides of the equation: i.e. what was done before should be changed to integrate with the innovation, just as much as the innovation should be changed to integrate with what was being done before. It is only at the stage of integration that the innovation ceases to be an add-on. At the final stage of creative integration – which only a few will achieve – the innovation is being used in ways that have not previously been envisaged. It is this creative potential that makes the process of innovation so appealing to some people. It is common for people to experience a sense of panic in trying out new things, but some people do get a buzz out of the adventure of innovation, and providing support for those embarking upon the use of ICT innovation is partly about trying to enable them to experience a buzz rather than panic.

Since 1990 my own research has focused upon the process of innovation in organisations, and in particular upon the management and facilitation of change. In Project INTENT (Initial Teacher Education and New Technology, 1990–2) we had the opportunity to research the ICT innovation in five initial teacher training institutions over a two-year period (Somekh 1993). We identified five key concepts in successful innovation (Somekh *et al.* 1997):

1   The first key concept is 'messiness'.
     Innovation requires individuals to employ 'situational understanding' (Dreyfus 1981) in 'a non-mechanical manner' (Fullan 1991). In other words, those who manage change have to understand the complexity of the situations they are in, the power structures, and the differing motivations of the people around them. Getting inside the motivations of different people ... who owes who what ... and who couldn't possibly do something because ... is the first component of 'situational understanding' (Dreyfus 1981). Good managers of innovation read the subtext of group interactions and work with colleagues to build on current opportunities as they arise and move in the desired direction in flexible ways.

2   The second key concept is the power of individuals to make a positive contribution to bringing about change.
     According to Giddens' 'structuration theory' (1984), power resides in the meshing of individual action with organisational structures; individuals can become 'extended professionals' (Hoyle 1969) and act strategically to make a positive contribution to bringing about change (Somekh and Thaler 1997). If you think of your colleagues you will probably be able to pick out the ones who always say, 'we tried this before and it didn't work', or 'they (i.e. the managers) won't let us do it'. There is always a tendency for those who feel trapped and disempowered to say it is the fault of the people above them in the organisational hierarchy. The people above may indeed appear obstructive and difficult, because they have different motivations and hold different assumptions. But the reality is that they will not be able to constrain those who do not construct themselves as powerless. The latter will always think who they could talk to, how they could take different action, how they might be able to re-frame their purpose to overcome barriers. The outcome depends upon both the individual and the organisation; pro-active individuals confident in their own agency, despite working in an organisation which is restrictive, may be able to get more done than those in more liberal, open, flexible organisations, who construct themselves as powerless.

3   The third key concept is partnership.
     Fullan (1991) stresses the importance of developing 'shared meanings' and bringing people together to create a 'critical mass'. In Project INTENT we supported change effectively by creating non-standard partnerships between key players (Somekh *et al.* 1992). To support the development of ICT in teacher

training institutions, Project INTENT paired very senior managers with staff development officers and each carried out action research into their own roles as change agents. We found that this kind of unusual alliance between the more powerful and the less powerful in formal organisational hierarchies, is extremely creative.

4   The fourth key concept is to make teacher professional development central to the process of planning and implementing change.

The key concept here is that involvement in the process of managing change is itself an effective form of staff development. Davis (1997) presents an analysis of this integrated process of staff development and institutional development to support ICT innovation, based on her work with Project INTENT. More generally, the importance of staff development needs to be re-stated because it was so startlingly neglected in the introduction of ICT to HE during the 1980s and 1990s. For example, the first phase of TLTP put no resources into it whatsoever; and although the JISC initiative launched in 1996 presented a coherent strategy for supporting the development of ICT, it placed very little emphasis on staff development issues (they were mentioned only in the last paragraph of The Aims).

5   The fifth key concept is the integration of theory and practice.

Fullan (1991) calls the integration of theory and practice 'the desirable, elusive goal'. In a paper drawing indirectly upon my work in Project INTENT (Somekh 1995) I argue that action research provides a methodology for achieving it. Encouraging participants to research the innovation they are introducing, even in a very small way, is a powerful means of supporting their development. Exploratory action can be monitored, and change introduced in response to feedback from data that has been collected purposefully. This pre-empts any tendency to try out something new unsystematically and reach a quick conclusion that it is not worth pursuing it. Involvement in research also makes it impossible for participants to feel satisfied with low-level, minimalist use of ICT and encourages them along the path towards 'creative integration' of the innovation (see above).

Insights into the innovation process from psychological research

Theories of the self provide fascinating insights into the process of innovation. It is people working with each other and talking to each other that bring about change. What is it about people that makes change complex and difficult? What is the nature of self? Can you know yourself? Mead (1934) provides us with a theory of the self that helps us to understand why change is often experienced as a threat. His threefold model of the self incorporates the 'I' or actor/problem-solver, the self-scrutinising 'me', and the 'generalised other' of socialised group norms. Only through 'engagement' of the 'I' and the 'me' with the 'generalised other', according to Mead, does the individual 'develop a complete self':

It is in the form of the generalized other that the social process influences the behavior of the individuals involved in it and carrying it on, i.e., that the community exercises control over the conduct of its individual members; for it is in this form that the social process or community enters as a determining factor in the individual's thinking.

(Mead 1934, p. 155)

According to Mead's theory, in all our interactions with people we are shaped by their responses to an extent that can only be understood by conceiving of the 'generalised other' as an integral part of the self. As a result, the lack of confidence that we experience when we are unsure about taking on something new has the effect of undermining our self-identity (Somekh 1994a).

Freud (1986) was, perhaps, the most influential theorist of the self in the twentieth century. His own threefold model of the self comprises the id (the sub-conscious), the ego (the conscious) and the super-ego (which loosely equates to the conscience). According to this model our actions are driven to a considerable extent by patterns of behaviour developed in response to the experiences of early childhood. Because they are driven by the unconscious these behaviours are often counter to the expressed values of the individual concerned. The behaviours are very difficult for individuals to change because they originate in an underlying undercurrent of drives that they do not fully understand. A first step is for the individual to recognise the discrepancy that already exists between expressed intentions and actual behaviours and this, in itself, can be traumatic.

In considering the question of the extent to which individual selves have control over their own actions we need to look, also, at the part played by routine. Most of us who drive cars have had the experience of finding ourselves on the road for home when we set out from work with the intention of going in a quite different direction. This phenomenon of unconscious, routinised action is explained in the work of Goffman and Giddens and it helps us to understand that the participants in an innovation may have relatively little control over their habitual behaviours, with the result that they may be deeply resistant to change at a subliminal level of consciousness. Goffman describes the complex systems of conscious and unconscious role play that are integral to all human action (1959, pp. 28–82) and Giddens recognises the relationship between routinised action and self-identity, for both individuals and groups, when he writes:

Routine is integral both to the continuity of the personality of the agent, as he or she moves along the paths of daily activities, and to the institutions of society, which are such only through their continued reproduction.

(Giddens 1984, p. 60)

These rituals of routinised action provide a secure framework within which individuals and groups have a degree of freedom to develop independent, creative gestures of speech and action. A huge amount of the teaching process is done on automatic pilot and this is of great importance in enabling teachers to function effectively in the face of multiple demands on their time and attention. As well as finding it difficult to change these routines, participants in an innovation experience a sense of disorientation and de-skilling if they succeed in doing so. Confidence is bound up in a feeling of doing the job well and this is undermined when it becomes necessary to abandon the security of routinised action and develop new ways of doing things (Somekh 1994b).

Polanyi (1958) develops a theory of 'personal knowledge' that explains the integral relationship between knowledge and self. For him, knowledge is bound up in culture and traditions. He describes (ibid., p. 207) how, 'the transmission of (the) immense aggregate of intellectual artefacts from one generation to another takes place by a process of communication which flows from adults to young people'. For him this whole process is dependent upon an 'act of affiliation, by which the novice accepts apprenticeship to a community which cultivates this lore, appreciates its values and strives to act by its standards' (ibid., p. 207). As a result, much of human knowledge is 'tacit' and integrally related to an individual's values and beliefs. As teachers we act only partly on overt and expressed views, and partly on tacit understandings which, for example, may go back to the way we were taught when we were students ourselves. These tacit understandings are part of each teacher's aggregate of personal knowledge and this makes it difficult for teachers to change how they teach in order to introduce effective use of ICT.

These ideas about the integral role of the 'generalised other' in the self and the personal and 'tacit' nature of knowledge are further explained by discourse theories. In the realm of human interaction, values and theories are constructed through language and power.

According to both Foucault (1972) and Kress (1985), through using familiar patterns of syntax and semantics we indicate to each other the existence of a shared discourse which signifies our values. The more we have a sense of belonging to a group, the more we assume a shared understanding of discourse without feeling the need to define concepts with any precision, with the result that, as we interact with other members of the group through language, our self-identity appears to be affirmed.

Other theories help us to understand the interaction between personal identity and public identity. There is an element of performance in filling all roles, but for professionals there is always a demarcation between private and public, with public roles being subject to more self-imposed constraints. Teachers have a professional need to appear confident and competent in the very public fora of lecture hall and seminar room. As a result, when adopting exploratory methods of teaching, for example when introducing the use of ICT, teachers experience stress related to some loss of self-esteem. Managers experience the same stress when they introduce exploratory strategies. Elsewhere, I have explored the concept of 'multiple selves' as an explanatory theory for coping with the complexity of managing change successfully (Somekh and Thaler 1997).

These theories all help us to understand some of the underlying barriers to innovation. When ICT is introduced, what does that actually mean in terms of what it is like to be a teacher? Most people who teach have some kind of love of the job – a sense of personal meaning in what they do. Some of that will relate to their discipline, to what it is they are teaching, and what counts as knowledge in that discipline. Some of it will be what they have found useful and successful to do over the years. They may actually enjoy the way that they enter the lecture room and the way that they stand at the overhead projector. Probably they experience an intellectual payoff from preparing a lecture, a buzz from feeling that this one is going to go really well tomorrow. Probably they get a buzz from their relationships with students, and depend to a considerable extent on watching students' faces, perhaps on seeing if they can get a laugh, to provide confirmation of their own value as a teacher. The move to ICT may be very disruptive to a lot of these things. So, in asking people to adopt the use of technology in their teaching, we may be asking them to abandon a lot of what, over the years, has made teaching rewarding for them. Moreover, institutions are very territorial places. Individuals often feel a sense of ownership of the rooms where they teach. Using ICT may require them to go into rooms which are part of a more alien culture. There may be some potential loss for them in terms of their formal or informal status in the organisation.

Very importantly, the introduction of ICT requires a high level of collaboration: collaboration in course design, teaching in teams, joint development of resources and sharing of resources (Laurillard 1993). The 'not invented here' syndrome has been well documented in much of the work of the Computers in Teaching Initiative (French *et al.* 1991); it is hard to lose that creativity of deciding what you are going to do and simply accept the resources produced by other people, especially if you perceive that ICT is going to be used as an alternative to your input as a teacher, rather than perceiving yourself as having a creative role. ICT is not value neutral. Computers look as if they came out of the science or engineering laboratory, which they did, and for some people in disciplines like sociology, anthropology, and English, that may be a not insignificant barrier. For them it may be very hard to feel good about using that kind of equipment in their teaching, and working in a space whose alien feel may be reinforced by the title of 'laboratory'.

In Project INTENT we were very conscious of the specialist discourse of ICT and tried always to be aware of how the words we used might be too full of technology, too jargon ridden, and act as a barrier for colleagues; and then a member of the INTENT team with an ICT background recounted how intimidated he felt, when working with English specialists, by the 'way with words that those people had' – he felt he was being tied in knots by their language. The ICT innovation cuts across the established patterns of discourse that give members of each group a sense of meaning and identity, of belonging to a club. People instinctively feel anxious about working closely with people who use a different set of words.

Pedagogical issues central to the ICT innovation

The ICT innovation in higher education has the potential – some would say the obligation – to challenge existing pedagogical practice. If ICT is to be used effectively there are many decisions to be made.

1   Resources
     What should be the level of resources available for students? What would be cost-effective now? Should every student be required to have a personal computer? Should every student have an Internet address? In some universities they already do, but not in all. Should they all have unlimited access to the Internet ? What would that cost? Who would pay for it? Can we really talk about effective use of ICT unless learners do have that kind of level of access?

2   Tasks
     What exactly are we doing with ICT? What is the nature of the learning task? Are we replacing lectures with some kind of interactive experience, or some creative experience, or some kind of information-seeking experience? If so, are those tasks really beneficial for learning, or is some of it time consuming and not as efficient, perhaps, as the lecture, which in some senses is a very efficient way of 'one to many' teaching?

3   Teaching
     How does ICT change the nature of the teacher's role? In what ways can ICT bring new kinds of job satisfaction to teachers? How can we integrate inter-personal support for students with teaching methods that make use of ICT? What is the impact on teaching and learning if students have problems accessing the course website?

4   Course organisation
     Should the organisation of teaching change to make better use of ICT? For example, should there be fewer lectures – more self-study – enlivened and extended lectures – tutorial support for self-study – occasional small group work?

5   Assessment
     Does ICT make it possible to change assessment practices radically, for example by an increase in machine-read tests, more use of multiple-choice approaches, and more formative self-tests in addition to summative assessment? How would changes of this kind be likely to effect the kind of knowledge that is tested?

In 1992, in my role as an evaluator of one of the TLTP projects, I visited around 20 departments of business and accountancy. Amongst a whole range of difficulties, two problems seemed particularly intractable because of the way in which they challenged institutional culture. The first related to course design. I found that very few departments were prepared at that time to contemplate a radical change in the whole organisation of their teaching. It was clear that individual lecturers who were keen on using ICT in teaching were not going to be effective unless the whole structure of the course changed. Without a high-level decision and agreement on collaborative action, it was inevitable that whatever ICT course-ware was developed would be an optional extra that students could or could not use if they wanted to, in addition to the on-going course. To introduce effective use of the kind of ICT resources becoming available necessitated radical change of a kind that most of those trying to promote the ICT innovation were powerless to bring about. The second related to the fundamental purpose of assessment. Is the purpose of assessment to give feedback to students and thereby enrich their learning experience, or is assessment mainly for credentialing purposes, to sort students and categorise their level of success or failure? Most of the work on the advantages of using ICT in assessment assumes the former, but the culture and traditions of universities are deeply-rooted in the latter. There is considerable enthusiasm among academic staff for computer-assisted assessment, because of the increase in the assessment load that has resulted from the worsening staff–student ratio and semesterisation. But when it is assumed that the purpose of assessment is to categorise students' level of success and failure, the practical problems often appear insurmountable. Can you really have people sitting in a computer laboratory doing assessment on screen and ensure that they will not cheat? Can you really assess students while they have all those resources on their laptop, including access to the Internet ? Again, they might cheat by just finding the references and reading them while they are doing the exam. It is very difficult to see how there can be any radical change to the nature of learning while university – and national – culture makes these assumptions about assessment. However, it is at least helpful that the introduction of ICT is challenging this culture by introducing ways of making formative assessment a more integral part of learning. The outcomes will probably be a more balanced approach with some assessment for both purposes, but it is important for those introducing ICT to be aware of the distinction.

Towards the successful use of ICT in Higher Education: the way forward

So what can we say is successful use of ICT? To begin to grapple with this question we need to consider at least five different structural 'levels' of increasing complexity: students; individual lecturers; course teams and departments; the university as a whole; and alternative, 'virtual' higher education organisations.

First there are the individual students. Is it sufficient for all students to have basic ICT tuition? A lot of universities now provide this and make some routine demands upon students to use ICT, for example to word process assignments. At the lowest level this means that there are no longer great quantities of hand-written texts to be assessed. But clearly this is not sufficient. There is a need for advanced ICT tuition for all, coupled with integrating ICT as a resource for students' self-study. The Dearing Report (NCIHE 1997) made it clear that, despite cost, this should be our goal. With regard to tuition, recommendation 21 of the report specified that key skills, including the use of information technology, should be a specified outcome of all HE programmes. With regard to students' access to equipment, recommendation 45 suggested that students should take over some responsibility for purchasing their own equipment, with HE institutions responsible for 'negotiating reduced tariffs from telecommunications providers on behalf of students as soon as possible'; and recommendation 46 suggested that 'by 2000/1 all students should have open access to a networked desk computer, and by 2005/6 all students should have access to their own portable computer'.

Next there are individual lecturers. Is it sufficient for individual lecturers to work alone, using ICT for some aspects of a module? Again, this indicates rather a low level of use. Recommendation 9 of the Dearing Report suggested that 'all institutions should, over the medium term, review the changing role of staff as a result of communications and information technology, and ensure that staff and students received appropriate training and support to enable them to realise its full potential'. But this too, in itself, is not sufficient. Dearing also recommended (no. 42) that 'all HE institutions should develop managers who combine a deep understanding of Communications and Information Technology with senior management experience'.

It is clear that, if there is to be any major impact upon the learning opportunities of students, the next structural level, the course team or department, must be involved. This is the level at which it will be possible to plan changes to integrate ICT skills with module outcomes, and to begin to release resources to enable radical changes in teaching strategies. ICT can never be effective as an optional extra to existing pedagogical approaches; to be effective, ICT-related activities need to become an integral part of the planned delivery of modules by a department or team, requiring students to carry out ICT-related tasks as an obligatory part of their learning.

This, in turn, has implications for re-structuring of universities. This is a matter not only for Vice-Chancellors and senior managers of universities, but for HEFCE and the other funding bodies. The MacFarlane report (CSUP 1992) recommended that there was a need for an overviewing body with the power to require individual universities to have action plans for using ICT effectively, in order to make radical changes to teaching provision and achieve significant gains in students' learning. Laurillard (1993) provides a comprehensive framework which involves everyone in the system working together to use ICT effectively to support learning. Its strength is that it allocates responsibilities to all the stakeholders, from HEFCE, Vice-Chancellors and key University Committees, through departmental heads and course leaders, to individual lecturers and students. A similar approach is suggested by Ford (1996), whose 'learning environment architecture', provides a very similar framework for managing change across a whole university.

The Dearing Report's recommendation to establish an Institute for Teaching and Learning in Higher Education went some way to enabling major structural and cultural changes of this kind to take place. To an extent, for example, it tackled the crucial issue of resources, recommending (no. 15) that the Institute should 'co-ordinate the national development of computer-based learning materials' and 'promote the development of computer-based materials to provide common units or modules, particularly for the early undergraduate years'. In this way ILTHE was intended to become the 'overviewing' body recommended by MacFarlane.

The TLTP Evaluation Report provided a measured assessment of what HE could expect to achieve, based on evidence from the TLTP experience:

Transferability and increased productivity are most likely to be met:
- where there are large first year classes
- where there are very different levels of preparation amongst students
- where there are common curricula across a large number of institutions

- where students can be exposed to something that they would not otherwise experience in their teaching
- where experiments require expensive equipment or are time-consuming in the use of facilities.

(Coopers and Lybrand et al. 1996)

The message is clear that, without the large-scale re-structuring and wide-ranging management of resources suggested by Laurillard (op. cit.), MacFarlane (CSUP 1992) and Ford (op. cit.), ICT will only be used in relatively minimalist ways. The TLTP evaluators pointed the way to those aspects of traditional university teaching where the benefits would be immediate and obvious: CAL software to deliver low-level teaching to large numbers of students, individualised courseware to cope with widely disparate educational needs within the same group, delivery of mainstream teaching in those exceptional cases where there is already agreement on a common curriculum across all universities (such as with professional accountancy courses), and simulations of various kinds to enable coverage of topics that would be too dangerous or expensive to be covered in any other way.

Undoubtedly, the TLTP Evaluation Report was realistic, given the complexities of the process of change outlined earlier in this paper. However, what is realistic is clearly also insufficient to meet the needs of a mass higher education system as envisaged by Dearing. In this article, I am suggesting that change of a much more radical kind is possible if we adopt strategies that build upon what we know about the successful management of change. In particular, the research literature on the process of innovation and related psychological and pedagogical factors provides powerful explanatory theories which should inform policy-making at every level.

Part III

Challenges of policy and practice

The exploration of the process of innovation now continues, but whereas Part II was concerned with looking at technology change for individuals, and the way they experience it in their organisations, Part III is concerned with the role of policy in introducing ICT to change the education system as a whole. Policy always has a difficult line to tread, between setting a vision which may be over-ambitious, or one which is over-cautious and reduces possible achievements to a low-level common denominator.

The two articles included in this section both present analyses of the state of ICT innovation in English education at the time of writing. The first was presented as a lecture soon after the election which brought 'New Labour' to power in 1997 and reviews policy visions and the extent and quality of their implementation from 1980 to the change of Government. It ends with a 'futuring' prediction of the changes ICT might bring about in schooling by 2010, if three barriers relating to cost of technology, the 'control' function of schools, and cultural reproduction could be overcome. The second was written for inclusion in a special issue of the *Technology, Pedagogy and Education Journal* on 'Research into Information and Communication Technologies' and is, perhaps, partly driven by frustration that by 2004 my predictions were not half way to being fulfilled. Nevertheless, its purpose is not to ridicule policy failure but rather to urge a more pro-active role for educational researchers in building scenarios for change and supporting the process of radical rather than incremental reform.

6   New technology and learning

Policy and practice in the UK,
1980–2010

Looking back ...

This article was originally written for presentation as my inaugural professorial lecture at the University of Huddersfield in 1998. In its original form it was illustrated with visual material, such as the Research Machines advertisement for multimedia work stations from the early 1990s, and demonstrations of software, for example talking books and an interactive simulation of dragster racing to teach calculus. These were replaced by written descriptions in the published version.

I had had personal experience of almost all the ICT policy initiatives between 1980 and 2000, for example as a teacher seconded to MEP to work on early software development for the BBC Acorn computer, as a training provider with NCET for ESG Advisory Teachers, and as an evaluator of the Department of Trade and Industry's Micros in Schools Schemes in the 1980s and the Education Departments' Superhighways Initiative (EDSI) in the 1990s. This made the interface between policy and practice an obvious choice of topic for my inaugural lecture.

Although a projection is given for spending on the National Grid for Learning (NGfL), the article does not really engage with the major shift in policy for ICT in education that took place after 1997. The report of the Independent Inquiry chaired by Dennis Stevenson, commissioned by the Labour Party prior to its election, recommended that all young people should have basic competence and confidence in using ICT for their learning and teachers should be able to use it routinely in their daily work. The vision was 'to see a society within ten years where ICT has permeated the entirety of education (as it will the rest of society) so that it is no longer a talking point but taken for granted – rather as electricity has come to be' (Stevenson 1997, p. 4). The National Grid for Learning was the flagship policy initiative between 1998 and 2002, responsible for major investment in new hardware and Internet connections in schools (Harrison et al. 2002; Somekh et al. 2002a). It was replaced by the ICT in Schools Initiative (2002–5) which focused more on integrating the use of ICT within classrooms, including the Curriculum Online Initiative which gave schools e-Learning Credits (NCSR 2006); the ICT Test Bed project which explored the impact of high levels of ICT resources on school improvement in areas of major social deprivation (Somekh and Underwood 2007); and the provision of Broadband connectivity (Underwood et al. 2005). There were two major initiatives to give teachers their own personal computers to assist with accessing resources, preparation and administration (IES 2002; Cunningham et al. 2003). Between 2003 and 2005 there was major investment in interactive whiteboards which were taken up enthusiastically, particularly by primary schools (Higgins et al. 2005; Somekh et al. 2007). At the time of writing this book, funding for ICT has been integrated with the main funding allocations to schools 'to increase schools' flexibility and autonomy, as well as reduce bureaucracy' (Becta 2006). In addition, ICT is a key component of the Building Schools for the Future (BSF) initiative which is investing around £3 billion in building new schools as well as maintaining and improving existing school buildings.

When this lecture was presented in October 1998 it was introduced by the music of Elvis Presley. I wanted to play Elvis's music because it illustrated the first of two revolutions that I feel myself to have lived through. As a small child, the difference between songs like 'Sugar bush I love you so' and Bill Hayley's 'Rock around the clock', followed shortly by the music of Elvis, was literally mind-blowing. And as an adult and a secondary English teacher, with virtually no education in science, the introduction of computer-based technology into my life, both at home and at school, was revolutionary. My first computer, purchased in 1981, was a BBC Acorn 8-bit machine with 32k of memory, onto which software had to be loaded from a tape-recorder. However, from the beginning there was a strong sense that something more powerful was just around the corner, and from 1984 onwards computers were to change the whole direction of my career.

My research on new technology and learning has been an obsession and a passion for over 14 years, so it was difficult to decide what to include in a paper that I intended should summarise my thinking. In the end, I decided to focus mainly upon issues relating to policy and practice in schools with some cross-references to higher education. The chapter is divided into three parts:

1   The politicised nature of policy for new technology in education in the UK.
2   Key issues from my research on new technology and learning.
3   Speculations on reorganising schooling with the help of new technology.

The term New Technology, which includes the full range of computer-based technologies and telecommunications, including telephone and fax, is used to avoid the difficulty of the current situation where different terminology is used for the same thing in different educational sectors and countries (e.g. IT, ICT, C&IT, NTIC, NICT, NIT). Perhaps the explanation for this variation is that we are constantly striving for terminology which expresses the newness and revolutionary nature of this rapidly developing technology.

The politicised nature of policy for new technology in education in the UK

The introduction of new technology into education has been a key component of government policy since around 1980. The ambition of Ministers for what new technology could achieve has been – and continues to be – on a grand scale. In 1995, when Michael Heseltine launched the Superhighways initiative, he said it 'would help with the vital task of keeping Britain competitive in the 21st century'. In 1997, when Tony Blair launched the National Grid For Learning, he said:

> Technology has revolutionised the way we work and is now set to transform education. Children cannot be effective in tomorrow's world if they are trained in yesterday's skills. Nor should teachers be denied the tools that other professionals are trained to take for granted. Standards, literacy, numeracy, subject knowledge – all will be enhanced by the Grid and the support it will give to our programme for schools improvement.

The persistence of this ambition has, perhaps, been one of the most interesting phenomena. David Blunkett and Tony Blair are just as committed to it as were Kenneth Baker and Lord Young in the mid-1980s. There have been achievements but they have never matched the dream. The dream has been no less than the solution to fundamental educational problems: how to individualise learning opportunities, to raise achievement for all to significantly higher levels, and to provide high-quality mass education at a cost the country can afford. Since educational achievement is linked to economic success, the ambition has gone beyond school itself to encompass the future economic well-being of the country. At a symbolic level, new technology has been attractive to politicians for its connotations of modernity, scientific advance, and the world of business and commerce. I believe it is not fanciful to say that politicians have taken possession of the new technology image and offered it to the electorate as a talisman. This has been both in the figurative meaning of a talisman as 'something that acts as a charm or by which extraordinary results are achieved' (SOED 1933) and to an extent as an object which it is propitious to possess – much as a Chief Executive of a company might wish to have a powerful computer on his or her desk, regardless of whether it is actually used. The point is illustrated by comparing a Buddhist prayer charm, taken from the Thangboche monastery, Solo Kumbu, in Nepal, with an advertising leaflet produced by Research Machines in about 1992. The prayer charm surrounds the central Buddha in the Stupa (or tower shrine) with auspicious symbols, syllables and deities. The advert, similarly, surrounds the central Multimedia Work Station with images of human aspiration and achievement. It plays to the politicians' dream, and the dream of all potential purchasers through these images which include a high-jumper in flight, a praying figure from a stained glass window, Shakespeare's famous words from Hamlet, 'To be or not to be', and a space rocket on the launchpad. It invokes the idea of obtaining the unobtainable by introducing multimedia with Neil Armstrong's famous words when he stepped onto the surface of the moon; and it invokes modernity and technological achievement by setting all the images against a backdrop of the world seen from space.

The development of policies, implementation strategies and infrastructures has taken place against this backdrop of political aspiration with its attendant urgency. The major initiatives for schools have been:

- The Microelectronics in Education Programme, 1980–6, £32 million.
- The Micros in School Schemes, 1981–4, £15.1 million from the Department of Trade and Industry. (Note: during the 1980s the DTI continued to provide funds for purchase of hardware, and occasionally software, on an annual basis from 'end of year' surplus.)
- The Technical and Vocational Educational Initiative, 1983–7, £240 million from the Employment Department. (Note: during this period the ED also co-funded occasional projects with the DES.)
- The Microelectronics Education Support Unit, 1986–8, later merged with the National Council for Educational Technology, 1988–98, £5 million annually.
- The Education Support Grant for England, 1987–93, £90 million. Further funding since 1993 within the Grants for Educational Support and Training (GEST) scheme.
- Multi-media computers in primary schools, 1992–5, £10 million.
- The Education Departments' Superhighways Initiative (EDSI), 1996–8, £10 million of sponsorship 'from industry and other sources', and an evaluation funded by the four education departments of the UK.
- Multimedia laptops for teachers: pilot project, 1996–8, £4 million to supply 1,400 teachers; main phase, 1998, £23 million to supply 10,000 teachers and heads.
- The National Grid for Learning, phase one 1998–9, £100 million for hardware, software and Internet connections for 8,000 schools. Predicted by 2002 to be more than £700m for infrastructure, services and content.
- Training for teachers and librarians, 1999–2002, £230 million from the New Opportunity Fund.

A considerable amount has been achieved. MEP, for example, was a major initiative with a national infrastructure. It developed software and training materials for distribution to all LEAs for sale at heavily subsidised prices, and established a base of personnel with expertise, either directly or through the support structures it generated in LEAs and the small software companies it spawned (Fothergill 1987). Although it illustrated all too well the destructive long-term impact on any industry – but perhaps particularly the software industry – of initial subsidy which creates false market expectations, MEP built a reputation for the UK in the mid-1980s as a world leader in the field of computer use in schools. The Micros in Schools Schemes supplemented the work of MEP by half-funding the purchase of BBC Acorn, RM or Sinclair computers by schools. I remember, at the time, that Jon Coupland of the College of St Mark and St John at Plymouth likened the initiative to asking teachers to climb the Eiger with only one 'pump' instead of climbing boots. Nevertheless, it got things started (MacDonald *et al.* 1988). Because of the DTI offer, all secondary schools and practically every primary school in the country had a computer by 1986. By 1994, primary schools had on average 10 computers compared with 2.5 in 1988; and secondary schools had on average 85 computers compared with 23 in 1988. More recently, the Superhighways Initiative (Scrimshaw 1997) was successful in interesting some major new technology companies in the potential commercial benefits of supporting schools' use of the Internet, and this resulted in the policy and early implementation of the National Grid for Learning (DfEE 1997), described by BECTA as 'a framework for a learning community designed to raise standards and improve Britain's competitiveness, and which embraces schools, colleges, universities, libraries, the home and the workplace' (BECTA 1998). By 1997/8, the average student:computer ratio in secondary schools was 8:1 and in primary schools 13:1, while Internet connections had leapt from 83 per cent to 93 per cent in secondary schools and from 17 per cent to 62 per cent in primary schools. Peter Scrimshaw, in a paper presented to the 1998 British Educational Research Association conference, likened New Labour's NGfL policy to a cross between 'Beef on the Bone[1]' and the Millennium Dome[2]', because on the one hand it sets out to control teachers and teaching through the production and dissemination of guidance documents and teaching materials (see for example The Standards Site and the Virtual Teachers' Centre), and on the other it promises to be 'big, very big' but without any clear idea of what exactly it will contain. Nevertheless, the NGfL is certainly currently one of the most ambitious policies of its kind in any European country.

Despite successes, mistakes have been made and, from my own point of view as a researcher, it has been disappointing that so little account was taken of research evidence when setting up the early initiatives. Many of the problems were predictable on the basis of research and evaluation work on similar initiatives previously undertaken (House 1974; MacDonald and Jenkins 1979). In particular, it was predictable that the over-emphasis on hardware at the expense of teacher training would greatly reduce the effectiveness of new technology use in schools. In some cases, such as the 1986 end-of-year windfall offer from the DTI of a modem with 1,200 baud rate to every secondary school,[3] money was certainly completely wasted. There was also a tendency to want tangible success in an unrealistic time frame and to blame project personnel when this did not materialise; this, in turn, led to a preference for funding those whose inexperience made them sanguine about taking on impossible tasks (Norris *et al.* 1990).

Meanwhile, the responsibility for developing policy and an infrastructure for its implementation, appears to have been an arduous one. Civil servants at the Department for Education and Science (DES) were apparently disappointed with the outcomes of MEP, since the Final Report of the Director was suppressed. The strain for the DES of failing to deliver what they had promised to Ministers continued to be manifested in bad relations with a series of Programme and Agency Directors over the next ten years. Key personnel were blamed for failing to deliver over-ambitious or ill-conceived policies and new, less-experienced people were brought in because they were prepared to offer more than could actually be achieved. The Microelectronics in Education Support Unit (MESU) was set up in 1987 but only a year later its Director was demoted when MESU was merged with the existing Council for Educational Technology to form the National Council for Educational Technology under the Directorship of a former civil servant at the DES. This Director was himself removed from office at short notice in 1994, after a lengthy period of dispute with the Department and the Council over the medium-term plan. The new Director, brought in from British Telecom, left office early in 1997, again after a period of disagreement with the Department (by then the Department for Education and Employment). A lengthy period of reassessment, following the change of government in 1997, led to the creation, in March 1998, of the British Education and Communications Technology Agency (BECTA) to replace NCET. We can only hope that its Chief Executive, who was formerly Head of an innovative, technology-rich primary school, will fare better.[4]

In addition to developing policy without drawing upon research evidence, during the 1980s the Department of Education and Science and, for the most part, the Department of Trade and Industry, avoided commissioning evaluation studies of their new technology initiatives (MacDonald 1992). The Department of Employment was the exception and in cases where they co-funded initiatives with the DES relations with the evaluators were strained (Norris *et al.* 1990). It was a case of 'shooting the messenger'. In the interests of public learning and ensuring good value for the spending of public money, the absence of evaluation was short-sighted in the extreme, if not negligent. Fortunately, however, the situation began to change in the new decade. Between 1989 and 1992, the DES funded 'an evaluation of the impact of information technology on children's achievements in primary and secondary schools' (Watson *et al.* 1993). In 1993, the National Council for Educational Technology, itself funded by the DES, called a meeting of researchers and invited our help to produce a booklet, *IT Works* (NCET 1994b), which presented the outcomes of research, supported by evidence. Thereafter, the NCET Research Consultative Group met two or three times a year at NCET to discuss policy and research outcomes. By this means, between 1993 and 1998, NCET built up trust with the research community and began to commission evaluations of all its major development projects. The stresses were not all removed – notably, the Chief Executive of NCET's formal endorsement of the outcomes of the evaluation of Integrated Learning Systems (ILS) (Underwood *et al.* 1994) was a significant factor in the disagreement with the Department that eventually led to her departure in 1997. However, the evaluation of the Education Departments' Superhighways Initiative (EDSI), 1996–7, provides us with a positive example of the Department and NCET working together with a large team of evaluators to produce results which appear to have genuinely informed and influenced policy development. As the evaluator of the two EDSI projects in Scotland, I experienced some of the stresses of producing a report to a very tight framework in a strongly politicised context that made it impossible to address properly the needs of local project teams. A great deal depended upon the skill and sensitivity of the synoptic evaluator, Peter Scrimshaw. Nevertheless, it was very pleasing to read the consultation paper on the National Grid for Learning and see all the major problematic issues arising from the EDSI evaluation clearly identified and analysed on the basis of EDSI evidence.

The same tensions, of course, arise when evaluating new technology initiatives in Higher Education. The discontinuity of policy between the Computers in Teaching Initiative (CTI) and the Teaching and Learning Technology Project (TLTP) ('we got the wrong people last time'[5]) and the long delay in appointing a co-ordinator for TLTP nearly a year after phase 1 projects were set up ('no need to waste money on support as CTI has done'), followed by his early departure and replacement by a civil servant ('these academics need sorting out'), and the failure to commission any evaluation of phases 1 and 2 of TLTP until the very last moment ('all we need to know is how many hours of bums on seats'), is all too reminiscent of what has happened in schools. In 1994 there was a grave danger that TLTP would never be evaluated, probably because of a fear that it might indicate a considerable waste of public money. If it was to be evaluated, who would have the credibility to produce an honest report which could not be side-lined by the Board, the Department and politicians. I was consulted at the time by someone from HEFCE and suggested that the only way of proceeding with confidence was to commission an evaluation by a team of two or three organisations, including at least one which was independent of Higher Education. The evaluation that was finally carried out by Coopers and Lybrand, the Tavistock Institute and the University of London Institute of Education provides a fair assessment of the problems of embedding new technology in the Higher Education system if insufficient attention is paid to bringing about cultural change (Coopers and Lybrand *et al.* 1996). It is clear that this evaluation was influential in Dearing's thinking about infrastructure and strategy when drawing up suggestions for making the best possible use of new technology in Higher Education (NCIHE 1997) (see Chapter 5 of this book).

Key findings from research on new technology and learning

The research I carried out in classrooms in schools between 1984 and 1990 was case study work, involving teachers as co-researchers, and using action research methodology. My first study was of children's use of word processing to write 'long stories' in my own classroom, using alternative keyboarding devices, called Quinkeys, that enabled four children to sit round the computer and write simultaneously on their own section of the screen (Somekh 1985). This work was carried out for my Masters dissertation in 1984. Shortly afterwards, between 1985 and 1987, I had funding for a small-scale project linking schools in Cambridgeshire with schools in Wellesley School District, Massachusetts (see Chapter 4 of this book). English teachers in two secondary and two primary schools worked with me to investigate the impact of email on children's writing. We focused, in particular, on whether writing in an authentic context, i.e. for 'a real audience', would improve the quality of children's work (Somekh and Groundwater-Smith 1988). International email connections in those days before the Internet were difficult, unless you had access to the Joint Academic Network, which the schools did not. We also attempted to link the Cambridgeshire schools to a kibbutz in Israel, but this proved, ultimately, to be impossible as the kibbutz did not have adequate access to the technology.

More recent evaluation studies of Argyll and Bute's Modern Communications for Teaching and Learning initiative and Nothern College Aberdeen's Superhighways Teams Across Northern Scotland (Hall *et al.* 1997), as well as a preliminary scoping study for the Apple Classroom of Tomorrow (ACOT) initiative in Scotland (Somekh *et al.* 1996a), have shown that some of the outcomes of this early research were generic, remaining just as true today, despite the enormous changes in the power of the technology.

First, the presence of new technology in a classroom has the potential to change the culture of the classroom and the relationship between teacher and students. In my very first study of word processing, I had to change the way in which I organised my teaching. The logistics of one computer, 30 children and five 40-minute periods a week immediately required the 'long stories' to be written by collaborative groups. Next I found I had to change my approach to the assessment of collaborative work, because this was more fully collaborative than previous so-called collaborative projects in which the contribution of individual children could be identified by their handwriting. Then, I had to abandon my practice of having periods of silent working because the four children writing at the computer needed to be in constant communication with other members of their group. I could, of course, have used the one computer for isolated work, with individual children working at self-contained programs that they could manage easily without assistance. Such an approach was often used in schools at the time, on the basis that 'hands-on experience' (simply touching the computer) was valuable skills training, but it was a trivial use of such a powerful tool. Any genuine attempt to integrate new technology with the learning tasks (work) that a teacher asks children to undertake, has the effect of changing the culture of classrooms. The effect can be negative, of course, as in many cases in secondary schools or higher education in which groups work in a specialist computer room for short periods of time on tasks that are unrelated to the rest of their course of study.

New technology's potential to change the culture of the classroom and the relationship between teacher and students is important, since traditional classrooms are not ideal learning environments. In the ideal learning environment teachers would work with individuals or very small groups. Teaching large groups involves skilled management and the exercise of power or charisma (which is a form of power). Jackson's seminal work, in the late 1960s, showed that teachers in classroom are primarily concerned with 'achieving and maintaining student involvement in (a set of) activities' while children learn early in their school lives to accept 'delay, denial, interruption, and social distraction' (Jackson 1968, p. 162). The focus upon learning is difficult to sustain. Doyle's work, in the late 1970s, showed that children become skilled at negotiating the tasks that teachers set them to do through a process of 'exchanging performance for grades' and that this leads to many classroom tasks being 'busy tasks' which do not involve any learning at all (Doyle 1979). It is, therefore, of major importance that new technology offers the opportunity to change the dynamics of classrooms. It changes the focus of attention, so that all eyes are no longer on the teacher and it offers the possibility of one-to-one interaction between child and screen, and a culture which is freer and less intense, in which the teacher can much more easily adopt the role of facilitator of learning. In this culture teachers' supervisory responsibilities are reduced because children take more responsibility for their own learning, and it becomes possible for teachers to engage in one-to-one discussion with individual children to take their thinking forward.

However, new technology tools require both students and teachers to work in new ways if they are to make any significant impact on learning. Word processors, for example, are powerful tools for supporting higher-order writing skills such as revising and refining a text organically, re-structuring it to maximise its impact, or tailoring it for different audiences, but the majority of students, regardless of age, will initially use a word processor only to correct spelling and punctuation and add more writing at the end. Despite the efforts of those who teach the Graves (1983) approach to writing, which emphasises experimentation, drafting and re-drafting, the habit of starting writing from the beginning and working through to the end without amendment, is deeply ingrained from an early age. A word processor can only become a useful tool when its special features (affordances as a tool, see Wertsch 1998, p. 29) are put to use. These features need to be taught to children, for example by a teacher demonstrating their power in group writing sessions around a big screen. Devoting more time to collaborative tasks is another change in the way of working that makes use of the strengths of new technology. Groups gathered around a vertical screen can compose together, with one at the keyboard, much more easily than they can do when using paper. Students in different schools, or countries, can produce and edit a single text, transferring it back and forwards between them sufficiently quickly for both to retain ownership and enthusiasm. However, collaboration depends not on technology but on relationships. Collaborative writing between children at the two ends of Cambridgeshire was initially just as difficult to establish as collaborative writing between children in the USA and Cambridgeshire (Somekh and Groundwater-Smith 1988). The big difference came when the Cambridgeshire children met each other. After one meeting, collaboration became much more meaningful. In exactly the same way, children in a year group of one in small primary schools on the Island of Mull could gain peer support from working collaboratively using video conferencing and other new technology, particularly in the year before they transferred to secondary schools, but a face-to-face meeting made all the difference as a starting point (Hall *et al.* 1997). Collaboration also depends upon planning, particularly when it is collaboration between whole classes of children and their teachers. A classroom is, as I have already said, a site for the exercise of power and negotiated agreements. Class and teacher, together, are a closely bonded group with loyalties and responsibilities to one another. For collaborative projects to be possible between groups of children in two different countries, the two teachers need to plan very carefully so that the project fits the needs of both environments (curriculum, learning outcomes, assessment system, teaching style). Such projects need to be addressed as team teaching initiatives (see Chapter 4 of this book).

Between 1988 and 1990 I led an action research project in 24 schools in Cambridgeshire, Essex and Norfolk, funded by the National Council for Educational Technology in collaboration with the three LEAs (Somekh 1997). The Pupil Autonomy in Learning with Microcomputers project (PALM) sought to combine computer-mediated curriculum development and teacher professional development in a single action research process. It had two aims:

- to work in partnership with teachers to research the role of IT in developing pupil autonomy in learning;
- to investigate the effectiveness of action-research as a means of teacher professional development in the IT innovation.

Action research methodology is particularly suited to studies of innovations that have only been partially implemented. Traditional research studies of the use of new technology in classrooms nearly always produce outcomes that appear to indicate its worthlessness, on the basis of very poor test sites. For at least three reasons, action research involving researchers working in partnership with teacher-researchers ensures that the test sites are worthy of study and the outcomes are useful. First, action research involves teachers in the design of the study, so that they are aware of the parameters of the research; there is, therefore, no possibility that they will misunderstand the purposes of the innovation, and the research can test in a meaningful way whether the envisaged outcomes are feasible and worthwhile. Second, action research allows teachers to use the initial outcomes of the research as the basis for making changes in the way in which they are using new technology; there is, therefore, an in-built process of improvement and staff development and towards the end of the study it becomes possible to evaluate the impact of changes in the teachers' implementation strategies. Third, teachers' participation as co-researchers ensures that the research is informed by teachers' practitioner knowledge (Elliott 1993), and is much less likely to reach conclusions that take no account of the culture of teachers and schools. Action research studies are, therefore, much more likely to be the basis for recommendations that can be easily put into practice (Somekh 1995).

The PALM research showed that new technology has the potential to transform the learning process, provided teachers adopt new ways of working. The 34 studies by teachers published in the Teachers' Voices series (PALM, 1990/1), together with the extensive data collected by the full-time research team, formed the basis for developing a dynamic model for a transforming pedagogy for IT. It contains seven 'dimensions of pedagogic change' and 29 teacher and student competences, the latter divided into general and computer-related competences (Somekh and Davies 1991). In writing this paper I have gone back to this framework and mapped it against the outcomes of my subsequent research into new technology and learning in Higher Education, specifically, the Initial Teacher Education and New Technology project (INTENT), 1990–2, funded by NCET in collaboration with five initial teacher training establishments[6] (Somekh 1993); and the evaluation of one of the first phase TLTP projects in Business Education and Accountancy, 1992–4, funded by HEFCE. I suppose I should not have been surprised to find that there is a considerable degree of overlap. To show this I will take six themes from the PALM framework, and discuss them in relation to learning in both schools and HE, illustrating them with brief demonstrations of new technology resources.

1   *On changes in the roles of teacher and learner*
    The teacher is no longer sharply separated from the student by role, with one imparting knowledge and the other imbibing it. Instead: 'There is … an understanding that teaching and learning are independent aspects of a single activity' (Somekh and Davies 1991, p. 156). Teachers 'cast themselves in the role of a learner or co-learner at the same time as that of a teacher' (op. cit., p. 158). This follows naturally from the power of new technology as a rich source of information. No longer able to control the information that enters

the classroom, teachers can no longer be expected to be experts on every subject that students may raise. In addition, they are frequently less knowledgeable than their students about the technology itself. The resulting shift in roles supports more autonomous learning and enables teachers and lecturers to become facilitators of learning which greatly increases the possibility of engaging in in-depth discussion with individual students on areas of conceptual difficulty. This directly supports the process of 'scaffolding' students' learning which enables students to move beyond their current level of achievement into their 'zone of proximal development' (Vygotsky 1986, p. 187). A good example of a new technology resource that supports this shift is the CD-ROM of the National Gallery complete illustrated catalogue (National Gallery 1997) which is also available on its website: www.nationalgallery.org.uk (accessed 8/8/06). In addition, there is some evidence that interactive software can itself take on the role of providing 'scaffolding'. To achieve this, software designers need to concentrate on developing an interactive environment that stimulates reasoning and is responsive, for example by displaying the outcomes of choices made by the student.

2   *On a new conception of the role of technology*
The teacher conceives of the role of technology in a new way: 'It is neither a tutor nor a tool (but instead) ... is part of a complex of interactions with learners, sometimes providing ideas, sometimes providing a resource for enquiry, and sometimes supporting creativity' (op. cit., p. 157). This new understanding of the technology itself is essential if it is to be used effectively in teaching and learning. Teachers in PALM typically went through a three-stage process of deepening their understanding of the role of new technology. They began by conceptualising the computer, with its software, as a tutor that would instruct students, with no additional role for the teacher. They moved on to conceptualising the computer, with software tools, as a neutral tool that students could use to carry out the same kinds of tasks that they could do with paper and pen. Finally, some but by no means all of them, conceptualised the computer as a cognitive tool that could be used by students in a wide range of different ways, enabling them to take on new tasks that could not have been done in the same way without technology. Action research, because of the emphasis it placed on experimentation and evaluation, was important in ensuring that they did not remain 'stuck' at one of the first two levels (Somekh 1997). In his role as evaluator of NDPCAL, my former colleague, Barry MacDonald, likened new technology to a Trojan horse, that comes into the walls of an educational organisation, and then without warning focuses attention upon learning and the effectiveness of teaching. In higher education, as in schools, many teachers initially assume that the computer is a kind of teaching machine. Moreover, we found clear evidence in Project INTENT that senior managers had initially little or no understanding that new technology had the potential to make a fundamental impact on the quality of learning. They tended to see it as an expensive luxury which was being promoted by enthusiasts out of self-interest (Somekh *et al.* 1997). While the enormous increase in interest in teaching and learning in higher education has

been led by teaching quality assessment, the CTI and TLTP initiatives have been very influential in raising awareness of the important ways in which lecturers can use new technology creatively to improve the quality of students' learning opportunities.

3   *On the changes that new technology enables teachers to make in the nature of tasks*
The teacher 'recognises the opportunities computers bring to shift the balance of students' activities from laborious tasks to higher level tasks' (op. cit., p. 158). This shift in the nature of tasks results from technology's ability to take on the time-consuming, inauthentic jobs that normally occupy students, happily, for long periods of time. Drawing graphs is a good example of such an inauthentic task. The computer's facility in producing graphs quickly enables much more time to be spent on the interpretation of the graph. This can pose a problem for teachers in traditional classrooms as the higher-level task of interpretation is more difficult for students and may not occupy them so happily for such a sustained period of time. This is, therefore, one of the areas where interactive software, supporting interpretation, could be particularly helpful.

We know that translating information between different symbol systems such as spoken and written language, number, algebraic expressions, various kinds of graphs and diagrams, is one of the most important skills that learners need, and one of the most difficult to acquire (Kozma 1991). Some young children have great difficulty learning to read, and talking book software, such as Living Books (1994) *Tortoise and the Hare* CD-ROM, can help them by synchronising the spoken text with sequential highlighting of the written words. A large number of students of science and mathematics of all ages have difficulty in accurately assimilating the meaning from equations, graphs and diagrams, and this is almost certainly a major factor in the large numbers that abandon study of these disciplines at an early age or drop out at university. New technology has been used with great success to produce dynamic graphs that change on screen when changes are made to the equation they represent. It seems that this is an area which is particularly helpful in higher education because of the difficulty that experienced mathematicians and scientists sometimes have in appreciating that students may not have already acquired these skills. A good example of software that supports the translation of concepts is *Calculus Connections* (Quinney and Harding 1996). This is a particularly interesting example as, in some sections, the learner can progress from an initial video demonstration of calculus 'in action' (e.g. of a dragster car accelerating and stopping with the aid of a parachute thrown out to the rear), to a trial-and-error learning environment in which one or two variables can be changed before each dragster 'race', to a dynamic display of graphs in which several variables relating to the moving car can be altered and the resulting changes observed.

4   *On the need for teachers to provide meaningful contexts for computer-mediated tasks*
The teacher 'interacts creatively with software by setting framing tasks (whether closely defined or very broad) in which the computer-mediated tasks can make the greatest contribution to students' learning (op. cit., p. 158). This is one of the most important roles for teachers working with new technology. Once new

technology tools/resources have been chosen, the teacher needs to find a way of making their use meaningful in relation to any other learning activities that students have or will be engaging in. The 'framing task' is the broader learning rationale that integrates new technology with the culture of the classroom and its relationships. This ensures that new technology tasks are not add-ons that have no meaning in the overall curriculum. In addition, provided they are an integral part of the curriculum, technology-based tasks may create a more 'authentic environment' for learning (Brown *et al.* 1989). These have been shown to be more effective because there is no layer of abstraction between the learner and the subject of study; no imaginative leap is necessary to make the subject meaningful. New technology is claimed to be able to create authentic learning environments through the use of simulations. This can never be entirely true, because the simulation is presented through a computer interface which the learner has to master, but *Calculus Connections* provides a good example of how authentic this kind of experience can be. Apart from simulations, the Internet provides access to a huge quantity of authentic information, for example stock exchange indexes and weather information. With this resource it is much easier for teachers to set assignments which allow students to engage in authentic project work.

5   *On the possibility of structuring learning to give students greater control*
The teacher moves 'from a sequential to an organic structuring of learning experiences' (op. cit., p. 156). PALM teachers sometimes expressed this as a move from a 'stepping stones' to a 'walled garden'⁷ approach. They were aware of the difficulty in judging the amount of structure to provide and the kind of structure that best suited the individual. The way in which a learning experience is structured is critically important because, assuming that learning is an active process of extending one's mental schema, the way in which material is structured either makes it easier or more difficult for the learner to link new concepts to existing mental schema (Bruner 1966, p. 2). New technology has the potential of being able to match structure to individual learners' needs, for example, by giving the learner some control over the order in which material is accessed. However, this is difficult. At present, much material is accessed from CD-ROM or the web at random and there is a well-known phenomenon of 'getting lost in hyperspace'. A package like the BBC Shakespeare CD-ROM of *A Midsummer Night's Dream* (BBC 1997), illustrates a walled garden concept at its best, with a wide range of images, video clips, sound recordings and textual information available to be accessed in any order, while remaining anchored to the chronology of the play itself, which provides a continuous linear structure.

6   *On greater student responsibility for learning within a supportive, interactive, organisational culture*
The teacher is able to use new technology to change students' attitudes to learning (op. cit., p. 157). The reduction in the need for teachers to exercise social control makes it possible to move towards the culture of a learning organisation (op. cit., p. 156). We know that motivation is fundamentally important to learning at any level. New technology is, in itself, highly motivating to some learners, but there is also evidence that it presents an initial barrier to other learners. For all

learners there is a problem when computer-based materials require considerable mental effort when the learner is working alone. Currently, a small number of educational packages, particularly some commercially produced instructional games, are highly motivating. The majority, however, are not. Gavriel Salomon (1992), whose own research has been in the field of developing intelligent tutoring systems, has identified the most important component in learning as AIME – Amount of Invested Mental Effort. A complex package like *Calculus Connections*, however good, requires a considerable investment of time and effort. It can be seen as providing much more support than a textbook, but much less than a lecture. New technology makes new demands, but it can also provide learning aids such as concept mapping tools and on-line note-pads that have the potential to raise students' level of AIME. In addition, once the web is speedy, easy to navigate and available in every home, some of the motivational problems arising from the technology itself are likely to reduce.

So far I have been talking about the positive gains from using new technology in learning. There are, however, some major pitfalls to be avoided, especially in the production of computer-assisted leaning materials. CAL material is easiest to design if it follows the pattern of teach, drill, test. However, much of this material is banal, requiring students to engage in low-level cognitive operations such as recognition and recall, rather than higher-level operations such as synthesis and analysis (MacDonald *et al.* 1976). This is helpful in the acquisition of basic skills and information, but does not result in deep learning (Martin *et al.* 1997). It is also easiest to produce CAL materials using standard authoring tools, with the result that it all looks much the same and students find it dull, especially by comparison with commercial products, such as games software. A major problem comes when CAL attempts to be a complete teaching package that replaces an entire lecture course. The sheer weight of information that has to be got across necessitates the incorporation of a large body of text. It is very difficult to integrate this with interactive material. In any case, students nearly always end up by printing the entire text. It is much better to limit CAL materials to a narrower focus on areas of conceptual difficulty. Reference can, of course, be made to books and other texts which can be made available on the web for students to download.

Computerised testing, incorporating computerised marking, is attractive to lecturers, because it has the potential to save time, but it is very time-consuming to produce test materials that can make accurate assessments of higher-level conceptual understanding (Elsom-Cook 1990). The basis for this kind of computerised testing is normally the multiple-choice question. In its most sophisticated form these test materials incorporate self-marking and advice, but this requires the designer to predict all possible variations of answers and match them accurately to a bank of advice statements. This takes time to produce and requires extensive piloting to ensure its adequacy. This is a job for professional instructional designers, not for lecturers developing course materials in their spare time.

Currently, there is enormous pressure on universities to expand their provision of indiviualised, open learning. This is partly a financial pressure to increase market share by recruiting nation-wide and globally and delivering by distance learning methods, and partly a pressure to increase the flexibility of access for part-time students by enabling them to study at home and in their own time. The first misunderstanding that is already prevalent is that this kind of course delivery is a cheaper form of provision. Students enrolled on distance learning courses need one-to-one email support from a tutor on a regular basis. Problems arise immediately if tutors are not allocated sufficient time or are not aware of the demands of this kind of teaching. The second misunderstanding, linked to the first, is to assume that the open learning materials can completely replace a teacher, or that on-line conferencing systems can provide the same level of support as a group of fellow students who meet regularly after lectures. The opportunity for discussion, that is for the creative process of framing ideas in words and interpreting the meanings of others, interactively, is crucially important to learning (Prawat 1991). We still do not know to what extent this can be replaced by on-line discussions. Asynchronous email exchanges are undoubtedly productive and provide a supportive learning environment for students working at a distance or in isolation, but it seems unlikely that they can ever replicate the creativity of hammering out an idea face-to-face. There will increasingly be an important role for video telephoning and video conferencing as a component of such courses. Many universities are supplementing distance delivery with intensive teaching blocks or summer schools, delivered either on campus or to groups of students in their local area. We are at a point when the explosion of need for individualised, open learning, needs sustained development work with the full backing of senior managers.

Speculations on reorganising schooling with the help of new technology

In America there is an academic pursuit called 'Futuring', and I have decided to conclude my lecture with some futuring of my own. I will present a scenario for a new way of organising schooling based on six assumptions:

1 The new technology applications that are already revolutionising the business world will soon be used to revolutionise many aspects of schooling.
2 The cost of the speed and power of new technology will continue to drop at a dramatic rate. (On the basis of Moore's Law, computer power increases tenfold every five years.)
3 The speed and navigability of the web will continue to improve, and full colour video and still images will soon be available without any perceptible delay. Through the National Grid for Learning, schools will have unlimited access to the Internet, including a selected range of commercial sites, for a single annual subscription. LEAs or regional groups of LEAs will have their own local grids.
4 In addition to its educative purpose, the system of schooling has a legal duty of care in loco parentis for the nation's children.
5 Schools have a socialising function that helps to prepare young people for adult life.

6   Changes to the organisation of schools need to build upon current policy trends but they also need to have a revolutionary element. Considerable beneficial change would be possible immediately with existing technology.

By 2010 all young people and all teachers will have personal, laptop computers incorporating a keyboard suited to their hand size, full colour, DVD drive (Digital Versatile Disc), integral Internet, fax and telephone, and a suite of software tools. They will have at least 3 Gbytes of hard disc, 50 Mbytes of RAM and a Central Processing Unit operating at 1 Ghz (roughly 1,000,000,000 instructions per second).

There will be plenty of room for resources of personal choice including material down-loaded from the web and intelligent 'biomorph' pets (sons and daughters of Norns from the current cult game Creatures – see Sharples 1998). These machines, which are best imagined as a cross between present day handheld games machines, mobile telephones and electronic notebooks or organisers, will be lightweight, fully portable, battery or mains operated machines, transported between home and school in waterproof heavy-duty shoulder bags. Classrooms, libraries and study centres will be designed around study carousels where six students will have access through a local area network (operating at 100 Mbits per second) to a wide range of resources (DVD and documents) and the Internet (with phone or cable connections operating at 100 Kbits per second), as well as to mains electricity.

All staff, students and their parents will have personal Internet addresses and their own websites, including password-protected areas. Every document, including students' written work, will be produced in electronic form. Students will send their work to their teacher's website as an attachment. Students and staff will automatically download their work to the central server on arrival each morning. All school information (e.g. the timetable, names of staff and students, organisational procedures) will be permanently accessible. Information on current assignments for each class, deadlines, resource lists, students' assessment records, progress reports, etc. will be available, as will the diaries of all teachers including the head. This resource base for the whole school will be automatically backed-up once or twice a day as a protection against crashes (because technology then as now will not be crash-free!).

Technicians will be crucial to the school's educative mission. They will, ideally, have specialist training which will include technical skills and people/support skills. Small schools will be able to call upon technician support from the LEA.

Teachers will organise their groups of around 30 students on the basis of agreed learning contracts and will normally work with groups of no more than ten at one time. The emphasis in these intensive teaching sessions will be on exploring areas of conceptual difficulty. From the age of seven, young people will spend part of their time at school in the library or a study centre, where they will be able to work either independently, using self-study materials, or on a group task in one of the group study rooms. Below the age of seven, children will work with teaching assistants and teachers in a classroom base, and basic skills in new technology will be taught integrally with literacy and numeracy. By the age of seven they will be competent users of their own personal computer as well as being well advanced in literacy and numeracy skills.

From the age of 14 young people will be able to work at home if they have written permission from both their parents and the school. Alternatively, they will work in supervised community study centres which may be based in community libraries and will be an extension of the current homework clubs. From both home and the study centres they will have access to a video-telephone advice line in the school library to assist with resource queries. Additionally, they will have telephone access to a national advice line for each subject which will be run along the lines of a call centre. The community study centres will be staffed by an experienced adult assisted by volunteers recruited from unemployed young people in the first instance. The national subject advice lines will be staffed by a mix of academic subject specialists and teachers.

Teachers will spend half their time on intensive teaching of small groups and half on the development of learning materials and/or continuing professional development activities. Some of this work will be co-ordinated by LEA support staff. All learning materials, including work sheets, PowerPoint displays and lesson plans, will be stored on the web and accessible to staff and students. Learning materials will be developed by teams of teachers, or downloaded from the National Grid for Learning and revised/refined by them.

A full range of software tools will be available on each student's mobile 'computer'. Learning materials will be available to students in both electronic and paper-based form. Books and a wide range of paper-based materials will be available in the library and resource centres. Materials stored on the web will be easily downloaded to high-quality printers. Intelligent tutoring software, or more basic CAL material will be used alongside paper-based materials and will focus, in particular, upon:

- drill and practice games to teach basic skills, such as arithmetical calculations
- interactive software and simulations to assist with the learning of difficult concepts
- simulations software and data-logging software to be used alongside experimental work in a science laboratory.

There are only three barriers to these developments happening immediately in schools. The first is cost of the available technology. Cost will reduce rapidly over a short period of time but much will depend upon production decisions made by commercial producers. A laptop computer with the specification included above would retail at the equivalent of around £200 to £300 in 2010. However, to stay in profit producers have so far found it necessary to produce ever more powerful machines and sell them at leading-edge prices. Deals may need to be struck between commercial producers and governments on an international scale, for example to guarantee purchases, to an agreed value, of lightweight mobile computers within this range over a specified number of years.

The second is resistance from those who may feel that schools run in this way would not be fulfilling their duty of care in loco parentis and might fail to socialise young people to become good citizens in the future. In fact, there is nothing in these proposals that would remove young people from the direct supervision of adults, under the age of 14, without their parents permission. In terms of socialisation, there is little evidence that schools currently find it easy to cultivate qualities of independence, self-reliance and responsibility in the majority of young people. I suggest that the kind of school organisation I am describing would be more rather than less likely to give young people a good preparation to be responsible citizens in adult life.

The third is the barrier of fixed assumptions and settled tradition. This is a formidable barrier, but we must overcome it. The traditions of our education system were mostly inherited from the Victorians. They belong to the era of the great mill and the production line and were better suited to preparing young people for that world than they are for our own world. Today we need self-confident, independent thinkers, whether team players or entrepreneurs, capable of acquiring a range of different skills and adapting to several jobs over a lifetime. Policy makers at the national and local levels have the power to make a difference in the way schools are organised. Those of us in higher education and schools, both teachers and researchers, need to work with policy-makers and business, parent and community partners to bring about these changes to learning practices and the culture of schools, teachers and schooling.

Universities will find a big change in their student intakes when schools all over the country are organised in this new way – which they undoubtedly will be at some point in the not-so-distant future. University students will arrive with a better level of basic skills. They will also have a wider range of abilities and much greater independence as learners, with more having taken the opportunity to pursue their studies at school to a higher level. Universities already need to revolutionise teaching methods along similar lines to those described here. It will make it much easier to do so if schools have already taken the lead.

7 Taking the sociological imagination to school

An analysis of the (lack of) impact of ICT on education systems

Looking back ...

In 2003, at the time of writing this article, I had been involved in the innovation of ICT in schools for twenty years, yet the barriers to embedding it in teaching and learning in the curriculum were still formidable. Little seemed to have been achieved and yet, at home, many young people were using ICT every day, very creatively, in ways that transformed their lives by comparison with previous generations. I believed that I had considerable insights from research into the reasons for this apparent failure for ICT to make an impact in schools and felt impatient of my inability to do anything about it. Surely there must be a better way for researchers to contribute to policy development and implementation. During the mid-1990s I had worked at the Scottish Council for Research in Education whose mission was to 'Improve Scottish Education through Research' and in much of my own work I had adopted an action research approach, combining the search for knowledge with support for the process of innovation through working in partnership with participants. I remembered that Cecil Wright Mills' book, The Sociological Imagination, *had given me theoretical insights with practical power to think about my own life in new ways, so this became my starting point in writing the paper.*

In his classic book *The Sociological Imagination* Cecil Wright Mills (1959) suggested that the job of a sociologist is to develop and use tools of analysis which allow the minutiae of everyday life to be understood in terms of theoretical frameworks. Actors in a social situation are able to perceive it only from their own point of view, trapped within the socio-cultural assumptions deriving from their personal life history and the organisational structures within which they live and work. Sociologists have the ability and public duty to analyse and make meaning from the apparently trivial in order to inform actors and empower decision-making.

The purpose of this chapter is to bring the sociological imagination to education systems and look at the impact Information and Communication Technologies (ICTs) have so far had on schools. For many sociologists looking at this area, the focus has mainly been on using the evidence of non-impact to challenge the unrealistic visions of policy-makers (e.g. Cuban 2001; Selwyn 2002). Adopting a different approach, I want to pose the possibility of radical change. My focus in this chapter is on the more generic issues that consistently mobilise resistance to ICTs within schools and education systems. Having spent many years trying to understand the reasons for this resistance, I want to set an agenda for researchers to work to circumvent it.

The impact of ICTs on young people's lives outside school

The first step in my analysis is to review the evidence that ICTs have had a radical impact on popular culture and the daily lives of children and young people outside school. In the ImpaCT2 evaluation, among a sample of 2000 students aged 10–16 in maintained secondary schools in England, home access to the Internet rose from 59 per cent in June 2000 to 73 per cent in June 2001 (Somekh *et al.* 2002a). During the same period, ownership of a computer in these students' homes rose from 83 per cent to 90 per cent. ImpaCT2 collected image-based concept maps to give insights into students' overall awareness of computers in today's world. These showed their extensive knowledge of how computers are used for communications (email and 'chat'), finding information, playing games, accessing music and images, controlling everything from supermarket stock to NASA's rocket launches, and for work in offices and schools. They also indicated that students were using computers for an extraordinary range of activities, although younger children generally called all these activities 'games'. In an interview with George about his concept map (see Figure 7.1) he confirmed that his main interest was in games. He then clarified that the buildings are part of 'a kind of game where you had to build your world and what these kind of things done was build computers and help developing a construction site so they can build all these'. Through playing this game he appeared to have developed an awareness of the links between computers and the world of work. In a log of her computer use kept for one week, a 16-year-old girl reported spending 5 minutes at school on word processing and a total of 25 hours at home on: word processing (4 hours), art packages (2 hours), CD-rewriter (2 hours), CD-ROM (2 hours), email (6 hours), surfing the Internet (3 hours), creating web pages (2 hours) and [a messenger service] (4 hours) (ibid., p. 11). The concept map by Fiona, aged 15 (Figure 7.2) vividly portrays the kind of social ambience that this wide-ranging computer use creates for young people, very much located in popular culture and the culture of the home as an integral part of their identity project. Other researchers have found similar evidence of young people using ICTs frequently and creatively in a way that has transformed the experience of childhood and adolescence by comparison with former generations, see for example Downes (1999) and Facer *et al.* (2003).

The (lack of) impact of ICTs on education systems

In a study of primary school classrooms in England based on extensive observations over a two-year period, Galton *et al.* (1999) found that computers were used so rarely that they did not include them as a main focus of their analysis of practice. This was despite the considerable investment in ICTs in education made by the UK Government since the early 1980s (see Chapter 6 of this book). Since Galton's study was carried out there has been further massive investment by Government through its National Grid for Learning (NGfL) initiative. Nevertheless, the ImpaCT2

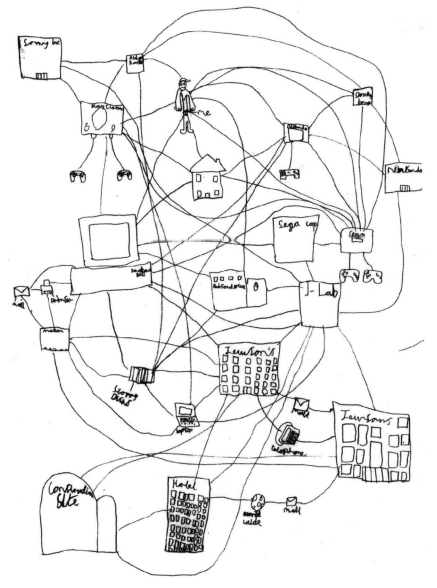

Figure 7.1 'Computers in My World' by George, aged 10

evaluation of the NGfL found that the most frequent use of computers by students in English, maths and science at school (inside or outside lessons) was by 10–11 year olds, of whom 24 per cent reported frequent use in lessons for English (most weeks or every week). However, more than 50 per cent of students in this age group reported that they used computers in maths and science lessons 'never' or 'hardly ever' and more than 50 per cent of older students (aged 13–14 and 15–16) reported the same

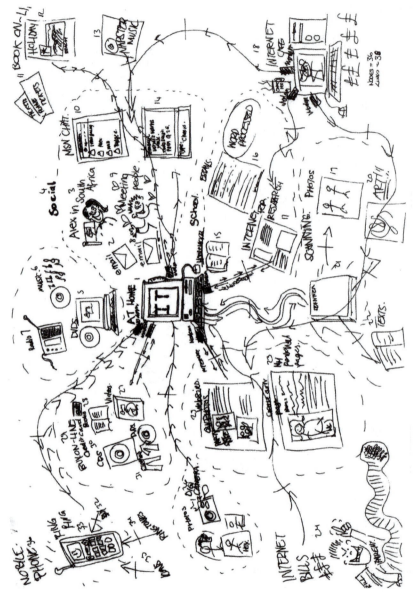

Figure 7.2 'Computers in My World' by Fiona, aged 15

very low level of use across all three core subjects in school, both inside and outside lessons (Harrison *et al.* 2002). This compares with Becker's findings from the 1999 Teaching, Learning and Computing Survey in the USA, which showed a very low level of use of technology in the teaching of academic subjects (Becker 2000). Had ImpaCT2 asked students about their use of computers in specialist ICT lessons the answers would have been different, because there was considerable evidence that ICT was being used by schools mainly to teach ICT skills. This is, in itself, a disturbing finding, particularly as the evidence suggests that much of this use in ICT lessons is for teaching low-level skills such as how to use office software (Somekh *et al.* 2002a, pp. 32–3). It is not surprising that Cuban (op. cit.) concludes that the money spent on computers might have been better spent on other resources such as 'smaller class size, higher entry-level salaries for teachers, renovation of decayed buildings' (ibid., p. 193) and further 'that computers in classrooms have been oversold by promoters and policy-makers and underused by teachers and students' (ibid., p. 195).

An intriguing piece of further evidence that ICT has had little impact on education systems, comes from the way in which it is largely ignored in most research in education that does not set out specifically to address it. For example, searches on 'computer', 'technology', 'digital media' and 'ICTs' revealed no entries in the indexes of either Arnot *et al.*'s *Closing the Gender Gap* (1999) or Alexander's *Culture and Pedagogy: International Comparisons in Primary Education* (2000). In the former text one might have expected ICTs to be addressed directly as a potential site of disadvantage for girls but this was not the case, presumably because the authors did not find that they were a significant characteristic of schooling. In the latter, the extent to which ICT had changed the classroom practice might have been expected to feature in the analytical framework used to compare pedagogies across the five countries in the study (France, India, Russia, the UK and the USA). But it was not so. A more detailed reading uncovered a reference in Alexander's study to the presence of computers in US classrooms (p. 337) and the use of the web as a means for the UK government to 'make entire standard lessons available on the web' (p. 339), but Alexander's comment that despite a wide range of resources, including computers, 'the everyday technology of teaching and learning in the Michigan classrooms was much more limited than [this] might suggest' (p. 337) is very significant. In general there was considerable commonality in the organisation of classrooms across the five countries and the presence of ICT in classrooms in the UK and the USA had not led to change.

Why the difference between the impact of ICT in the home and at school?

The difference between children's experience of ICT at school and at home is very extreme and immediately raises the question why. Such a very strong differentiation of use can only be accounted for in terms of the institutional functioning of schools and education systems as a whole. Mills (1959, p. 29) in a paraphrase and explication of the ideas of Parsons (1951, pp. 38–9), explains the inter-relationship of people in institutions in terms of role-playing governed by 'mutual expectations' called 'standards' and 'expected reactions' called 'sanctions'. On this basis, Mills defines institutions as 'a more or less stable set of roles'. Through enacting these roles, individuals establish and consolidate the authority structures of the institution.

Gamoran is one of many writers to comment upon the extraordinarily 'stable structure' of the school and the 'persisting process' of classroom organisation and pedagogy:

> Dominated by textbooks, lecture and recitation, instruction has remained fundamentally unchanged even though new tools have made other approaches to class work, homework and teacher–student interaction feasible.
>
> (Gamoran 2001, p. 136)

Bidwell argues for the need to understand resistance to change in schools by adopting an integrated approach, combining 'network-based analysis of the faculty workplace in schools ... with a neo-institutional analysis of the formal organization of the school' (Bidwell 2001, p. 102). Drawing on Waller's classic analysis of schools as sites of struggle in which faculty (teachers) attempt to motivate students to learn 'a collection of dessicated subjects that are far from students' experience' (Waller 1932, p. 10), Bidwell suggests that schools should be analysed in terms of how their organisational structures impact on their 'production – that is, the processes by which schooling results in the cognitive development or moral socialization for which schools are formally responsible' (op. cit., p. 101). His basic premise is that the institutional structure of schools, consisting of a hierarchy of bureaucratic roles and divisions of the teaching force into sub-groups according to subject discipline and age phase, combined with the strength of external threats (e.g. high-stakes testing and inspection regimes), constructs the informal networks of teachers as mechanisms that are increasingly expert in adapting externally imposed innovations to existing practice.

According to Bidwell's analysis, ICT can be seen as yet another example of an innovation which has failed to penetrate the forces of socio-cultural reproduction built into the institutional structures of schools. Bidwell's theory leads me to conclude that schools are locked into mechanisms of mutual constraint: the formal authority of the head teacher (principal) and policy-makers to bring about radical change through the introduction of ICTs is rendered powerless by the capacity of the informal networks of teachers to adapt such changes to traditional practices; while, at the same time, teachers are equally constrained by the predicament of working within an institution which, in Waller's terms, is 'a despotism in a state of perilous equilibrium' (Waller 1932, p. 10), and as a result are unable to use the potential power of their informal networks to engage in creativity, experimentation and risk-taking. This analysis fits well with Giddens' theory of structuration in which individuals within an institution are active co-producers of its structure and integral to its power relations:

> According to the notion of the duality of structure, the structural properties of social systems are both medium and outcome of the practices they recursively organize.
>
> (Giddens 1984, p. 25)

Giddens' theory does not suggest that institutional structures are easy to change, rather its main contribution is to shed light upon the process of institutional formation. The institution is formed, maintained and sustained as much by the assumptions and routine behaviours of those who work within it as by the larger system which gives it legitimacy. Teachers, parents and the community – students even – can be said to be complicit in the un-reformed institution of the school.

What is it about ICTs that discourages their integration into teaching and learning?

The nature of the Internet is inherently individualistic, anarchic, exploratory and disruptive. It gives control to individual users to access vast quantities of information which have not been subjected to quality control; because there is no process of quality control there is *de facto* no oppressive control of the flow of information to anyone who seeks to access it; there is no formal division between knowledge consumers and knowledge producers, so that any individual can establish a web page and place material in the public domain; channels of communication are open between users, anywhere in the world, and there is an impetus to invent fictitious identities since there are no mechanisms to cross-check against 'true' identities; there is no division between communication (characterised as 'talking' in schools) and information retrieval (characterised as 'work' in schools); multi-tasking with several 'windows' open at the same time is increasingly part of the routine practices of users, particularly since they have not been encultured like older generations into the importance of 'concentrating on one thing at a time'; the process of seeking information is not subject to time-constraints, but rather invites open-ended exploration and a certain degree of discovery by serendipity; information is not ordered into disciplines or differentiated according to the capabilities of the user (age or level of education), and hence the power differentials embedded in formal knowledge structures are removed (e.g. medical knowledge is available equally to medical practitioners and their patients); there is sound accessible both as an integral part of specific websites and downloaded to be played and stored on home computers; there is a merging of genres in a new genre of the web, so that moving images and commercial advertising impinge on areas of knowledge that have traditionally been presented only through text within non-commercial cultural settings; there is a merging of technologies so that the production of digital images is an integral part of both communication and web-publishing, and the Internet can be accessed through cell (mobile) phones and personal digital assistants (PDAs).

It is not difficult to argue that every single one of the features of the Internet and ICTs more generally listed in the previous paragraph is antipathetic to the culture and traditional values of schools. At an apparently superficial level ICTs have the potential to disrupt the routine procedures of schooling and challenge some of the basic principles which it symbolically upholds (Sharples 2003). At a more fundamental level, following Bernstein (1971), schools and education systems can be seen as sites for both strong classification and strong framing of knowledge, which are fundamentally challenged by the destabilising impact of ICT on concepts like knowledge, teaching, the disciplines and rationality.

Institutionalised resistance to the radical changes made possible by ICTs

In line with the approaches to analysis put forward by Bidwell and Giddens, it seems clear that the formal bureaucratic structures of the school and the informal micro-networks of teachers come together, subliminally and powerfully, to defend the school against this fundamental attack on all that it stands for. This resistance on the part of teachers, head teachers and educational officials consists partly of assumptions that run so deep that they are barely recognised formally (e.g. the division of knowledge into separate subjects, and the division of the school day into short time periods), and more explicit invention of new rules to contain and constrain ICTs (e.g. by forbidding the use in school of cell phones, on-line games, and websites considered by the teacher to be trivial). It is resisted where possible by young people by means such as using the 'mute' facility of their cell phone and text messaging each other silently; or multitasking with several windows open on the computer at the same time, enabling quick transition from one to another with a flick of the hand, using the ALT+TAB command.

To illustrate this process of institutionalised resistance to ICT, which operates largely subliminally and therefore without acknowledged intentionality, I will put forward just four examples: the implications and operational outcomes of constructing ICT as a discreet subject in the national curriculum; the assumption of 'starting from scratch' in teaching ICT skills; the exacerbation of the 'second digital divide'; and the constraints placed by schools on children's access to the Internet. Each of these springs from the fundamental values embedded in the education system and has far-reaching, unexpected, negative outcomes.

The implications and operational outcomes of constructing ICT as a discreet subject in the national curriculum

ICT has the status of a discreet subject in the English National Curriculum and the accompanying paraphernalia of specified knowledge components, 'level descriptors', 'attainment targets' and national tests. It is largely taught by specialist ICT teachers, who in primary schools are called ICT coordinators; in both primary and secondary schools these specialists are responsible for preparing students for national tests and public examinations. The curriculum specifications are translated into classroom practice with the help of 'guidelines' drawn up by the Qualifications and Curriculum Authority (QCA) and the quality of the school's ICT teaching is perceived by many teachers to be judged by inspectors (OFSTED, the Office for Standards in Education) on the basis of adherence to these guidelines. The guidelines give examples of lessons in which ICT is embedded in an activity; however, although these activities are nearly all oriented towards another curriculum subject (e.g. skills of using email are taught within communication activities which have a relationship to the literacy curriculum), the fact that they are taught by an ICT specialist, often in a specialist ICT suite, means that they are scarcely ever integrated with subject teaching. The effect of this was very clear in the outcomes of the ImpaCT2 evaluation which showed only a very marginal improvement in test and examination scores in some core subjects at some levels as a result of using ICT; specifically, the only gains that were statistically significant were in English and to a lesser extent maths for 10–11 year olds, science for 13–14 year olds, and science and design & technology for 15–16 year olds (Harrison *et al.* 2002). As mentioned earlier in this chapter, these disappointing results can best be understood in terms of the very low levels of use of ICT in English, maths and science lessons recorded by students in the sample in questionnaire responses.

The assumption of 'starting from scratch' in teaching ICT skills

The national curriculum for England specifies learning in a series of levels which proceed on a linear basis from KS1 (Key Stage 1) for 5–7 year olds to KS4 for 15–16 year olds. Although it is nowhere so stated, the national curriculum is based on the assumption that all learning will take place in the school, or as directed by the school, and it is the responsibility of the school to ensure that students are given their 'entitlement' of teaching to enable them to progress from one level to the next. The school system is, therefore, unprepared for wide variations in students' prior learning of the kind now typical in terms of ICT skills as a result of frequent and sustained use of ICTs by many young people in the home (Lewin *et al.* 2003). As a result, teaching largely proceeds on the basis of covering the whole of the specified curriculum 'from scratch' with all students regardless of the skills they have already acquired. Several studies have shown that this results in some students being, at best, very bored by ICT at school and, at worst, 'hating it' (Somekh *et al.* 2002a, pp. 31–3; Facer *et al.* 2003, pp. 205–11). Tellingly, Facer *et al.* quote Huw, aged 12, summarising what he sees as good teaching in a situation where some students have more highly developed ICT skills than the teacher: 'Then a good teacher like Miss Andrews would … take on your information that you inputted into the lesson. She learns from you and you learn from her. So it's like a two-way system. It's not like some teachers who, you know, pound it into you, try to just get information into you …'.

The exacerbation of the 'second digital divide'

Embedded in English schools there is a very strong 'fairness ethic' by which teachers always try to ensure that no student is given an unfair advantage over any other student. No doubt this is strongly linked to a reaction against the naked injustices embedded in the still-enduring divisions of social class, and the former tripartite system of schooling (in place during 1947–70 approximately, but still persisting in a small number of local education authorities) whereby children were selected according to ability at the age of 11 for schools which offered different curricula, resources and career opportunities. In relation to ICT the fairness ethic has the effect that teachers are reluctant to ask students to use ICTs for homework, first because they often underestimate the proportion of their students who have access to ICT at home, and second because they see this as irrelevant anyway, since the principle would be the same even if requesting ICT use only discriminated against one student. However, there is now a considerable body of research evidence that shows that in addition to a divide in terms of access to ICT in the home, there is a 'second digital divide' which operates through the choice of the kinds of use of ICTs that students make in the home (Natriello 2001). This is merely another manifestation of the well-established phenomenon by which students are differentially advantaged or disadvantaged according to the cultural capital available to them in the home. Lewin *et al.* (2003) have shown that when teachers make no specific requests for students to use ICTs for homework, those in homes with high cultural capital are much more likely to choose to use ICTs for school work than other students with similar access to ICTs at home; moreover, children are less able to argue their need with parents and siblings for access to a shared resource if teachers have not made a specific request for them to use ICTs.

The constraints placed by schools on children's access to the Internet

In relation to this issue the term 'children' is used more often by the mass media than 'students' because of its 'fit' with the discourses of anxiety and threat. All the points raised here, however, refer equally to all students up to the time of leaving school.

It is very difficult to untangle all the issues relating to constraints placed on children's access to the Internet, but some things are becoming clear. First, that the dangers of children inadvertently accessing unsuitable material are real but relatively small; and that similarly the dangers of them being approached and 'groomed' on-line by paedophiles seeking to meet them are also real but relatively even smaller. Second, that we live in an increasingly risk-averse society in which few children are permitted to play in the street or the park, or walk to school. In England (and undoubtedly in the USA too) children's lives are increasingly circumscribed and constrained by adults, and anxieties about the dangers of the Internet have to be seen in the context of this national panic. Third, that we live in an increasingly litigious society, in which teachers are at risk of prosecution in the case of an accident happening to a child in their care. Rather than being *in loco parentis* and taking reasonable decisions in the knowledge that if something goes wrong they will be given credit for doing their best in the interests of the child, they are increasingly blamed for mishaps. This creates a context for Internet use in schools in which parents and the public greatly overestimate the dangers and teachers cannot afford to take any chances. Fourth, that, as a result of these anxieties, in some schools access to the Internet is severely hampered by 'screening software' that prevents access to a large number of websites and slows access to all. It is common for researchers to be told by children that they prefer to use the Internet at home where their access is much faster than at school (partly also, of course, because in school there may be multiple users seeking access at the same time through the same cables).

The points above are, however, only the context for a deeper-level issue relating to control over individual action and responsibility for learning. It is in relation to these issues that ICTs have the maximum potential to disrupt the traditions and routines of schooling. Schools are notoriously sites of control in which students are required to conform to a regime of practice which places the teacher in the role of an authoritative individual and students in the role of members of an ignorant and potentially oppositional group. Waller's analysis from the early twentieth century (op. cit.) locates the imperative for control in the school's focus on a mandated curriculum of little interest to its students. Today, with the urgent need for radical change in schooling to prepare students for a radically different world in the twenty-first century, and the resources of the Internet available to allow coverage of a far wider range of material and on-line support which could be used to give students far greater responsibility for their own learning, it is both highly desirable and possible to radically change schools. Unfortunately, the anxieties surrounding Internet use are joining forces with the institutionalised resistance to change within the education system to prevent this from happening.

New medium, new message: time for the end of school as we know it

In the UK, Stephen Heppell and his team at Ultralab (http://ww3.ultralab.net/projects/notschool, accessed 7/8/2006) have successfully demonstrated a new approach to education through their NotSchool initiative. NotSchool works with school refusers, long-term truants and those excluded from school for bad behaviour, and has shown that by giving them access to a computer in their own home, removing all the structures and discourses of school (buildings, roles such as 'teacher' and 'student'), naming them as 'researchers' and working with them in non-coercive relationships where they are sometimes asked to take on the role of teaching adults, they are able to reconstruct their identities and respond positively to the respect they are being shown. NotSchool might be seen as a twenty-first century enactment of Illich's (1971) vision of Deschooling Society, made possible by the new digital media. In both the USA and the UK, Alan November (2001) has challenged schools and policy-makers to place the empowerment of students at the centre of their vision and practice. Cuban gives the reason for the failure of education policy-makers' visions for technology-induced radical change as originating from the fact that there has been no fundamental change in the system of schooling:

> For such fundamental changes in teaching and learning to occur there would have to have been widespread and deep reform in schools' organizational, political, social, and technological contexts.
>
> (Cuban, op. cit., p. 195)

Whereas, in the past, Cuban's accusations might have seemed unreasonable and Illich's vision unrealistic and unaffordable, NotSchool has actually demonstrated that, with the Internet and other ICTs, fundamental changes to teaching and learning and the whole institution of schooling are both achievable and desirable. The only pity is that it is seen by policy-makers as a radical solution to the otherwise no-hope situation of school-refusers, rather than a model of fundamental change for the system as a whole.

Three bodies of theory enable the sociological imagination to reach a deeper analysis of the reasons why ICTs cannot be introduced into education as superficial additions to the existing system, but need to be located in radical institutional and systemic changes. All three focus upon the inter-relationship between ICTs and users which fundamentally changes the experience of being human and makes ICTs an indispensable part of that experience. The first is McLuhan's (1964, p. 7) explanation that 'the medium is the message' at the heart of which is his theory that media are 'extensions' of ourselves. Writing at the time when the era of mechanisation was being replaced by the era of cybernation (or 'automation') McLuhan saw the telegraph as an example of 'the electric form, that ... ends the mechanical age of individual steps and specialist functions'. Telegraph technology – which I am taking here to be the forerunner of contemporary ICTs – is seen by McLuhan as a force which has brought about seismic change in the world of journalism and information management:

> Any innovation threatens the equilibrium of existing organization. ... the outering or extension of our bodies and senses in a 'new invention' compels the whole of our bodies and senses to shift into new positions in order to maintain equilibrium. A new 'closure' is effected in all our organs and senses, both private and public by any new inventions. ... Naturally the effects on language and on literary style and subject mater were spectacular.
>
> (McLuhan, op. cit., p. 273)

McLuhan's use of the language of the body and physical functions is not merely metaphorical, it expresses his understanding that a new medium in use becomes an extension of the body of the user and hence fundamentally changes the body's functions and means of expression. Rejecting any simplistic dichotomy of mind and body, he sees new media – of which for us ICTs are the contemporary example – as having fundamental personal and social consequences because they are extensions of ourselves.

The second body of theory is the work on the impact of ICTs on the self and identity formation carried out by Turkle (1984, 1995) over a period of more than 15 years. In her early work she probed the way that users of all ages – from young child-novice users of electronic games to post-doctoral students of computer systems and artificial intelligence – vested something of their own identity in the machine, seeing it as a 'second self' or responsive mirror. In her later work she focused on the relationship between users in the virtual world of 'cyberspace' and their playful construction of fantasy identities as a means of self-liberation and exploration of what it means to be human. Her descriptions of individuals constructing and re-constructing identity through 'living in the MUD' (Multi-User Domains) of on-line interactive simulation games provides fascinating insights into the ontology of human experience (Turkle 1995, p. 11). She concludes that 'in the past decade, the computer culture has been the site of a series of battles over contested terrains' (op. cit., p. 267) and categorises the computer in three different ways: 'as tool, as mirror, and as gateway to a world through the looking glass of the screen'. The allusion to Lewis Carol's topsy-turvy world of an alternative psychological reality signals both creative power and loss of traditional certainties. Like McLuhan, she does not conceive of ICTs as separable from the identity of their human users.

The third body of work is activity theory, which embodies the Vygostskian concept of tools as mediators of human activity. The most powerful description of this fundamental inter-dependence of tools and human agents skilled in their use is Jim Wertsch's metaphor of pole vaulter and pole, neither of whom/which is capable of clearing the high bar without the other (Wertsch 1998). In a notable edited collection, Nardi (1997, pp. 17–44) refocuses activity theory specifically upon the analysis of human interaction with ICTs, presenting it as a 'potential framework for human–computer interaction research'. The chapter by Christiansen (1997) in Nardi's book draws upon the imaginative insights of sociology and cultural psychology to characterise the special nature of ICTs as lying in their capacity to be loved by their human users.

> Of course, an artefact cannot have feelings. It is the relationship between artefact and user that creates a feeling inside the user, which in turn is projected to the artefact. The tool relationship becomes a kind of filter through which the user experiences the artefact.
>
> (Op. cit., p. 176)

She goes on to explain that this relationship between tool and user lies at the heart of the conceptualisation of activity as defined by Leont'ev, following Vygotsky. Just as it was for McLuhan and Turkle, technology is seen as inter-dependent with human experience and action with the power to radically change the nature of human activities. But activity theory goes further to explain the way that institutional structures within national systems, with functions as diverse as education and the postal service (Engeström and Escalante 1997), construct and constrain the inter-relationship of humans and ICTs in mediated activity.

When the explanatory power of these three bodies of theory that show that to be transforming ICTs need to become an integral part of human activity is put alongside the practical example of NotSchool's success, the case for radical change of the school system becomes incontrovertible. The mutual constraints that render school leadership powerless to direct effective change from above and the informal networks of teachers powerless to produce creative change from below are clearly indicated in the evidence of (non-)impact of ICTs on education systems over a period of more than 20 years of high levels of investment by policy-makers. It is time for the end of school as we know it.

An agenda for research to promote radical change

Natriello ends his analysis of the unintended failures of ICTs to have any impact on schooling with a challenge to sociologists of education. It is not enough, he contends, to say as Attewell does, 'We must wait to see whether "Let them have Pentiums" is more practical than "Let them eat cake".' Rather, he argues, 'Sociologists of education can play a significant role in designing the educational institutions of the digital age. Failure to engage at this defining juncture may appropriately lead to forfeiture of the right to criticize in the future' (Natriello, op. cit., pp. 263–4).

In the UK and the USA there are currently a number of significant initiatives aimed at radically changing aspects of schooling. These range from radical designs for new school buildings, to innovative deployment of mobile ICTs for use both at home and at school, and experimental formations of curriculum and pedagogy. They are all still considerably constrained by the technologies of national/state curricula, high-stakes testing and traditional pedagogies, but many are supported by funding from commercial partners who bring with them none of the assumptions embedded in the culture of schooling. The dissatisfaction with the education system which is leading increasing numbers of parents in both the USA and the UK to remove their children from school and educate them at home, drawing on the services of Internet-based providers of educational materials, is a strong signal of the imperative for change. Educational researchers should draw upon the tools of sociology and use their sociological imagination to play a leadership role in scenario building to assist policy-makers in the transformation of the education system.

Part IV

Research methods for ICT in education

I now turn to the process of research – its methods and methodological foundations – to explore the role that researchers can play in supporting the process of innovation. I have been strongly influenced by working at the start of my career at the Centre for Applied Research in Education (CARE) at the University of East Anglia, and over the last eight years at Manchester Metropolitan University with four colleagues who share that background. This has shaped my work as a researcher in two ways: first, in showing me that high-quality research is dependent upon continuous investigation into research methods, exploring new approaches to the collection and analysis of data to suit them as closely as possible to the focus of study; and second in giving me a high regard for carrying out evaluations of innovative programmes, since it is through evaluation work that researchers have the best opportunity of making an informed, responsible contribution to civil society (Wildavsky 1993). Methods for both research and evaluation studies, rather than being procedures to be implemented in any kind of routine manner, are contingent on context and dependent on deeper methodological considerations of the nature of knowledge and the nature of being. These epistemological and ontological underpinnings are grounded in a researcher's values, but develop over time with knowledge and experience. Hence in the three papers presented here, the influence of my reading in cultural psychology and activity theory can be seen to extend and deepen my practices as a researcher over time. Chapter 8, first presented at a conference in 1998, does not draw on these theories but they figure prominently in Chapters 9 and 10.

All three chapters are about ways of contributing research knowledge to policy formation. Two are position papers and fairly wide-ranging: Chapter 8 presents a model of 'supportive evaluation' developed especially for working with innovatory ICT initiatives, Chapter 9 reviews how methods for researching knowledge construction and the process of coming to know need to draw on theories from both cultural psychology and philosophy, especially when ICT is a component of the learning context. Chapter 10 exemplifies the socio-cultural method in a presentation of an image-based, hand-drawn concept mapping method used to research children's mental models of ICT in their world.

Policy-makers are impatient of research knowledge, especially when it focuses too heavily on 'discovering the unintended consequences of purposive, political action' (Lauder *et al.* 2004, p. 11), for as Johnson (2004, p. 25) points out 'when they know there is a problem, inaction is rarely an option for policy-makers, particularly for politicians'. Policy-makers operate within a politicised arena in which the time-frame is too short to allow the long-term planning and preparation needed to give 'ownership' of change to all participants (Fullan 1982). In these chapters I begin to explore the possibilities for a new kind of relationship between research and policy-formation, in which researchers build scenarios for future development on the basis of knowledge generated from evaluation of recent and current initiatives. The vision is for a new kind of research in which analysis of the drivers of 'unintended consequences' of current initiatives generates explanatory theories that could be useful in planning new, more successful initiatives.

8 The role of evaluation in ensuring excellence in communications and information technology initiatives

Looking back ...

This paper was written for presentation at the New Technologies for Higher Education Conference, University of Aveiro, Portugal, sponsored by the European Union in 1998, and again, under the title 'Effective Evaluation: Why it is important and how to do it well' at an EU Concertation Meeting in Brussels in 1999. It was then revised and extended for publication in 2001. Its origins explain its focus on higher education and the wider context of EU policy rather than UK policy as is the case in other chapters. Shortly before writing it I had heard Frank Coffield present his paper, 'A tale of three little pigs: building the learning society with straw' (Coffield 1998) and this gave me interesting insights into the inter-relationship between European and UK education policy.

The world has moved on a bit in the nine years since the paper was first presented. The context for both research and evaluation work has changed considerably in the USA, as a result of the neo-conservative policies of the Bush administration. In the UK, New Labour has invested heavily in social services, including education, and looked for research evidence to inform policy development, making this an interesting period for evaluators. Technology has moved forward rapidly, especially with regard to the speed and functionality of the Internet, the rapid development of interface protocols and user conventions for web browsing, and the very welcome shift towards involving professional designers in the construction of websites. With broadband connectivity the Internet is now part of everyday life in the UK. However, many of the issues for innovative ICT programmes in education remain as problematic as ever, so there is little that I would change were I to be writing the article today. (CIT, rather than ICT, was the term used in HE at the time.)

We have reached a point in time when it is possible to envisage that Communications and Information Technology (CIT) could begin to deliver some of the educational goals which have been promised for the last two decades. The technology itself is now much more user-friendly; the community of software engineers and developers has the benefit of experience; the Internet has given us an accepted international platform for delivering and accessing material; and, despite disappointments, EU and national policy-makers and politicians are still providing substantial funding (compared with the funding available for other initiatives).

However, we should not be lulled into underestimating the difficulty of the task. In this chapter, I will argue that evaluation is an essential, integral component of all innovative programmes, and is particularly important in the field of CIT because of its complexity and the technical demands it makes on users. I will begin by outlining the many purposes for which evaluations are commonly commissioned. I will then go on to discuss the characteristic problematic features of development work in CIT. And I will finish by putting forward a model for evaluation that can help to ensure excellence in CIT programmes. The model involves both a formative support role and a summative role for the evaluator and I will argue that, because of the problematic nature of CIT initiatives, both roles are essential if the evaluation is to assist in ensuring excellence.

The purposes for which evaluations are commissioned

Evaluation in the social sciences is a form of research that differs from other forms of research because it is commissioned by a sponsor. The evaluators work under contract to pursue objectives that relate either to a funded development programme or to some phenomenon of human activity observable in present-day society. Evaluation, therefore, differs from other research in its inescapably politicised nature, deriving from the need to manage the inter-relationships between the sponsor and other stakeholders and feed into the process of decision-making.

Although it may appear that the purpose of evaluations is obvious, they are in fact commissioned for many different reasons. They are always concerned with judging the value of what has been achieved, but the basis for judgements, the uses to which these judgements are put, and the range of stakeholders who have a right to know the outcomes of the evaluation, may vary considerably. An important part of the evaluator's role is to discover the sponsor's purposes, both explicit and hidden, and take these into account when designing and carrying out the evaluation.

Ideally, an evaluation could be said to be primarily educative. Its purpose is to find out what has gone well and what not so well, in order to learn from this. This educative purpose may focus mainly on the future, by drawing out lessons at the end of the programme and making them available to inform the design and conduct of future programmes. Or it may focus more upon the current programme, drawing out lessons during the course of the work and feeding these back to those concerned so that the work of the programme can be continuously improved while it is on-going. The former are sometimes called 'summative evaluations' and the latter 'formative evaluations'. In practice, most evaluations have both summative and formative elements, which are inter-related, but they usually have a stronger orientation to one than the other. The notion of an educative evaluation fits well with the concept of a 'learning society' but sponsors often find it an unexpected approach. House *et al.* (1996, p. 139), in a study of evaluation practice in the US National Science Foundation, identify the importance of 'establishing an evaluation culture'. I would argue that educative evaluation is essential to a genuine learning society (DfEE 1997; NCIHE 1997), but is antipathetic to the 'technocratic model' that Coffield argues underpins the rhetoric about the learning society in many European and UK policies (Coffield 1998).

Evaluations nearly always have a second purpose: to satisfy the need for accountability for the spending of the sponsor's (often the tax payers') money. Has the money been spent wisely, have the outcomes been sufficient in number and of sufficiently high quality? Can the programme be said to have been cost effective? The sub-agenda here is who should get the credit if things go well, or bear the blame if they do not go well? Accountability is always layered in a hierarchy of responsibility: the programme director and team(s) are held accountable for their work on the programme; and the officials who hired them are held accountable for choosing them for the job and keeping them on track; politicians, in their turn, are held accountable for the actions of their officials; ultimately, accountability in a democratic state is to the electorate, and politicians who are seen to preside over the waste of public money are unlikely to be re-elected. In the UK, the Audit Commission carries out evaluations wholly to serve the need for public accountability. The focus of their work is entirely upon value for money and they claim an authority for their findings that is grounded in facts and figures, without taking account of the value-laden assumptions that have determined what facts and figures should be collected (see for example Audit Commission (1990) which presents a case for closing small rural schools based on calculations which do not take account of the impact of closure of its school upon a rural community).

These two main purposes of evaluation are, therefore, in tension with one another. In order to learn it is important to acknowledge failures, as well as successes, and explore the reasons for both, openly and honestly, but this will be difficult to do if individuals feel that their future careers will suffer as a result. Programme directors may not get further funding; officials may be side-lined or passed over for promotion; politicians may lose their seats in government. In practice, a lot depends on the prevailing culture set by those in positions of power, and the way they handle publicity and the media. If there is a strong blame culture at the top this will be passed down the line and make it difficult to learn from the evaluation. If, however, those at the top have trust in their officials and encourage open public debate, they can set the tone for a learning culture that will permeate through all the levels. This analysis is too simple, since a strong personality in a powerful position can, to an extent, act as a protective layer against blame and enable a learning culture to grow among subordinates. There is also a role for an evaluator in mediating between sponsors and the programme team(s), providing explanations for problems, often in terms of the contextual factors such as policy decisions that have constrained the possibilities for action. MacDonald developed a model of democratic evaluation in which equal rights are accorded by the evaluator to all the participants (MacDonald 1974). In democratic evaluation, successes and failures are explored in relation to the policies and structures put in place by the sponsors rather than simply in terms of the programme's outcomes. MacDonald found that this was frequently a surprise to those who had commissioned the evaluation, who assumed an alternative model of 'autocratic' evaluation in which those who hired the evaluator were themselves above judgement.

Another frequent reason for evaluation is largely symbolic. It may be a condition of setting up a programme that a proportion of the funds should be set aside for evaluation. In this case, the sponsors may not be greatly concerned with the evaluation's outcomes, provided there is a report and the evaluation can be said to have been commissioned and carried out. Alternatively, evaluations may be commissioned in order to promote the programme, and sponsors may expect the evaluator to engage in advocacy on behalf of the programme. Stake (1998) provides a case study of work in the USA, which goes some way to explaining the differences in values and motivations which lead to this kind of grave misunderstanding and the ethical implications for evaluators.

It is common for evaluators to be led to believe that an evaluation has been commissioned to feed into decision-making when, in fact, the decision-making time-frame is too short to wait for the evaluation report. If this is the case, interim reports or meetings with the sponsor part-way through the course of the evaluation may be much more influential than the final report. An additional complication is that policies often begin to change and shift after the evaluation has been commissioned and begun work; and evaluators are often pressured to introduce new elements or shift the focus of the study. Although this can normally be resisted by citing the contract, many evaluators prefer to take on board the new focus in order to produce a report that is more likely to have an impact on future policy.

There are, in broad terms, two kinds of question which can be the focus of evaluations:

1   *Questions which seek factual information*
    These questions start with words like 'how much/many ... ?' and 'how quickly ... ?' In terms of hardware and software development this kind of question includes: 'does it function ... ?' and 'how robust is it ... ?' These include questions asking people for their opinions, in order to find out how many people hold one opinion and how many hold another. The latter involve administering structured questionnaires (e.g. using Likert scales) to a representative sample which can be compared with 'a control group'. The resulting quantitative data can be analysed statistically (using probability theory) and the outcomes treated as facts, subject to a margin of error. These questions are designed to provide dependable, factual data to inform judgement. These data are sometimes called 'hard data'.

2   *Questions which seek reasons and explanations*
    These questions start with words like 'why ... ?' and 'how ... ?' For example, 'how effective was this piece of software?' and 'what strategies for collaboration proved most successful and why?' These questions explore issues of quality and seek informed judgements and in-depth explanations. They are designed to generate data which can form the basis for explanatory theories. Data are normally collected using methods such as observation and interviewing or open-ended questionnaires. These data can be analysed using methods of qualitative data analysis, which will involve coding the data in some form and then interpreting the outcomes. Theorists of qualitative methods sometimes use terms such as 'theoretical sensitivity' (Strauss and Corbin 1990) to describe the most highly developed interpretative skills of the qualitative researcher or evaluator. These data are sometimes called 'soft data'.

Learning cultures which place priority on the educative purposes of evaluation give a higher priority to the second kind of question, whereas accountability cultures give a higher priority to the former. The terms 'hard data' and 'soft data' are primarily used by those who favour quantitative methods as a means of undermining the credibility of qualitative methods – who after all wants to base judgements on something 'soft'? If possible, evaluators should avoid relying completely on either one kind of data or the other – both quantitative and qualitative data are essential so that the evaluation can produce reliable information and robust explanatory theories. Arguably, without the latter an evaluation cannot be educative.

For various reasons politicians and policy-makers often place higher reliance upon quantitative methods. This is partly because there is always pressure on them to be able to claim certainty in justifying how they have spent public money, and they can do this more easily with research based on the methods of the natural sciences because they command a high level of public confidence. Quantitative measurements of empirical studies have enabled the amazing technological progress that has led to the production of CIT resources; and statistical analyses of large bodies of data collected in controlled, experimental conditions have produced knowledge about illness and the human body which has revolutionised medical practice. However, a group of human beings interacting with one another to work collaboratively or learn new skills – say for example, a group of computer users – is subject to irrational responses and unpredictable behaviour in a way that the human body, as a functioning system, is not. The social sciences, of which evaluation is a sub-set, have adapted quantitative statistical methods to apply to group behaviour and human interactions, but the results of this kind of analysis are much less reliable than is often claimed (see House 1980, p. 71 who refers to the conclusions of an extensive study by Cronbach). It is particularly important to remember this when evaluating CIT initiatives because technologists may tend to privilege quantitative methods with which they are familiar in their own research. Paradoxically, qualitative methods may be essential to enable technologists to understand the complex emotional and cultural factors which make it difficult for non-technologists to become confident and competent users of technology (see Chapter 4).

Most evaluators now accept the need to use mixed methods in evaluating CIT initiatives, combining the collection of both quantitative and qualitative data (e.g. Greene and Caracelli 1997). However, the point is that many policy-makers and sponsors continue to have an unthinking preference for quantification and measurement. Evaluators need to continue to argue the case for mixed methods very persuasively.

Characteristic problematic features of CIT programmes

In this section I will outline the problematic features of CIT programmes, for two reasons; first, because it is helpful for all stakeholders to understand the ways in which such programmes may differ from other innovatory initiatives; and second, because such programmes can easily be undermined by these problems and, in the next section, I want to suggest a role for evaluators in preventing this from occurring.

CIT programmes are defined here as any that involve either developing software or infrastructure, or developing the use of CIT systems by individuals or groups, or integrating CIT into organisational structures and practices.

In the final section I will be outlining a model of programme evaluation that contributes to ensuring excellence in CIT initiatives, by combining both formative and summative roles. To undertake this dual role, evaluators need to pay attention to both the products of CIT programmes and the processes by which the programme teams carry out the work. Both feed into the success of the programme's outcomes because, for the products to be successful, the team needs to work together effectively – as a genuine team.

Process problems

Collaboration

> Technological innovation, and its diffusion, reflects complex collaboration between different stakeholders, typically involving partnerships between the State, universities and business.
>
> (Cullen *et al.* 1993, p. 117)

It is in the nature of technology projects that they require a high level of collaboration between disparate groups. This requires a mixing of cultures, in which each group brings its own assumptions about what counts as valuable embedded in the language they habitually use and their working practices. Geertz (1973) provides a metaphor for culture as 'webs of meaning', perfectly describing the apparently insubstantial nature of our deeply rooted allegiances to a range of cultural identities. The purposes of the state, universities and businesses are very different but they frequently come together to work on technology projects. The time-frames of politicians and businesses are shorter than those of academics, so there is a tension between the emphasis on short-term as opposed to medium to long-term goals. There are also issues of commercial secrecy, essential for business partners, which conflict with both the ideal of academic freedom and the obligation to share knowledge developed with public money provided by the nation state or federal government or the European Union. The overt differences overlay the hidden cultural differences and the two reinforce each other.

Collaboration is, in any case, a much more complex and difficult process than is generally recognised (Somekh 2006a). One of the great benefits and pleasures of working on EU programmes is the requirement to work as part of an international team. For Europeans this is culturally enriching and the strengths, in terms of skills, of each national group are made available to others through collaboration. Nevertheless, there is a price to pay for these benefits of European integration. Teams often come together with little prior knowledge of each other. Usually one or two of the partners will have worked together in the past, but the others will be strangers. Even if we all spoke the same language – heaven forbid – there would be inevitable misunderstandings because meaning is constructed by groups on the basis of interaction and shared experience. Meanings become even less precise when the team is working in several languages on a day-to-day basis and operating at different levels of familiarity in an agreed common language for meetings and reports. There are also inevitable stresses in working together to tight deadlines to produce high-quality 'deliverables'. There may be different expectations of what counts as quality; there will certainly be different understandings of how best to manage time. Overlaying the deep-rooted differences in national culture there are differences of research culture. One group may be more practical and pragmatic and focus wholly upon the contractual outcomes and deliverables; another may believe it to be essential to begin by developing the theoretical and philosophical knowledge upon which to base the practical work. Political ideology may also be a factor. In the UK, between 1979 and 1996, we were led by a government that emphasised competition rather than collaboration and set the tone for a blame culture rather than a learning culture. For many of us this has made it a particular pleasure to work on EU collaborative projects, but we have also been unable to avoid our association with a country that has been perceived by other Europeans to be 'isolationist' and often 'arrogant' and 'difficult'.

Mixed skill teams

To be successful, CIT projects in education need to bring together researchers and practitioners from different disciplines. Software development is the province of software engineers and computer programmers; despite the increased availability of advanced software tools and libraries of routines there is and will continue to be a need for specialists who can maximise the power and flexibility of the technology. At the same time, the development of learning materials is the province of the educational specialist; what appears on the screen is the province of the electronic designer; and the content of the material is the province of a relevant subject specialist.

In practice, this means that individuals from different disciplines have to learn to work together. The social process of such projects is grounded in, and constructed by, conflicting paradigms and discourses. What Foucault says about society in general is equally applicable to groups working in specific disciplines with their own distinctive cultures:

> Each society has its regime of truth, its 'general politics' of truth: that is, the types of discourse which it accepts and makes function as true; the mechanisms and instances which enable one to distinguish true and false statements, the means by which each is sanctioned; the techniques and procedures accorded value in the acquisition of truth; the status of those who are charged with saying what counts as true.
>
> (Foucault 1972, p. 131)

These differences affect every aspect of the project from fundamental beliefs (e.g. what kind of research needs to be carried out) to day-to-day working practice (e.g. the frequency and purpose of meetings).

Over-ambition

Perhaps it is the rapid pace at which technology has advanced that leads to the unrealistic aspirations which are often characteristic of technology-based projects. The origin of the problem lies with the unrealistic demands of sponsors. Technological innovations are often seen as having the potential to bring about major change at the system or state level (see Chapter 6 of this book), and in this way they seem to offer the kind of high profile, system-wide, 'magic solutions' so dear to politicians (House 1974, pp. 213–14). This phenomenon originates in the fact that technology projects are usually shrouded in a certain mystique. As Cullen *et al.* also point out:

> Technological innovations do not draw on an unbounded pool of knowledge available in society at large, but rather focus on an existing technological base which may reflect the goals and objectives of institutions (Mackenzie and Wajcman 1985).
>
> (Cullen *et al.* 1993, p. 117)

This dependence of technology projects upon specialist technological knowledge also makes it difficult for non-specialists to judge their potential at the stage of the grant proposal. In the highly competitive business of bidding for funding, the temptation for those writing grant proposals to oversell the benefits of the proposed initiative is always strong. In the case of technology initiatives, because sponsors and the public in general are ill-informed, it is possible to succumb to this temptation and remain credible.

CIT programmes are, therefore, often in the position of managing the disappointment of sponsors as the work progresses towards completion. This phenomenon was particularly apparent in the first phase of the UK Teaching and Leaning Technology Programme in which some projects (but certainly not all) achieved considerably less than had been promised (Coopers and Lybrand *et al.* 1996).

Another problem of over-ambition is that technology projects sometimes rely upon technology too much as a means of communication. Telephone systems in all the participating institutions or countries may not be adequate to meet the demands of the programme; hardware may be delivered late; software may take time to install; local needs may conflict with programme needs, leading to problems with differences in protocols, particularly with the transfer of files as attachments in electronic mail. Sponsors expect far-flung CIT programmes to communicate electronically and may reduce travel budgets accordingly. This can lead to serious difficulties.

Delay

What a programme director – or a sponsor – expects to be possible at the time of designing the research is often not possible when work actually begins. As long ago as 1984 I found out to my cost that if you ask most ICT technical personnel in general terms if they can do something they will say yes, but if you ask them again three months later to do it now they will say, well not now, tomorrow ... Things are always promised for the near future, but unexpected problems constantly arise and delay implementation. One reason for this is, of course, that it is unacceptable to carry out development work with yesterday's technology. Hardware and software rapidly become out of date, so it is a difficult challenge for a three-year CIT programme to produce state-of-the-art products. This makes it essential to use the newest technology for development tools, but this makes the programme vulnerable to late delivery and/or software bugs. Installation also usually takes much longer than planned. Sometimes buildings have to be adapted, electric wiring has to be changed, new furniture has to be purchased, telephone lines have to be installed. I have never yet evaluated a technology project which was not subject to some delay at its inception. In one case, involving colleagues rather than myself, the delay was so extensive that, combined with the unrealistic time-frame for the work set by the sponsors, some of the software products never reached user groups for trialling because they still did not run at the end of the funded period (Norris *et al.* 1990).

Product problems

Lack of established conventions for effective communication

It is still much more difficult to design high-quality learning materials for electronic delivery, via multi-media, CD-ROM, or the Internet, than it is to design paper-based materials. This may partly be because there is no notion of a professional publisher for electronic materials. The process of publication is incorporated with development and the product is produced by the technologists. Perhaps it is hardly surprising that many of these materials lack professional polish in their finished form. However, the problem is a more fundamental one. A book or a journal follows an established format, the reader knows what to expect, the author can use established conventions such as chapters, bibliographies and indexes. More elaborate paper-based learning materials, such as those produced by the Open University in the UK, have been designed with the benefit of years of experience to be easy-to-use and readable, incorporating the right balance of text and 'white space'. By contrast, we are still learning how to communicate effectively in electronic form. There are relatively few established conventions and we are still at the stage of exploration. The pull-down menu, the hot button, the switch from pointer to hand as it hovers over the button, and the change of colour after a text button has been clicked on, all seem to be established conventions, but there are relatively few others. Developers are still experimenting with navigation systems to provide structures which are flexible without causing the user to get 'lost'; the interface between the software development tool and the learning environment it has created is often discordant; and there is little agreement about how much text it is reasonable to put on the screen. The proportion of images to text on Internet screens has changed dramatically in response to increased speed of accessing images and user preferences for pictures and colour, but our long habit of privileging textual representations makes it difficult for those designing educational materials to make creative use of more visually rich environments. It is claimed that one of the great benefits of CIT materials is their interactive components in which the user engages with the materials which change in response to user-inputs. However, in practice it requires considerable skill to design interesting and challenging interactive materials. We still lack sufficient models of how to do this in effective and varied ways. Indeed, the expectation that electronic learning materials will communicate with users effectively without the supportive intervention of a teacher is so far proving untenable in practice.

The medium constrains the content

A major difficulty is the way in which the electronic medium constrains the way that the content can be presented. This is partly to do with digital memory constraints. Text is less memory-hungry and (despite the improvements in accessing images noted in the previous paragraph) is accessed more quickly over the Internet, hence most learning materials use more text than diagrams, photographs or moving images. Rather more worrying, because more fundamental and long-term, is the way in which computerised tools for analysis impose a logic on the storage of information. There is a tendency to categorise information so that it can be sorted and counted, rather than storing it in an uncategorised form and using it holistically. There is also a tendency to produce text in screen-sized chunks with simplified vocabulary and syntax. The small size of the screen is thus beginning to have the effect of creating a tabloid-newspaper style of on-line communication, with a tendency to simplify ideas and concepts, and present them in a fragmented or partial way. This kind of reductionism is balanced by the ability to down-load whole documents for printing and it may be that screen-reading will never become the accepted norm for lengthy documents.

It is in the area of traditional testing and assessment that the constraints of the medium are most apparent. CIT learning materials often have built-in assessment, but very few styles of format are possible. The only method which is reasonably simple to produce is the multiple-choice question bank. These can be designed to test understanding of concepts at a deep level, but this requires the person setting the test to have considerable skills in test design as well as in-depth understanding of the subject matter. At present, many of the tests incorporated with CIT learning packages are rudimentary and simplistic. If this kind of testing becomes the norm it could have the effect of reducing knowledge to information, as predicted by Roszak (1986), and its acquisition to a technical process much less challenging to the learner than constructing knowledge – and fundamentally less educative.

The halo effect and tolerance of poor quality

There are worrying indications at the present time of an explosion of higher education teaching materials on the Internet. There is some evidence that this is leading to poor-quality materials being accepted uncritically because of the medium in which they are being presented. The web has a halo effect, which lends an unwarranted value and respectability to minimal products. For example, some university tutors are simply placing the 'bullet point' PowerPoint presentations from their lectures on the website, together with reading lists. While these are useful supplementary resources for students who have attended the lectures, they are arid in the extreme for anyone who was not present on the day. The next step is to put learning materials on the web. Unfortunately, easy-to-produce electronic learning materials, constructed from one of the existing 'open shell' software products, tend to be highly repetitive in format and dull for the learner to use. In many cases the authors could have produced far more interesting, better-quality materials, in another media. The greatest potential for on-line learning in HE seems to lie in interactive websites. One approach is to use software such as CBCM or WebCT, where groups of students engage in dialogue with each other and/or their tutors, but such sites need careful management and are most successful where they are set up as an integral part of the formal course structure. In an extensive study of project-based collaborative group work in courses at the University of Twente, Collis (1998) concludes that affective factors relating to human–computer interaction continue to cause some intractable problems.

There is, however, pressure from higher education managers/administrators to teach students 'on-line', with an assumption that this is less time-consuming than teaching in a conventional manner; at its worst this leads to no more than audio-taped lectures being added to the PowerPoint presentations on the website. Without proper time-allocation for teaching 'distance-learning' students enrolled to take such a 'course', university tutors are soon overwhelmed with a flood of email queries that prove much more time-consuming to deal with than they had anticipated.

Inappropriateness to users and inappropriate uses

The biggest problem for designers of CIT materials remains the difficulty of matching users' needs. This is a dual problem – partly one of judging the level of difficulty of the content correctly, but partly too of creating a user-interface that makes it possible for all learners to participate with ease and confidence. The computer environment remains a technological environment. The human–computer interface problem is still not solved (Collis, op. cit.). In the end, the lone user contributes the essential element to his or her learning that Gavriel Salomon (1992) calls AIME (Amount of Invested Mental Effort) (see Chapter 6 of this book). CIT materials are more dependent upon AIME than most other kinds of learning materials because they are more likely to be used without the support of a teacher. It is always crucial to involve members of potential user groups in the development of the materials and to pilot their use with learners. In practice, many CIT development programmes find it difficult to do this effectively because they are working to a tight time-frame and running behind schedule.

The quality of the learning materials is of paramount importance, but this can only be determined in relation to theories of effective learning. There is no one right theory, but too many CIT products are developed without taking account of any learning theory. Elsewhere I have reviewed some of the learning theories that seem to me to be worth taking into account (Somekh 1996). Another study by Koppi *et al.* (1998) explores the role of technology in enabling five desirable learning outcomes: holistic appreciation of where the subject fits into a global context, active experiential knowledge, collaborative communication and team work, problem-solving and critical thinking, and control over one's own learning in order to become a life-long learner.

Another problem for designers is that they have no control over the uses to which the materials will be put. Users may spend little time on those parts of materials designed for concentrated work; they may use strategies to accelerate progress on the task which circumvent the learning 'track' (e.g. giving deliberately wrong answers to test questions in an ILS system). Many studies show that teachers play an essential role in supporting learners in using such materials (e.g. NCET 1994a), yet in cases where the materials are mediated by school teachers there is the possibility for investigative work to be trivialised (e.g. by the teacher partially supplying the answer), and, in higher education, there may be an assumption that no teacher support is needed. When authoring tools are made available for use with open-ended resources, many teachers reduce the potential interactivity of the materials by creating electronic work sheets (Norris *et al.*1990).

The role of evaluation in ensuring excellence in CIT programmes

As a result of the problematic features of CIT programmes, outlined in the previous section, their evaluation makes special demands on evaluators. In this section I will put forward an approach to the evaluation of CIT programmes which is largely derived from my own experience, but also draws upon the evaluation literature.

During the last 25 years considerable research has been done to develop robust strategies for evaluating programmes. In an early study, House (1980) defines eight separate approaches including 'systems analysis', 'behavioural objectives' and 'case study'. He does not recommend any one approach, but concludes (ibid., p. 256) that, 'Public evaluation should be democratic, fair, and ultimately based upon the moral values of equality, autonomy, impartiality, and reciprocity.' Ultimately evaluation is about making value judgements but doing so on the best possible evidence. After 30 years experience, Cronbach came to the conclusion that:

> The evaluator should almost never sacrifice breadth of information for the sake of giving a definite answer to one narrow question. To arrange to collect the most helpful information requires a high degree of imagination, coupled with the flexibility to change plans in midstudy.
>
> (Cronbach 1982, p. xii)

Currently, there is a preoccupation with the tension between the educative and the accountability purposes of evaluation that I referred to in the first section of this paper (Greene 1999). McEldowney (1997, p. 176) refers to these more explicitly as the 'control' model and the 'helping' model of evaluation. He explores the concepts of 'deadweight', 'displacement' and 'additionality' as means of judging the value for money of a programme, but concludes that although this is a useful approach:

(It is) often without regard to the difficulties and limitations that exist in measuring these concepts (and is often at the expense of) a consultative style where a transfer of learning should occur based on timely feedback to program managers about the effectiveness of patticular interventions or measures and about the achievement of the objectives set for the program in question.

(McEldowney 1997, p. 186)

Those who see evaluation as primarily an educative process place emphasis upon its utilisation (Patton 1986). Others such as Stake (1998, pp. 203–4) see their role as 'finding and understanding quality' and warn against becoming 'collaborators in redevelopment'. The tension between these two approaches is now one that evaluators frequently need to address, since currently there is considerable interest in approaches to evaluation which take into account the needs of multiple stakeholders (Somekh *et al.* 1999).

Some of the most interesting recent work has reported on various approaches to evaluating multi-site programmes. In the case of European Social Fund programmes, evaluators have the opportunity of looking at similar initiatives implemented in different countries, with the possibility of determining the effects of adopting different strategies. Barbier and Simonin (1997, p. 396) look at two levels of imple-mentation: 'the political, administrative and financial level' and 'the street level' but cite Hall (1996) in concluding that comparisons are difficult as 'all actors involved have objectives of their own; the more numerous they are, the more objectives and points of view there are'. In the case of CIT projects funded by the EU each partner normally contributes in different ways to each work package and takes responsibility for different deliverables. Nevertheless, there is potential for much greater depth of understanding when working with more than one partner. Large-scale multi-site evaluations require good organisation and good communication. The numbers of partners involved at meetings can pose problems, hence some evaluators have developed tools for structuring discussion and consultation (Beywl and Potter 1998). The Kellogg's Foundation's 'cluster evaluation' approach is of particular interest. It has four key characteristics:

1   It looks for common threads and themes across sites.
2   It seeks to learn why things happened as well as what happened.
3   It is highly collaborative, encouraging all players to participate.
4   It maintains confidentiality between the external evaluators and the projects (i.e. project teams had enhanced control over the release of information beyond their project).

(adapted from Worthen and Schmitz 1997, p. 303)

Evaluations of CIT in education fall into two broad categories: evaluations of funded programmes and evaluations of general uptake as a result of on-going policies and accumulated spending on CIT within the education system. An important evaluation of the general uptake of CIT in the US education system was the 1998 national Teaching, Learning and Computing (TLC) survey (Becker 2000), which provided rich contextual information on teacher beliefs and attitudes, usage in teaching and the location of equipment, as well as information on the numbers of computers in schools. It achieved a response rate of 75 per cent. A very early evaluation of a computers in education programme was House's analysis of the PLATO programme which began in the USA in 1960. According to House (1974, p. 188), the political imperative for PLATO to succeed was so great that the reality of the technical problems, poor-quality 'lessons' and excessive time demands upon the teachers developing materials were not acknowledged, and it continued to receive funding for a number of years. During the 1990s the focus of CIT evaluation in the USA was on meeting the requirements of the 1993 Government Performance and Results Act (GPRA) for performance measurement (Greene 1999, p. 161). This led to the production of materials to assist administrators/managers in evaluating initiatives in-house, such as the 'framework of 7 inter-dependent dimensions' for planning, implementing and evaluating initiatives, produced by the Milken Exchange on Education Technology (1998); and the 'evaluation tool kits that can be used to support local and national studies of the educational uses of computers, video and telecommunications', produced by the Flashlight project supported first by the Annenberg Foundation and later by the American Association for Higher Education (Ehrmann 1997). To ensure quality in a field increasingly open to newcomers, the Joint Committee on Standards for Educational Evaluation, sponsored by 15 national associations of researchers, teachers and education officers, including the American Evaluation Association, produced Program Evaluation Standards setting out 'how to assess evaluations of educational programs' (Sanders 1994) and these were updated and re-titled, Guiding Principles for Evaluators, in 2004 (see below).

In the UK, a large number of projects were funded in higher education within the Teaching and Learning Technology Programme, and many of these included funding for an evaluation. Data for section two of this article is partly drawn from my own work as evaluator of a project funded to develop courseware to teach accountancy in Phase One of TLTP (Somekh 2001). A typical example of a more recent TLTP evaluation is given by Hall and Harding (2000), who report on a project implementing the use of computer-based teaching in a university History Department. The shift from the development of materials to in-house support for implementing their use is partly the result of the recommendations of the 1996 evaluation of TLTP by Coopers and Lybrand *et al.* (op. cit.) which found that uptake of TLTP resources had been disappointingly low. A year later, the report on IT and Teaching and Learning in Higher Education (ITATL), commissioned by the Dearing Enquiry into Higher Education, was inconclusive in its findings, mainly because the sponsors demanded a large element of cost–benefit analysis for which the data were not available from universities (Boucher *et al.* 1997). Within the school system in the UK, strong political interest in Success Maker and other Integrated Learning Systems (ILS), as 'solutions' to under-achievement, led to a series of three major evaluation studies (NCET 1994a, 1996; Wood 1998). The conclusions of these studies discouraged any major national investment in ILS. Other evaluations during the 1990s also had a significant impact on policy. The Superhighways Initiative (EDSI), an innovative initiative to encourage commercial sponsorship for networked technology projects, incorporated a government-funded evaluation involving five teams of evaluators and a synopter (Scrimshaw 1997; Somekh *et al.* 1999). The EDSI findings led directly into a major programme to establish the National Grid for Learning and provide system-wide training for teachers in ICT. The evaluation of the Multimedia Portable Computers for Teachers pilot project, funded by the National Council for Educational Technology (NCET) (Harrison *et al.* 1997), has been important in confirming the efficacy of giving teachers powerful portable computers for their own use. A major national initiative to provide all teachers with this technology resulted.

Evaluation to ensure excellence: towards the effective evaluation of CIT programmes

I want now to recommend an approach to evaluation as an essential, integral component of achieving excellence in innovative CIT research and development programmes. The approach presupposes principles, goals and contributions from the evaluators to both the development of the produce and the working processes of the programme.

Principles of the evaluation

The evaluation should:

- build trust with the team(s)
- remain independent of the team(s) and other stakeholders
- operate within agreed ethical guidelines.

Evaluators are in a position of power in relation to the programme director and team(s). Their access to information and the quality of the information they collect is dependent upon establishing trust. They need to form good working relationships with the director and team(s) so that they have access to the informal, as well as the formal, working processes of the programme. Evaluators need to understand problems. In my view their privileged position places them under an obligation to provide advice and assistance where they can, within the limits of their remit. The evaluators' active engagement with the purposes and working practices of the team make this approach somewhat akin to the kind of 'participatory evaluation' recommended by Cousins and Earl (1995) in which 'trained evaluation personnel (or research specialists) and practice-based decision makers (work) in partnership' (p. 8). However, I am not here suggesting that the project participants take on any of the function of the evaluators, because a large part of the evaluators' usefulness results from their independence. They need to maintain a distance from the programme director and team(s). Striking the right balance between independence and informality is important. In my experience you need both, with some formal procedures to distinguish between different purposes for different occasions. Once trust and informal relations have been established it can be helpful to formalise some of the data-collection events and meetings, perhaps by linking them to formal written feedback.

The evaluation must operate within clear ethical guidelines which give all concerned control over access to information and its clearance for publication. A good starting point is the codes of practice that set ethical standards for evaluation practice that have been produced by the American Evaluation Association and the British Educational Research Association (AEA 2004; BERA 2004). However, each evaluation needs to develop its own code of practice customised to the institutional and political context of the programme. It is best to negotiate these guidelines with the programme director and team(s) early in the life of the project and produce an agreed written statement. The team(s) needs to be assured that any written reports will be fair and accurate, that they will be asked to comment on draft reports and play a part in improving their fairness and accuracy, and that where they disagree with an interpretation made by the evaluators they will have the right to have their own alternative views included in the report. An example of guidelines of this kind, developed for an action research project, are given in Somekh (1997). The guidelines have at least three purposes:

- to ensure that the evaluation is able to report fully and fairly on the work of the programme, which is important to ensure accountability for public spending;
- to protect the rights of the programme director and team(s) and place reasonable limits on the power of the evaluators, which is important to ensure social justice;
- to ensure that the evaluators have access to full information, without the team(s) feeling the need to conceal anything potentially damaging, which is important to ensure quality.

Aims of the evaluation

- Identify and address the various purposes of the evaluation.
- Address both the formative and the summative aspects of the evaluation.
- Meet the needs of stakeholders.
- Generate both quantitative information and explanatory theories.

It is very important for the evaluators to begin by exploring the various purposes of the evaluation, to ensure that they are able to address any purposes that may have been intentionally or unintentionally concealed as well as stated purposes. House (2000, p. 80), for example, warns that important values issues may be hidden from sponsors and participants if the evaluation employs methods such as cost–benefit analysis without careful investigation of embedded assumptions. This process of clarification is important in identifying the partisan interests of different stakeholders so that they can be taken into account, while ensuring that the evaluation takes a non-partisan view. This might involve adopting what Datta (2000, p. 2) calls the role of 'an advocate for pluralism'.

Evaluations are always politicised, sometimes strongly so. The development of policy for CIT in education is contested because it is costly and because it is often the source and focus of aspirations. Power is exercised at different levels. Evaluators need to make judgements about the extent to which different players have power, and monitor the shifts in the political context. Inevitably, therefore, evaluation is itself a political activity. It is better to acknowledge this than try to ignore it. Evaluation is an inherently moral activity that involves the evaluator in wielding power, however large or small, according to ethical principles (see the previous section).

Programmes developing CIT for education always have multiple stakeholders, including national or EU policy-makers, the programme team(s), commercial partners and users, such as teachers, students and local policy-makers. All these stakeholders have rights and all are likely to have different needs. It is a matter of democratic principle to address all their needs; but it is also a matter of professionalism and efficacy, since the stakeholders all have the potential to assist or to block the take-up of products. Clarifying the sponsors' purposes enables evaluators to get some understanding of the time frame for decision-making, so that they are in the best possible position to influence future policy: for example, sometimes an interim report may have more impact if it is produced by a particular date. It also helps in deciding on the balance to be struck between the formative and summative purposes of the evaluation: for example, if the purpose of the evaluation from the sponsor's point of view is mainly symbolic, there is little point in placing the main emphasis upon a detailed summative report; instead time can be better spent on producing more detailed formative feedback for the team(s).

Depending upon the purposes of the evaluation and the needs of the various stakeholders, the evaluators will need to make different judgements on the right balance between quantitative measurement and the development of qualitative understanding. Both are important in the evaluation of CIT programmes which always involve stakeholders from technological or business backgrounds, who place a high value on statistical measures, as well as 'users' who fail to respond as positively as expected to CIT. User's problems often arise because they find CIT confusing or threatening, and understanding the reasons for this requires the exercise of careful judgement on the basis of qualitative data, for example from observations and interviews. There is a duty to provide both factual information about, and explanations for, progress/success that can provide the basis for future action. To ensure that the programme remains on track to achieve excellence, there is also a duty to include formative elements in the focus of the evaluation. Bhola (2000) gives an example of a form of 'impact evaluation' which addresses both of these needs by including three types of impact: 'impact by design, impact by interaction and impact by emergence' and requires the evaluators to use subtle, skilful, professional judgement in reaching conclusions that take a wide range of factors into consideration:

The evaluator will have to learn to listen and then to go beyond people's utterances. The unsaid will have to be heard; the invisible will have to be seen; both shadows and foreshadows will have to be registered. The evaluator will then have to 'hypothesize' plausible connections between the initial intervention and the impact by emergence and, in John Dewey's words, 'seek appropriate warrant to assert the reality of impact that emerged in people's lives' (Bhola 2000, p. 165).

Contributions of the evaluation to the development of the product

- Alert the team(s) to what has been learnt from previous projects of a similar kind.
- Monitor progress on the multiple tasks of the programme.
- Provide feedback on the products as they develop.
- Trial products with users, thereby assisting the programme to meet user needs.

The evaluators' contributions to ensuring excellence in a CIT programme need to include a direct input into the development of any CIT products. Normally, the first need is for the evaluators to contribute ideas from the wider educational research literature, much of which may be unknown to the programme team(s). For example, as an evaluator of a TLTP project developing courseware, one of my contributions was to review the literature on learning theory and feed this into the development process (Somekh 1996). Decisions that followed about the software development could then draw upon this knowledge which was not previously available to the project team. To be effective, this kind of input needs to be an integral part of established trust in working relations, rather than a one-off input. Evaluation is, unavoidably, an intervention; so it makes sense to acknowledge this and ensure that it is a positive intervention. A good example of a recent European evaluation of a CIT programme that adopted this kind of approach is the evaluation of the Telematics for Teacher Training Programme (T3). The T3 Evaluation, which was directed by Wim Veen from the University of Technology, Delft, The Netherlands, used the Concerns-Based Adoption Model (CBAM) developed by Hall *et al.* (1975).

> The foci of the evaluation effort was on:
> formative evaluation of the development and implementation of the new teaching practices using Telematics within the partner universities involved, and
> summative evaluation of outcomes and impact of the project as a whole and of the development of pedagogical approaches for Telematics learning environments.
>
> (Davis *et al.* 2000)

Honest feedback is of enormous value to programme directors and teams. My own preference is for very open preliminary feedback within a confidential framework that ensures that the focus is upon learning rather than upon judgement. I often distinguish between a draft report that I feel will make a good preliminary discussion document with the team(s) and the report that ultimately I write for publication. They have different purposes and can be dealt with differently.

The evaluator often acts as a broker of judgements on the products through collecting a range of data including stakeholders' perceptions. They can observe usage, interview users, count frequency of use, issue questionnaires, as well as trying the product out themselves as users. They have a particularly important role in feeding information back to the team(s), especially if the different stakeholders have different responses. Because of their relatively powerless position, students' views may be given less credence without the mediation of an evaluator. Without the evaluator they might not even have been asked for an opinion, but their views may be the ones that are most critical to the eventual success of the uptake of the product.

Contributions of the evaluation to the working process of the programme

- Mediate between the programme team(s) and multiple stakeholders.
- Mediate between team members where differences in attitudes and values exist.

Evaluators can also make very helpful contributions to the working processes of team(s). The separation of tasks into discrete units of responsibility, or work packages, means that individuals are often working in isolation; and personality differences or differences in disciplinary background or national culture between team members may lead to misunderstandings and escalating stress. The evaluators' monitoring function can help to keep everyone motivated and evaluators can also serve a useful role in keeping different partners aware of the work being carried out by others. This is particularly useful when dealing with several teams engaged in different aspects of a large programme. CIT programmes are pressured working environments. Deadlines have to be met; there are likely to have been delays; team members have their own purposes which are not necessarily the same as those of the sponsor, nor indeed of each other; they are usually working with the uncertainty of a fixed-term contract and future employment may depend upon pleasing the sponsor or pleasing the programme director (which are not necessarily the same thing). When colleagues are working under pressure misunderstandings can easily arise and evaluators can play a positive role in team building. Likewise, the programme director will be working under stress: responsible for delivering to target, needing to ensure that the reputation of the institution remains high, mindful that national policy-makers will be watching the outcomes of the project. Evaluators need to be good listeners and act as mediators between the programme director, the team(s) and various stakeholders, or between different members of the programme team(s). This again underlines the moral nature of the evaluator's role. They are in a position of trust and must act responsibly.

Postscript

Having set out my own ideas for the kind of evaluation that could enable excellence in CIT initiatives, I want to ensure that no one goes away under the illusion that I am putting this forward as a definitive answer, or that I have found it easy to implement this model unproblematically in my own work. People often mistake 'models' for 'blue-prints' that ensure quality through the mere implementation of procedures. This is certainly not the case. The value of models is that they provide a simple outline that can be adapted to complex situations through the exercise of judgement. There is no doubt that the approach I have put forward enables evaluators to make a substantial, positive contribution to the quality and productivity of the work of CIT programme teams, but every evaluator will need to renew it through the exercise of careful, informed judgements, suited to the particular programme to be evaluated.

Evaluation is a fascinating, socially useful, morally demanding and highly politicised activity. Its future depends upon the uses we put it to, and the role it is given by sponsors and politicians. As Ernie House says in the introduction to his book, *Professional Evaluation*:

> Evaluation has been shaped and continues to be shaped by powerful and complex social forces. Exactly what shape the institution, profession, discipline, and practice will take in the future is impossible to predict. What is clear is that the fate of evaluation will be bound to the government and the economic structure and will be determined in part by its own history and traditions. Part of the destiny of evaluation lies within the control of evaluators themselves; part does not.
>
> (House 1993, p. xvi)

9 Methodological issues in identifying and describing the way knowledge is constructed with and without ICT

Looking back ...

The initial ideas for this article were presented at a seminar at the University of Warwick sponsored by the Economic and Social Research Council (ESRC) in May 1999. However, its gestation spanned a two-year period and it was only completed and published in a special issue of the Journal for IT in Teacher Education *on ICT and Pedagogy in 2001. At the time when I wrote it I had recently moved to Manchester Metropolitan University and, relieved of management responsibilities, had been able to spend time exploring socio-cultural and activity theory. The article draws on these ideas and other theories from philosophy and psychology as well as my practical experience from research projects over the previous fifteen years. Writing it gave me an opportunity to locate my research practice in a clear methodological framework and provided a firm basis for taking my work forward in subsequent years.*

Little has changed in the education policy context I describe in the article, except that the ESRC Teaching and Learning Research Programme has continued to attract major funding. In 2006 it announced a new joint initiative of the ESRC and EPSRC (Engineering and Physical Sciences Council) in Technology-Enhanced Learning, and funded seven preliminary projects for six months to prepare proposals for future 'million-pound plus projects'. ICT is still at the heart of UK policy-makers' vision for transformation of the education system and TEL is intended to develop on-line materials and virtual environments to take the vision forward.

> Education, in its deepest sense and at whatever age it takes place, concerns the opening of identities – exploring new ways of being that lie beyond our current state. Whereas training aims to create an inbound trajectory targeted at competence in a specific practice, education must strive to open new dimensions for the negotiation of the self. It places students on an outbound trajectory toward a broad field of possible identities. Education is not merely formative – it is transformative.
>
> (Wenger 1998, p. 263)

The methods a researcher uses to identify and describe any element of human activity are dependent upon epistemological and cultural-political factors. The quotation with which this paper opens, for example, gives opposing definitions for 'education' and 'training' which have been derived through this socio-cultural process. To be precise, 'what counts' as knowledge for different interest groups, including politicians, policy-makers – and, in relation to educational research, teachers, parents and children – plays a major part in determining the social practices of human activity at any particular time, as well as shaping the likely response to the research when it is made public. And what counts as knowledge is determined by all the varied factors of the cultural-historical tradition, together with the current contests for power between the individuals and groups that make up society. At the same time, decisions to use particular methods are guided by the methodology that is an integral part of the researcher's practice, located in her/his personal and professional values. In addition, since research has the aim of generating knowledge, the research process involves construction as well as identification and description. It is an active rather than a passive process involving making informed judgements and using creativity and 'sociological imagination' (Mills 1959).

The methodological issues addressed in this paper reflect this meshing of epistemological and cultural-political factors, as well as deriving from my own experience as a researcher centrally concerned with the introduction of ICT in education, and its effectiveness as a tool for learning, since 1984.

Cultural political factors that influence the choice of research methods

The influence of cultural-political factors is particularly clear at the present time, since educational research has a high public profile as it emerges from an extended debate that has involved considerable negative criticism of researchers, their practices and their products (Freedman *et al.* 2000). The criticisms have related to the alleged irrelevance of much educational research to the practice of teaching, and in particular the esoteric language of academic publications, its small-scale nature, and the lack of generalisable outcomes which would 'demonstrate conclusively that if teachers change their practice from x to y there will be a significant and enduring improvement in teaching and learning' (Hargreaves 1996). The process of scrutiny, and in particular the report commissioned by the Department for Education and Employment, *Excellence in Research on Schools* (Hillage *et al.* 1998) has led to a considerable increase in funding for educational research, in particular through the £12.5 million Teaching and Learning Research Programme, funded by the Higher Education Funding Council and administered by the Economic and Social Research Council. The latter has closely defined aims and through a highly competitive selection process (in Phase II, 9 projects were funded from 94 proposals submitted) has defined what counts as knowledge and acceptable methodologies within a publicly funded programme of educational research. In particular, preference was given to projects which would lead to clear outcomes likely to have an impact upon practice, rather than those with a more exploratory, open-ended focus. There was an emphasis on 'measurement' and the use of control groups to establish a certain kind of evidence. The close links between the recent critique of educational research by powerful players in the political scene and the kind of projects funded within the programme is clear. In this sense, the choice of TLRP projects can be said to exemplify the processes of the sociology of knowledge.

It is, I believe, the responsibility of an educational researcher to contribute to the improvement of education. The methodological issues relate to judgements about how best to make this contribution in the light of one's own values. Given my own long experience of working closely with teachers using action research methodology, and my increasing interest in theories from cultural psychology that illuminate the process of change for individuals and groups, I adopt socio-cultural research methods which involve close participation with participants at all levels of societal or institutional hierarchies of power. A critically interesting methodological issue is how, then, to work in a positive synergy with policy-makers – who are important participants in the education system – while at the same time providing robust critiques, on the basis of research evidence, of those aspects of policy that are not working. Currently, we are all participants in an education system that is grounded in Wenger's definition of 'training' rather than 'education'. Since the Education Reform Act of 1988, through a wide range of policies including the establishment of a National Curriculum, the reduction in the power of Local Education Authorities, league tables of pupils' test and examination results, and a new regime of public inspection of schools, this has led, in the words of Barry MacDonald, to 'recalcitrant and alienated pupils' and 'a crisis of teacher recruitment' (MacDonald 2000, p. 23). Wenger's definition of 'education' has 'the opening of identities' as its central aim and this resonates well with Elliott's analysis of the underlying reasons for under-achievement in our current education system. Drawing on Fukuyama's book, *The End of History and the Last Man* (Fukuyama 1992), Elliott explores the twin motivations for human endeavour: first 'the desire for recognition' and second 'desires that stem from rational self-interest'. He argues that under-achievement in our schools is the result of policies that assume young people are motivated by the latter, whereas the prime motivation in a liberal democracy, after 'the end of history', is in fact the former. A sense of personal recognition is an essential part of the development of identity. Elliott asks:

> Could it be the case then, that the key to 'improving' schools in the liberal democratic societies of the West lies in the extent to which the curriculum, and the pedagogical processes by which children are engaged with it, provides students with opportunities to secure recognition of their worth as individuals, in a form which is congruent with the basic values from which people derive their sense of worth? The emergence of the liberal democratic state expresses the need of individuals, in the absence of traditional forms of social authority, to have not just their material desires satisfied but also their desire for recognition as autonomous and free agents capable of shaping the conditions of their existence in civil society.
>
> (Elliott 2000, p. 179)

By adopting a stance of interactive engagement with policy-makers, I can use insights such as Elliott's to build a positive critique of policy that remains incisive and independent but goes beyond detached deconstruction. That at least is the aim. I can try. The methodological issue is how so to do without compromising research so that it becomes a kind of collusion with power.

The nature of knowledge and coming-to-know

I now want to turn to epistemological factors relating to knowing and coming-to-know. The choice of research methods to identify and describe the way knowledge is constructed, and develop new knowledge to inform policy and practice, depends upon the way a researcher understands and defines the nature of knowledge and the learning process. Theories to explain the human capacity of knowing (knowledge) and the process of coming-to-know (learning) have been posited and debated since before the time of Plato, so that our own understanding of them is interlaced with the history of the development of western thought. In this sense, concepts of knowledge and learning are cultural artifacts which, rather than being stable constructs, have been defined and re-defined in every generation. We are fortunate that a considerable body of work has been produced over the last two decades which gives present-day researchers excellent conceptual tools to inform the choice of methods. My own methodological choices are informed by theories and insights from this work which I will outline here.

There are clear differences between the way that philosophers think about knowledge and the way that psychologists think about learning. Although knowledge and learning are closely inter-related they tend to be respectively the province of one or other of these two disciplines. It is true to say that much of philosophy is concerned with distinguishing between different kinds of knowledge and the relative value of the kinds, whereas psychology is concerned with how learning takes place and is much less concerned with ascribing more or less value to the things that are learnt.

Knowledge and the curriculum

In the early 1970s in the UK, the school curriculum was strongly influenced by the work of the philosophers Peters and Hurst. They put forward a view of subject disciplines based upon different 'forms of knowledge' (Peters 1966) each with their own 'tests for truth' (Hirst 1974). By the mid-1980s the school curriculum was shifting towards a more integrated approach to knowledge, with an emphasis upon grouping subjects to prevent both fragmentation of knowledge and unnecessary overlap in teaching between subjects. At a time when there was no National Curriculum, secondary school teachers were closely involved in developing the new examination curricula that emerged as part of both of these 'movements'. The 'tests for truth' for the social sciences became embedded in the new Schools Council History course for 14–16 year olds which included the analysis of original documents, and the recognition that evidence was differentially reliable, depending on its sources, and needed to be interpreted before it was used as the basis for decisions. Stenhouse's Humanities Curriculum involved adolescents in debating sensitive moral issues under the guidance of a teacher acting as 'neutral chairman' (*sic*) in order to develop moral understanding and a sense of individual worth and responsibility. These curricula were derived from the philosophy of knowledge, but they also constituted an explicit attempt to design curricula that would prepare young people for the challenges of their future lives, both at home and at work. They were conceptually-based curricula that were intended to stimulate thinking. By contrast, the current National Curriculum is specified in terms of traditional subject knowledge. It involves the transmission of a very large quantity of facts and reified concepts within each separate subject area. Since it was largely drawn up by non-specialists selected by government ministers, it draws heavily on the traditional curriculum of the public schools and post-war grammar schools and at the time of its introduction constituted a conservative backlash from the innovative curricula developed in the educational reforms of the 1970s and 1980s. A functionalist, market-led ideology was then added on to this academic foundation. Schostak, in referring to this, notes:

> It is no accident that the school efficiency 'movement' came to dominate political discourses of schooling in the 1990s, since the political definition of mainstream schooling is all about the engineering of children as raw materials to fit the needs of economic and administrative powers. Its language is one of benchmarking, standards, standardization, comparisons with competitors and engineering children in ways similar to those for the engineering of aircraft.
>
> (Schostak 2000, p. 38)

Young (1998) sees the current school curriculum as an example of socially organized knowledge (see the discussion of the Teaching and Learning Research Programme earlier in this paper). He clarifies this process. Knowledge is differentiated and accorded higher or lower status as a result of 'the power certain groups have to restrict access to certain kinds of knowledge, the opportunity for those who have access to knowledge to legitimize its status and the beliefs they have about the relations between knowledge and society'. He goes on, 'the high value of some knowledge is institutionalized by the creation of schools, colleges and universities to transmit it as the curriculum and to produce it as research'. Young sees the current school curriculum which has resulted from this interplay of powerful interest groups, as inappropriate to today's needs and predicts transformation to a less specialised, more integrated, curriculum in the future: '(My) general hypothesis ... is of a shift from "curricula of the past", which were insulated, narrowly specialised and highly stratified to "curricula of the future", which I predict will need to be connective, broader and with low degrees of stratification' (Young 1998, p. 15).

Learning: the process of coming to know

In the 1990s considerable innovative work was carried out by psychologists developing new understandings of the process of learning. In addressing the methodological issues relating to researching how knowledge is constructed, I will draw mainly on the work of psychologists like Bruner, Cole, Engeström, Lave, Salomon, Wertsch and Wenger, all of whom have built upon the work of Vygotsky to develop the new sub-discipline of cultural psychology. The origins of their work lie in the cognitive psychology that replaced behaviourism in the early 1970s, but they have gone beyond simple ideas of mental schema developed 'in the head' to an understanding of mind that is socio-culturally embedded.

A good summary of the approach of cultural psychologists is provided by Lave as 'four premises concerning knowledge and learning in practice' that were agreed upon by participants in a two-part conference who later contributed to the book she edited with Chaiklin:

1. Knowledge always undergoes construction and transformation in use.
2. Learning is an integral aspect of activity in and with the world at all times. That learning occurs is not problematic.
3. What is learned is always complexly problematic.
4. Acquisition of knowledge is not a simple matter of taking in knowledge; rather, things assumed to be natural categories, such as 'bodies of knowledge,' 'learners,' and 'cultural transmission,' require reconceptualization as cultural, social products.

(Lave 1996, p. 8)

Chaiklin and Lave's edited book *Understanding Practice* and Engeström and Middleton's (1996) collection *Cognition and Communication at Work* both build upon and considerably extend the concept of 'situated learning' (Brown *et al.* 1989). The understanding that learning is always either supported or constrained by its context is now reinforced by a considerable body of evidence. In particular, there is strong evidence that schools do not provide supportive environments for learning, but may provide the structures which cause many children to develop a 'failing' identity. Lave, in her introduction to *Understanding Practice*, which separates case studies of learning in the workplace from case studies of learning in formal educational settings, writes: 'Paradoxically, learning craftwork may appear easy in the chapters in Part II (i.e. the workplace settings) whereas in Part III it often seems nearly impossible to learn in settings dedicated to education' (my addition in brackets; Lave, op. cit., p. 9). She goes on to say that the case studies in educational settings:

provide evidence of the sociocultural production of failure to learn. ... They are about how people learn identities and identify the situated meaning of what is to be learned, and the specific shaping of people's identities as learners. ... Students who fail (and perhaps the most successful as well) are the sacrificial lambs whose fates give material form to legitimate knowledge.

(Lave, op. cit., pp. 10–11)

Wenger offers the 'reification' of knowledge as one explanation of the problems learners face in schools. The stratification and codification of knowledge in a textbook or a curriculum 'creates an intermediary stage between practices and learners'. He cites the use of grammatical categories to teach language as an example and goes on,

'Because of this additional step, making sense of the reification becomes an additional problem that may not exist in practice. ... There is a pedagogical cost to reifying in that it requires additional work – even, possibly, a new practice – to make sense of the reification' (Wenger 1998, p. 264). In the UK, Lings and Desforges report on research into subject differences in primary children's application of knowledge to learn and conclude that the classroom creates a context in which the children's goal becomes 'the efficient completion of tasks' rather than the application of subject knowledge:

> Children are not lacking cognitive skills; on the contrary, from an early age children appear to be extremely competent thinkers ... and from the findings appear to be adept at managing themselves in relation to the perceived demands of the classroom. But if the view is taken that the application of knowledge should be subject-specific in classrooms, then while children appear to adapt to work efficiently, educational goals may be achieved as a lucky by-product rather than as the result of intentional or deliberate learning.
>
> (Lings and Desforges 1999, p. 218)

In the USA, Page reports on detailed case studies of school science, including one in 'an academically prestigious high school' in which he identified 'a veritable absence of science in science classes' (Page 1999). He goes some way to explaining what he calls 'the muddlement of knowledge in US schools' in terms of:

> the extraordinary reach, or complexity, of ordinary school lessons ... that move from teacher plans to student responses, beyond events in classrooms to the culture of a school, across contemporary hybrids of divergent curricular rationales to long-past historical debates, while traveling between subject matter knowledge and status politics.
>
> (Page 1999, p. 590)

There are so many different influences impacting on the classroom that teachers are unable to focus on clear educational objectives. In particular, Page believes that the general ambivalence in society towards school knowledge, and the sense that school is no more than a transit camp to higher education, has undermined students' motivation and made the job of the teacher nearly impossible.

Together, these studies of learning in educational settings show that there is little relation between what is specified as the formal curriculum and the actual learning that takes place in educational settings. In the UK today, when curriculum specification is tight and assessment and inspection are used to create a competitive, public system of accountability, at best pupils focus upon 'task completion' rather than the acquisition of knowledge. At worst, they become alienated or disruptive of good order in the classroom, leading to the problems we are experiencing in high rates of truancy and exclusion.

One of the features that distinguishes those learning environments where learning flourishes is purposeful activity. In activity theory, the word activity has a specialist meaning. It may refer to actions or to a range of other behaviours, including talk (inter-mental activity), thought (intra-mental activity), and knowledge construction (likely to involve both inter-mental and intra-mental activity). It always involves the use of mediating tools (Wertsch 1998), either artifacts such as books, pens or computers or cognitive tools such as language, numerical tables, or scientific concepts like Newton's laws. Cognitive tools include representations of the artifacts themselves which Cole, following (Wartofsky 1979), calls 'secondary artifacts' that 'consist of representations both of primary artifacts and of modes of action using them' (Cole 1999, p. 91). Engeström (e.g. 1991, 1999), with Cole and others, has developed a model of human behaviour, derived from Vygotsky and tested in research settings, that incorporates mind, mediating tools and tasks into an activity system. In this system individuals and/or groups engage in activities with purposeful outcomes, assisted or constrained by the unique features (affordances) of the tools themselves and the rules, structures and divisions of labour that govern the micro and macro social groupings in which the activity occurs. Learning is an integral part of the outcomes which may be predominantly practical or cognitive but will include elements of both, except in the case of conceptual understanding developed on the basis of reified knowledge.

Engeström illustrates activity theory in a model comprising an extended triangle (Figure 9.1). The elements are linked to form a system or net, so that each constrains or facilitates the operation of the others. If this model is applied to learning in classrooms, it can be seen that the setting of classroom tasks (a code of behaviour) by the teacher (a role) to meet the specifications of the National Curriculum (an organisational tool), shapes and constrains the purposes (tasks and outcomes) of individual or group work. (It should be noted that the tasks/outcomes which are the focus of the activity system may not be congruent with classroom tasks which are frequently pre-specified and routine.) Educational transformation, therefore, requires changes in rules, structures and roles which would unlock pupils' motivation by supporting them in the construction of identities (Wenger, op. cit.) and offering them the opportunity to achieve recognition as autonomous and free agents (Elliott,

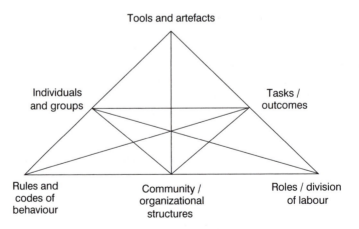

Figure 9.1 The activity triangle, adapted from Engeström (1991)

op. cit.). Based on the case studies in *Understanding Practice* (Chaiklin and Lave, op. cit.) we can conjecture that, to be effective, the models for new rules, structures and roles would need to be drawn from locations outside formal educational settings, such as the workplace (which offers a wide range of models) and the home.

Another of the features that distinguishes those learning environments where learning flourishes is that they support a process of 'distributed cognition'. Cognition and ability have until recently been seen as located exclusively within the individual. In fact, in the UK, the entire system for assessing ability and the acquisition of knowledge to select those suitable for higher education or employment is predicated on this assumption. Hence assessment normally takes place 'under examination conditions' which means in silence, without conferring in any way with others, and with the use of only a limited number of specified tools and resources (primary artifacts). It is now recognised, however, that learning is not usually a fully autonomous process and it is much easier to learn – and to demonstrate knowledgeability – in environments that promote talk, interaction and shared activity (Prawat 1991). The case studies presented in *Cognition and Communication at Work* (Engeström and Middleton, op. cit.) illustrate this process very explicitly. The chapter by Hutchins and Klausen on 'Distributed cognition in an airline cockpit', goes beyond the notion of mutual scaffolding of learning through talk to describe an activity system in which it was impossible for the researchers to locate all the relevant 'cognitive properties' by observing or interviewing any one of the individual pilots. Not only was the pilots' knowledge distributed between themselves with variations in understanding and expertise, they also relied upon the representational instruments that were available for their shared use. The researchers needed 'a unit of analysis' that 'must permit us to describe and explain the cognitive properties of the cockpit system that is composed of the pilots and their informational environment. We call this unit of analysis a system of distributed cognition' (Hutchins and Klausen 1996, p. 17). In this kind of system, technology becomes an indispensable part of the understanding and decision-making (coming-to-know) of each individual and the group, but is not in itself intelligent since it is only of value when it is used by experts. The integration of ICT tools with the process of learning in a system of distributed cognition is becoming an increasingly important part of coming-to-know. However, Salomon (1993a, p. 135) argues for distributed cognition to be seen as additional to individual cognition rather than replacing it: 'One should regard situations of distributed cognitions not only as ends in themselves but, more important, as means for improving mastery of solo competencies.' He retains an important place for those situations, like the writing of an academic paper, in which the individual wrestles with ideas and constructs knowledge autonomously. When it comes to the design of situations in which ICT tools enable distributed cognition, he argues that 'such situations should be designed to promote or scaffold, rather than limit, the cultivation of individuals' competencies'.

There is, however, a kind of knowledge that does not fit easily into the kind of learning environments which appear to be most supportive of learning. This is the knowledge which forms the foundation for our present-day way of life because, for example, it enables planes to fly and telephones to function and gives us Shakespeare, the Beatles and the languages of the world: the science, sociology, philosophy, psychology – and all the other systematised, formal knowledge that is located in subject disciplines. When philosophers focus upon ways of distinguishing different kinds of knowledge, their different functions and their relative values, they are addressing the fundamental problem of education. What should a society pass on to its next generation? How do we distinguish those cognitive tools and cultural artifacts, including disciplinary knowledge, which will provide our children with the capability of becoming 'autonomous and free agents capable of shaping the conditions of their existence in civil society' (Elliott, op. cit.)? And, given their need to negotiate their own identity and their desire for recognition, how can we create formal learning environments (schools of the future) in which pupils will engage with teachers in cognitive apprenticeship, acquiring the valued knowledge of our cultural heritage? It is clearly important that we step back from that very traditional curriculum which privileges only formal, generalisable, de-contextualised knowledge (Lave, op. cit., p. 23), and which gives high status exclusively to literacy, individualism, abstractness and unrelatedness (Young, op. cit., p. 19), but ultimately a socio-cultural analysis of knowing and coming-to-know must include interaction with the knowledge and understanding of our socio-cultural heritage. Shakespeare, for example, must live for our children, but we need an education system that enables them to engage with his work actively, through performance, rather than as de-contextualised text-to-be-struggled-with, without any purpose or desire to understand it. To this, Saljo adds the 'psychological tools' (what I have called earlier 'cognitive tools') that are essential resources for all kinds of learning and problem-solving. These include language, writing, spelling and number work which are complex for young children to learn and 'have taken humankind a very long time to develop'. He goes on, 'Psychological tools in the form of concepts, definitions and procedures are not to be opposed to practical knowledge as is commonly done when discussing the alleged conflicts between "theory" and "practice"' (Saljo 1999, p. 150).

ICT provides us with a range of new tools that are already making substantial changes to all aspects of communications and information storage and retrieval in the business and commerical world. The economies of the world are moving into new relations with one another and multi-national companies are re-grouping. In particular, media companies are merging to forge new alliances capable of capitalising on the opportunities of merging technologies. In some cases, so-called 'ordinary people' have been able to exercise power in unprecedented ways by creative use of the Internet (e.g. in the demonstrations against the G8 meeting in Seattle in 1999 and the defence against the MacDonalds' law case). In terms of learning, a large number of websites offer open access to expert knowledge and in fields like medicine this is having a significant impact on patient–doctor relationships. In higher education the impact of new technology is clear with the development of some specialist on-line universities and several large international co-operative groupings of universities committed to on-line provision of some part of their courses. These very substantial changes to the structures of so many sectors of human activity are easily explained by activity theory. They are the result of the development of new tools which are changing human capabilities by mediating tasks and outcomes in new ways. It is impossible to believe that schools will not also change in radical ways. Yet, currently in the UK, despite an ambitious programme of investment by government in ICT resources, infrastructure and teacher training, there is no evidence of change of the radical kind observable in the commercial world. It is almost certainly because the structures, rules of behaviour and division of labour (roles) in schools are rooted in long-standing traditions and authority structures, that the potential for ICT to have a significant impact on learning has not so far been realised (see Chapter 7 of this book). Researchers have an important role in working in partnership with teachers, pupils, parents and communities to track the impact of changes and provide feedback and evidence to inform and encourage more radical change.

Methodological choices: research as a contribution to the improvement of education

Research can only identify and describe knowledge construction if its methods fit what we know about the process of knowledge construction and the learning environments in which it occurs. I have already said that my own experience as a researcher has involved working co-operatively with teachers and other participants at all levels in educational institutions and the education system. The research on learning reviewed in the previous section confirms that this approach is a good one since it would be difficult to gain insights into the complexity of contexts, individual biographies, rules, roles and organisational histories, let alone the process of distributed cognition, without working in close co-operation with the participants whose involvement in knowledge construction is being researched. So, my starting point is participatory methods. I adopt a socio-cultural stance, and in particular see my own research as located within many overlapping activity systems including those I am researching. I, therefore, need to go beyond independent deconstruction and detached critique and find robust research methods capable of encouraging and informing re-construction in the light of critique. This means understanding the values, assumptions and imperatives that underpin the aims and objectives of policy-makers, since these are part of the context I am researching; and it means contributing to their understanding with the aim that research should be educative to all participants in the system, from pupil to policy-maker. The research process includes explaining and recommending changes that might lead to improvement in knowledge construction, as well as identifying and describing it.

It is of particular importance for researchers not to be circumscribed by the assumptions of the education system. For example, it is assumed to be a matter of 'common sense' that learning takes place in schools, whereas there is considerable research evidence, some of which I have referred to earlier in this paper, that schools are not good environments for learning. Therefore, to identify and describe the way knowledge is constructed, it is essential to focus on environments which are not formal educational settings as well as focusing on schools. One could even argue that it is not worth doing any more research in schools since they are fundamentally uneducational. However, I would see this as counter-productive and prefer to engage with those (e.g. teachers, pupils, managers, parents and policy-makers) who are involved in constructing the socio-political processes through which education has the potential to be transformed. At present there is a real opportunity that ICT might enable us to change the structures of schools so that educational transformation might become a reality.

In focusing on learning outside formal educational settings one is struck by the importance in learning of exploratory play. This is a cherished principle of nursery education which has been long forgotten by teachers of adults and adolescents. Its value is clearly demonstrated in any observation study of accomplished computer users surfing the Internet. This is just one example of why researchers need to focus on a wide range of behaviours and activities, without invoking preconceptions about what constitutes valuable use of time or 'waste' of time. Computer games, for example, may be important vehicles for learning a range of skills and strategies (cognitive tools). For the researcher to have a genuinely open mind implies a grounded theory approach to the collection and analysis of data. Unstructured participant observation, combined with 'think aloud' protocols may be the best way to capture self-directed learning. Theories about the inter-relationship between purposeful and serendipitous learning can then be generated by allowing analytical categories to emerge from the data.

Another important issue for researchers is to recognise the valuable role of formal education in bringing students into interaction with the knowledge and understanding contributed to our society by all those who have lived before us. Everything we know about knowledge construction shows us that this enterprise is fraught with difficulty – because it is simply not possible for every concept to be introduced to pupils in a 'situated' context. However, there is a body of knowledge that needs to be passed on. Researchers need to retain Polanyi's vision (1958, p. 17) of young people learning alongside adults through a process of 'passionate participation in the act of knowing'. The researcher's mission might be to work with schools where this vision could be put into practice. Again, there seems a real opportunity that ICT might enable us to move towards educational transformation.

The most obvious methodological problem when researching knowledge construction is that the cognitive processes of any individual mind are hidden, private and personally unique. To communicate what has been learnt to a researcher, or anyone else, the individual must translate the knowledge and process of coming-to-know into language (written or spoken), or visual representations, or demonstrate it through actions or the completion of tasks. This is a complex process for the learner and the less open-ended the tasks (e.g. a closed task like a multiple-choice test), the poorer the match is likely to be between the knowledge that has been constructed and what is demonstrated through the task. It is only when knowledge has been codified and tightly specified in advance that it can be tested by means of closed tasks. For such knowledge, which includes a wide range of scientific concepts, closed tasks are an appropriate way of identifying what has been learnt, but here too they may not be good at allowing learners to demonstrate that they can use the concepts to solve problems. And they remain a poor way of identifying and describing the process of coming-to-know (learning), which is more rather than less likely to be fraught with difficulties when the knowledge to be learnt is codified and tightly specified.

Participant observation is, of course, obtrusive. However, this is not necessarily a disadvantage when researching knowledge construction, since the best source of information is the learners themselves: for example, a shared classroom experience makes a good starting point for an interview. 'Think aloud' protocols depend entirely on the co-operation of the learner, who is asked to provide a running commentary on internal thought processes while engaged in an activity. Another way of getting an account of a learning process, provided it has involved making something or following a procedure (e.g. conducting an experiment in science), is by taking a series of photographs at timed intervals (say, one every two minutes), and using these to 'stimulate recall' during a follow-up interview. Observation can also be used in this way, by noting events, actions or words which the researcher conjectures might signal a learning process and using these as the focus of a follow-up interview. Interviewing can be an excellent way of gaining insights into another person's knowledge and understanding: for example, 'pre' and 'post' interviews can give insights into both knowledge gains and the learning process. It is important, though, to keep the interviewee focused on the actual event rather than seeking more generalised opinions. In the latter kind of interview, which is designed to collect a different kind of information, there is the problem of getting only the views that are commonly expressed among peers, or the views that are an expected part of the person's formal role (say, as a principal), instead of accessing the deeper reflexivity that can direct attention to the uncertainties and micro-political issues that make the work of professionals complex and challenging. Deeper reflections can often be reached if the researcher can ask an unexpected question that genuinely catches the interest of the interviewee, and this may mean that the researcher needs to express an opinion and engage in a more interactive conversation rather than attempting to remain detached.

The concept of mediated action, described earlier in this chapter, places tool-use at the centre of the learning process. To research the nature and extent of mental representations that enable us to use tools creatively, various forms of mind mapping or concept mapping are very useful. This alternative to written text fits well with the enormous increase in visual forms of communication in contemporary society. Film and images are ubiquitous in our access to news and information. Iconic representations, too, surround us, whether to identify commercial retail brands or to offer us choices on our computer screens. Written language, which is a complex, abstract form of representation is being replaced to a considerable extent on the Internet by still and moving images. The REPRESENTATION Project[1] used image-based concept mapping as a means of capturing children's representations, or secondary artifacts, of ICT. The invitation to draw enabled 10-year-old children in REPRESENTATION to produce much richer representations of 'computers in my world' than they were able to produce in written form (although writing was also collected to enable comparisons). In some other countries participating in the project, children found it difficult to draw quick sketches as opposed to careful 'finished' pictures. In the UK, however, children appeared to find drawing a natural means of communication and many were able to convey more of their knowledge through drawing than through writing. It seemed to make the task more unusual and less akin to a 'test', and some children displayed considerable creativity as well as wide-ranging knowledge of ICT. Two kinds of computer-based concept mapping were also used later in the project (*Inspiration* and a prototype developed by the REPRESENTATION project itself) but these appeared to be more suited to the presentation of ideas, or as tools for sorting objects in hierarchies or categories, rather than as a means of collecting data on the user's own mental models. Selecting and linking pre-prepared images was not such an intuitive process as drawing pictures of objects and their links on paper.

Visual, graphic and diagrammatic forms of data collection are particularly valuable ways of recording knowledge construction. The SLANT project (Mercer *et al.* 1991) used a video camera, together with a simple 'dribble file' to construct split-screen presentations of children's key presses together with video recordings of their interactions. The tapes were also transcribed, giving a rich data set from which to produce an in-depth analysis of the nature of children's talk. Other possibilities include the use of software such as *Prism*, *Netmap* and interactive psychometric testing software to manage, interpret and display data sets, either as the basis for group interviews with participants or to communicate ideas more effectively to non-participants.

ICT provides researchers with other new resources. Of particular interest are those ICT tools which make it easier to track the process of knowledge construction. Electronic communications of all kinds have the potential to be easily stored and recaptured for analysis. Electronic mail, interactive websites such as *WebCT*, text conferencing systems such as *First Class*, chat rooms and simple email 'lists' are all on-line environments in which people lodge communications that are quasi-permanent but have the feel of the informality and ephemeral nature of speech. These communications lie on the borders of speech and writing and can be thought of as 'written speech' since they are often written with a speed and spontaneity that is not characteristic of other forms of written communication. Their status as texts should, therefore, be treated with caution and researchers should negotiate their use as records with their authors. Nevertheless, they give researchers access to a large amount of interaction that would previously have taken place in phone calls, and been unrecorded. They have also replaced letters and memos to a large extent, and have created a different kind of informal exchange which gives more direct communication access to all members of an organisation, regardless of their formal position in the hierarchy. ICT also offers research tools which can be used to manage the interactions of learning communities and support the process of knowledge construction explicitly. Examples of these are the *Knowledge Forum* developed for use in schools by (Scardamalia and Bereiter 1996), and the Advanced Meetings Systems software (http://www.webex.com/webex/webex-company.html, accessed 7/8/2006), although packages like *WebCT* and *First Class* can also be used in similar ways with an active manager sorting and organising contributions.

In my early research into ICT and learning I used action research methodology because it was very soon obvious that traditional, more 'objective', research methods were only capable of providing evidence that the outcomes of the innovation did not in any way match the original aims of policy-makers. Action research in the PALM Project enabled professional development of the teachers to become an integral part of the research process. This meant that the research was able to track the development process while at the same time supporting fuller implementation and adaptation of the innovation. Teachers were also much better motivated to use computers to the best of their ability when they adopted a research role to explore whether or not computers could be useful tools to support pupils' learning (Somekh 1997). The work of Whyte (1991) on participatory action research, as well as Fullan's work on change in organisations (Fullan and Stiegelbauer 1991), and John Elliott's TIQL Project (Elliott and Ebbutt 1986), influenced the design of the Initial Teacher Education and New Technology Project (INTENT) which used two-tiered action research: IT co-ordinators researching their role as supportive change agents and senior managers researching their role as managers of change (Somekh *et al.* 1997). In this case, participatory action research was a mechanism for motivating participants and increasing involvement, as well as supporting the development process, monitoring its progress and providing feedback to keep the development on target.

As an extension of these participatory methods, but much more carefully designed to manipulate the levers of change directly, activity theory offers a radical methodology to support educational transformation through research. Currently, the extraordinary changes being brought about by ICT in many sectors of society make it possible that similar changes could be brought about in schools. So far there is no research evidence to show that this is happening. However, the need for radical change in schooling is overwhelming. The curriculum is too rigid, too many adolescents are alienated and teaching is no longer an attractive profession. Most worrying of all, studies of classrooms confirm again and again that they are not environments in which learning easily occurs. Activity theory not only explains the link between radical societal changes and new technology tools, it also provides a model for how similar changes could occur in schools. The urgent need now is for intervention studies, involving groups of innovative schools with very high access levels to ICT for pupils and teachers, working with policy-makers, parents and local communities to make radical changes to rules of behaviour, roles and structures, in order to maximise the use of ICT in new approaches to learning. Such studies would test the value of exploratory play, the negotiation of identity (Wenger, op. cit.) and ways of giving young people recognition as autonomous members of a civil society (Elliott, op. cit.) and they would reconstruct the curriculum as well as abandoning the traditional structures of schooling by replacing classroom teaching with an alternative regime (see the futuring scenario in Chapter 6 of this book). The intervention studies would follow the method described by Engeström which embodies three principles:

> First a collective activity system can be taken as the unit of analysis, giving context and meaning to seemingly random individual events.
>
> Second, the activity system and its components can be understood historically.
>
> Third, inner contradictions of the activity system can be analyzed as the source of disruption, innovation, change, and development of that system, including its individual participants.
>
> (Engeström 1996, p. 65)

The unit of analysis in each case would be the school and its community, including parents, local companies and policy-makers at both the local and national level. Ideally, the QCA and one of the examination boards would also be involved as consultant partners. Research would focus initially upon analysing the history and current practice of the school and its extended community as an activity system, working with all participants to make visible the rules, structure and roles which act as constraints or facilitators of new styles of learning using ICT. Following Engeström's method, the first stage would culminate in a workshop at which this initial analysis, including the sources of disruption, innovation, change and development, would be presented in narrative and diagrammatic form and discussed in depth. The second stage would involve the participants working together to design new structures and working methods, involving the replacement of classrooms with an alternative regime such as that described above. The third stage would involve implementing the plan. The researchers' role would involve 'the dual task of documenting and analyzing on the one hand, providing feedback and interventions on the other hand' (Engeström 1996, p. 75).

Conclusions

Writing this article has convinced me that there is little difference between the methodological issues in researching knowledge construction with and without ICT. There are differences, however, in the processes of learning that are made possible by ICT. Just as the invention of writing reduced the need for humans to memorise everything. and the printed book made it possible to pass on knowledge, information and stories to a much wider audience than was able to access manuscripts, so ICT provides new ways of accessing information and communicating ideas. As they become easy to access, these new tools change the fabric of the culturally patterned ways in which we undertake scholarship and work, and extend our capabilities through the process of distributed cognition; and it is only a matter of time until access to powerful, portable technologies is available to all teachers and students. In their structures, universities still have the vestiges of the community of scholars gathered at the feet of Peter Abelard in twelfth-century Paris, and schools are still organised as they were in the days of Dickens and Thomas Arnold. It is time for a change, however. The production line no longer exists in modern factories and production-line education is also obsolete. ICT tools make it possible to customise education to individuals. There is a role for research in working with schools and communities to transform education by making the knowledge of individuals visible to all so that a learning community can begin to take decisions in the best interests of all its members. Without external support, and access to evidence of new ways of going about things, our schools may be let down by a failure of imagination resulting from the reproduction of old cultural patterns fossilised in structures of power and authority.

Today, the main barrier to researching the way knowledge is constructed with ICT is the lack of access to technology, any time, any place, for all teachers and students. It is only when new technology tools become an integral part of human activity that they can have their full impact in changing cognitive processes. Although this kind of access is rare at the present time, there is evidence of its impact on the learning of some students who own networked technologies at home. Given the extensive evidence that currently schools are not places where learning easily occurs, there is an urgent need for intervention studies in which researchers work with schools where this kind of access to ICT is the norm. Such studies would involve schools in working with their wider communities and local and national policy-makers to develop new radical structures, making use of the affordances of ICT to enable these structures and transform the processes of learning. ICT has already brought about radical changes in the structures of our society, for example in banking, business and industry. It is clear that similar changes could occur in education with the likelihood of beneficial outcomes.

10 Mapping learning potential

Students' conceptions of ICT in their world[1]

Looking back...

This chapter gives a more detailed account of the concept mapping method which was described briefly in the previous chapter in relation to Project REPRESENTATION. The focus here is on the analysis and interpretation of the 4,000 maps we collected from students aged between 9 and 16 during the ImpaCT2 evaluation of the National Grid for Learning. Two other maps from this large data set appear in Chapter 7 where they are used along with other data collected from the same students to give a rounded picture of their use of ICT at home. In Chapter 3 a slightly different kind of concept mapping exercise is described which we used to gain insights into the kind of 'community of practice' that children experienced when using the GridClub 'edutainment' website.

This form of data has proved particularly useful for our research. It does not, of course, give an exact representation of a mental model, but then neither does any other form of data. Students' responses to being asked to draw appear to be culturally shaped by their previous experiences, hence French students in Project REPRESENTATION, who had been taught drawing formally in school, were reluctant to produce rapid drawings without paying attention to their form or accuracy. English children generally loved 'communicating with the researchers through drawings' and seemed to feel that this kind of data was appropriate in relation to ICT which itself uses so many iconic representations. We have found we learn more about young people's socio-cultural understandings of ICT from hand-drawn than from computer-generated maps although we realise the latter would be very useful for collecting more precise data on mental processes. Maps made with words rather than drawings, in the manner originally developed by Novak and Gowin (1984), provide rather different insights from drawings because words can represent abstract concepts as well as physical artefacts. We used these with older students in ImpaCT2 because we anticipated that they might be reluctant to draw and it had the advantage of giving us insights into their passions, excitements and anxieties. However, mixing the two forms of representation had disadvantages, too, as it made it impossible to make any systematic comparisons between their maps and those produced by younger students.

The rationale for using concept mapping in ImpaCT2

This chapter discusses the use of a particular form of image-based concept mapping to explore how students aged 10–16 conceptualise the role of computers in today's world. It is based on the work of the ImpaCT2 project, 1999–2002,[2] funded by the Department for Education and Skills (DfES) for England and Wales. The aims of ImpaCT2, specified in the invitation to tender, were:

1   to identify the impacts of networked technologies on the school and out-of-school environment;
2   to determine whether or not this impact affects the educational attainment of students aged 8–16 in English schools;
3   to provide information that would assist in the formation of national, local and school policies on the deployment of ICT.

A mixed methodology was adopted which would combine quantitative measurement of students' gains in national tests (at ages 11 and 14) and examinations (at age 16) with qualitative research into young people's use of ICT at school and at home, and the nature of their learning with ICT. To measure attainment the project looked for differences between students' actual and expected test results, using the University of Durham's PIPS and YELLIS data on individual students in the sample (Fitzgibbon 2002), and correlated these with the extent of their use of ICT during the previous 18 months (Harrison *et al.* 2002). From the start, however, the evaluators were mindful that this approach might fail to identify new kinds of learning made possible with ICT which might not be measured by traditional tests. For example, the innovative work of the Apple Classroom for Tomorrow project (Sandholtz *et al.* 1997) and the creative, exploratory pedagogies advocated by Heppell (1993) do not employ the kind of close focus on learning pre-specified subject matter and concepts that is likely to lead to high scores in tests. These case studies of classrooms using technology as an integral part of innovative pedagogies provide evidence of very significant changes in the nature of students' learning, in particular in their autonomy, creativity and high levels of motivation. It was important for ImpaCT2, therefore, to collect other data which would provide a different kind of evidence from test scores. The impact of networked technologies on the school and out-of-school environments was investigated primarily by collecting students' accounts of where, how, how often and when they used them. In addition, a concept mapping task was used to capture students' knowledge and understanding of current uses of computers in their world. The assumption, drawing upon the work of Project REPRESENTATION[3] (Pearson and Somekh 2003), was that students whose concept maps showed that their conceptualisation of these new tools was complex and extensive would be very well prepared to acquire skills easily and use ICT creatively. This assumption was based on a tradition of research in socio-cultural psychology which extends the Vygotskian concept of a mediating tool to include the interior cognitive representations of the tool that are essential pre-requisites to using the tool itself effectively (Cole 1999, p. 91). In the project proposal we suggested:

Such data could be crucial in the final analysis of attainment in relation to school factors, and could offer a much more subtle account of the ICT-attainment relationship than has been available from earlier statistical research studies.

(ImpaCT2 Proposal to the DfES, November 1999)

Evidence to suggest that ICT might support kinds of learning not reflected in national tests

My action research with teachers during the 1980s suggested that technology can be used to transform children's learning experiences but that this depends to a considerable extent on the way the curriculum is specified and how it is enacted through the processes of teaching and learning. The critical factor is the extent to which teachers and students are able to adopt cognitively active roles 'since knowledge is constructed and reconstructed through a heuristic processes of creative thinking and interaction, as well as the acquisition of appropriate information' (Somekh and Davies 1991, p. 154). The main findings of my research, carried out before the national curriculum had been implemented in schools (Somekh 1997) can be summarised as follows. The use of ICT tools in classrooms shifts the focus of attention away from the teacher to the computer screen, which begins to undermine the traditional authority role of teachers: when teachers respond positively to this as an opportunity it can have an empowering effect for both them and their students by making it easier to work together as co-learners. Moreover, when a genuine attempt is made to integrate the use of ICT with the learning tasks that students undertake, the culture of the classroom changes significantly, in terms of its organisation and how students learn. Students can work more effectively either alone or in small groups because their interactions with the computer keep them on-task for longer. Once they have some skills, they can work more autonomously in the sense of being freer from the teacher's direction, better able to find the information they need without help, and able to produce products unhampered by poor spelling and handwriting, in which they appear to take greater pride. More time can be spent on tasks which involve cognitive engagement and less on low-level, time-consuming tasks.

However, the school curriculum in 1999 when the ImpaCT2 project began, with its emphasis on teaching pre-specified knowledge to ensure that students reached 'attainment targets' and frequent practising for national tests to reach the school's targets for numeracy and literacy, did not suggest that the use of ICT was likely to be transforming students' learning experiences. This made it possible at the start of ImpaCT2 to envisage that the impact on students' learning of the introduction of networked technologies into schools might be negligible. If this proved to be the case, it would be important for the evaluators to provide recommendations in response to Aim 3 for changes in the deployment of ICT to enable it to have the transformative impact that policy-makers envisaged. Data to support the claim that ICT had the potential to be transformative if the curriculum and pedagogy changed would not, however, de facto be available in the schools. These data would need to draw on students' use of ICT outside the school environment. In addition, through concept mapping methods we could collect data on young people's conceptualisations of ICT in today's world, from which we might be able to imply their potential to use ICT creatively and autonomously if practices in schools were to change.

Using concept maps to assess students' potential for transformative learning with ICT

Socio-cultural learning theories developed over the last 20 years are particularly useful in helping us to understand the reasons for the repeated failure of ICT to transform students' learning experiences in schools (see Chapter 7). Learning happens most easily when the learner is situated in a context of use (Brown *et al.* 1989) where s/he is able to learn alongside expert practitioners through a process which Lave and Wenger (1991) call 'legitimate peripheral participation'. Schools are not ideal learning environments because they necessitate a wide range of extraneous learning that acts as distractions from authentic learning: see for example the body of evidence that Engeström presents to show that diagrams in school textbooks require students to learn that size is notional rather than actual in diagrams; without this knowledge diagrams showing equivalent sizes for the sun and the moon systematically and persistently confused students so that they failed to understand the reasons for the phases of the moon, muddling the concept of 'phases' with the concept of eclipse (Engeström 1991). The point here is not that it is unimportant to learn how to interpret diagrams, but that these diagrams were needlessly confusing. The power relations that govern the behaviour of teachers and students in schools, and schools' own powerlessness in all countries to move outside the structures and practices of education systems, encapsulate them in a time warp. As Papert has come to realise, teachers are not resistant to change but are caught in a constant tension between the technicist demands of the system and their instincts to assist children to learn by engaging actively with ideas and concepts:

> The institution of School, with its daily lesson plans, fixed curriculum, standardized tests, and other such paraphernalia, tends constantly to reduce learning to a series of technical acts and the teacher to the role of a technician. … What is important for thinking about megachange is that this situation places the teacher in a state of tension between two poles: School tries to make the teacher into a technician; in most cases a sense of self resists, though in many the teacher will have internalized School's concept of teaching.
>
> (Papert 1993, p. 55)

'Megachange', as Papert calls it, is what most of us have experienced over the last ten years in our patterns of living and working practices as a result of ICT. For example, communications, shopping, banking and access to information have been transformed by the arrival of the Internet. Arguably it is only when megachange arrives in schools that the patterns of learning will be transformed for children. Meanwhile, the enormous socio-cultural changes brought about by technology in today's world have destabilised the way we conceptualise knowledge, teaching, the disciplines and rationality (see Chapter 7):

The circumstances, conditions and the very status of knowledge, learning, teaching and researching are currently in a state of profound upheaval under the double impact of rapid and far-reaching technological changes and the massive assault on longstanding narratives of foundation and legitimation.

(Lankshear *et al.* 2000, pp. 17–18)

The difference between information and knowledge has become blurred as Roszak (1986) warned it might and knowledge, according to Lyotard (1979), is commodified as packages to be acquired and exchanged rather than something of value in its own right. Lankshear *et al.*, drawing on Lyotard, describe this as resulting from 'the impact of technological transformation' which has undermined long-established practices for legitimating knowledge through concepts such as 'meaning, truth and emancipation' (op. cit., p. 22). They point to the impact of the Internet which has resulted in a 'superabundance of information', mainly 'presented' uncritically (pp. 26–7), the destabilisation of the ideas of curricula divided into subject disciplines, and the blurring of the underpinning concept that education involves both learning knowledge and learning how that knowledge was produced and justified historically (pp. 34–5). Knowledge in the new age is 'multimodal' involving a 'radical convergence of text, image and sound' (see also Kress and van Leeuwen (1996), and, in the context of postmodern society, rather than being something that already exists, knowledge becomes transformed into the basis for action: 'an ability to perform' (Lankshear *et al.*, op. cit., pp. 35–6). These vast changes in society's practices of knowledge construction and consumption should be reflected in changes in assessment practices within education systems. The individualistic notions of individual knowers whose knowledge can be tested within the confines of a lone mind, without reference to a community of practice or tools/resources other than pen and paper, belong to the past rather than the present. Yet none of these shifts has touched the practices of schools or the technologies of curriculum and assessment enshrined in our education systems. More fundamentally, and therefore more seriously, schools which have the key role in preparing young people for life have not begun to grapple with the tensions and problems created by these megachanges in how knowledge is defined and used in contemporary society (see Chapter 7).

Children, however, spend a significant proportion of their time outside school. They are used to leading multiple lives at school, at home and beyond, straddling the cultures of youth, family and school. They inhabit different activity systems and use a variety of ICT tools, which are an integral part of many of their lives, and have a significant mediating impact in the home. Much research has been carried out in the last ten years into children' use of ICT in the home (Downes 1996, 1999; Sanger *et al.* 1997; Livingstone and Bovill 1999; Furlong *et al.* 2000; Sutherland *et al.* 2001; Somekh *et al.* 2002a). These studies show children using technology for a variety of purposes, nearly always rather autonomously, often several times a week and sometimes for long periods of uninterrupted use. ImpaCT2 was to provide substantial further evidence of the variety of ways in which young people use ICT at home, finding also that the time spent using ICT at home for the average 10–11 year old is around three times, and for 12–16 year olds around four times, that spent at school (Somekh *et al.* 2002c, p. 6).

Concept mapping as a means of capturing students' conceptions of ICT in their world

The concept mapping task was designed to give the evaluators insights into young people's conceptualisation of computers in their world, whether it was derived from home use or shaped by the more general process of enculturation through a range of media (newspapers, television, radio, advertising, labelling of goods, etc.) and social interactions (with parents, peers, the icons of youth culture, etc.). The method draws directly on Vygotsky's conception of 'instrumental' psychology (Vygotsky 1978, p. 44) by which 'higher functions incorporate auxiliary stimuli, which are typically produced by the person himself (*sic*)'. In other words, our efforts to achieve any outcome are supported by cognitive tools which are an integral part of our skilled use of actual artifacts. First the ICT tools mediate the leisure (and in Lave's sense (1996) also learning) activities of the child, making it possible for new objectives to be achieved which would otherwise be unattainable, in a manner that Wertsch (1998, pp. 27–8) compares to the pole's mediating enhancement of the pole vaulter's capacity to jump (see the top section of the triangle diagram in Figure 9.1). Second the child's ability to use ICT is mediated by the 'auxiliary stimuli' of his/her own capacity to imagine the possibilities for ICT use. These ideas are clarified in Wartofsky's account (1979, pp. 198–203) of the role of representation in human perception. For Wartofsky, perception is always an active process, rooted in our cultural history and experience, whereby we use tools (primary artifacts) and are enabled to do so skillfully by our 'representations of modes of action' based on our past awareness and experience with these tools (secondary artifacts) and are further able to create 'possible worlds' mediated by the tools through our ability to imagine and reorganise these representations of the tools (ibid., pp. 206–7). Although Wartofsky grounds his theory of perception in the Aristotelian distinction between 'making' and 'doing' within a unifying concept of human 'praxis', Cole (1999, p. 91) is clearly right in seeing it as complementing and clarifying Vygotsky's ideas of higher order auxiliary stimuli. Wartofsky also placed emphasis on the importance of images in perception and characterises imagination as 'internal representation' or 'picturing in the mind' of alternative forms of action.

The concept mapping task was developed as a means of exploring the children's conceptualisations of ICT, or to describe the process more specifically in terms of the theories of Vygotsky, Wertsch and Wartofsky, to explore their internal representations (secondary artifacts) of ICT by collecting their maps/drawings which gave insights into how they conceptualised ICT objects and the links between them at a particular time. Evidence of well-developed and/or complex secondary artifacts of the role of computers in their world would suggest that they either had skills in ICT use or were well placed to acquire these skills readily, and more likely to be motivated to use ICT autonomously by imagining possible uses and anticipating interesting or useful outcomes.

The concept mapping task was administered to the whole sample of around 2,000 students in ImpaCT2 on two occasions, June 2000 and June 2001. Teachers gave their class a brief introduction to the idea of producing drawings (icons) to represent their ideas/'things'[4] and drawing lines between them to show which ideas/ 'things' they saw as linked. The task itself was then introduced by teachers reading aloud a prepared 'script' so that, as far as possible, all 2,000 students were doing the same task. Students were told that the purpose of drawing their 'mind maps' was to communicate with the ImpaCT2 researchers and that the researchers wanted to know their own ideas: the quality of the drawings was not important so they should try to draw quickly, and not be influenced by other students' drawings. The total time given for the task was 30 minutes, including time at the end for listing the items drawn. The maps suggest that students enjoyed doing this task and took great care with it. They provided the evaluators with a very large amount of information presented in a visual form which was readily accessible to analysis. Although there was some degree of ambiguity in the drawings and links, other problems such as anxieties over spelling and handwriting might have inhibited students in a writing task; although students were inevitably influenced by recent experiences to include some objects and not others, this phenomenon would have occurred in the same way in their writing; furthermore, drawing and writing enable different conceptualisations to be communicated (Kress *et al.* 2001). Some advantages of collecting drawings rather than writing appeared to be: the students' positive attitude to the task; the amount of information that they were able to give the researchers in a very short time; and the ability of all students to participate equally without some being disadvantaged by poor spelling and handwriting.

The drawings were analysed using a framework that built upon and considerably extended the earlier work of Project REPRESENTATION (Pearson and Somekh 2003). There was no attempt to assess the correctness of the images or the links as the aim was to access students' conceptualisations not to test their formal knowledge. The number of objects (nodes) drawn, and the number of links between objects were counted. The latter were counted in two stages, first by counting the number of links emanating from each node, and second by totalling the number for all nodes. This enabled us to count extremely complicated maps accurately. The ratio of nodes to links (the 'connectivity' score) was then determined by dividing the number of links by the number of nodes. This resulted in a ratio of 2:1 for the two simplest structures of maps (one central node linked to all other nodes; and all nodes linked to two others in a linear or circular form) and up to 7:1 or higher for maps with complex linkages between multiple objects. The latter could be said to bear a greater resemblance to the actual structure of networked technologies, suggesting more developed knowledge. The contents of the maps were then coded within two categories which emerged from an initial qualitative analysis of a sample of 60 maps carried out by two researchers. The analysis was grounded in the phenomenographic approach developed by Marton and Booth (1997) and involved the classic 'grounded theory' method of in-depth study of individual maps, followed by listing of conceptual labels, and constant comparisons between maps as further conceptual labels were developed and then grouped into categories (Strauss and Corbin 1990). The two category codes that emerged were: 'spheres of thinking' (SoT) and 'zones of use' (ZoU). The SoT included sub-categories of 'information', 'communication', 'advanced control mechanisms', 'technical details about computers', 'games', 'music', 'images' etc. The ZoU included 'home', 'school', 'workplace', 'shopping', 'transport' etc. Drawings were allocated to these sub-categories by the researchers and SoT and ZoU scores awarded to each student on the basis of the number of sub-categories identified within each. The list of SoT and ZoU was revised during the first phase of analysis to include, as far as possible, all types of drawings produced by the students. Since the variety of the drawings was very considerable, the category 'other' was retained for any which might still be outside the predicted categories. The team worked together to develop rules to ensure reliable coding, following which inter-rater reliability was checked across the six researchers and surpassed the level recommended by Marton and Booth (90 per cent agreement of ratings on first coding and 90 per cent agreement on the remainder second time around; Marton and Booth 1997).

Validating the concept mapping method

The validity of the concept mapping method was tested by means of quantitative analysis. Although it was only possible to reveal trends in the data between year groups and over time, and correlations between these data and other data, the outcomes strongly suggest that the concept mapping method was a valid indicator of the extent of students' conceptions of networked ICT (although the exact nature of their experience could not be determined).

The maps varied considerably in numbers of nodes, links, connectivity scores and numbers of SoT and ZoU. Considering they were produced in 30 minutes the amount of detail contained in some exceptional maps was extraordinary (see Table 10.1). In June 2000 there was a consistent trend of increased detail and complexity across the age groups (KS2: 10–11 years; KS3: 13–14 years; KS4: 15–16 years).

There was also a clear trend towards increasing scores over time by those students in Key Stage 2 (KS2) and Key Stage 3 (KS3) who produced a second concept map in 2001. This was not the case with the KS4 students where results were either comparable or very slightly lower, but this may have resulted from students' lower motivation to engage with the task at a time when they were in the middle of national examinations.

Table 10.1 June 2000 concept mapping descriptive statistics

	Key Stage 2			Key Stage 3			Key Stage 4		
	Min	*Max*	*Mean*	*Min*	*Max*	*Mean*	*Min*	*Max*	*Mean*
Nodes	2	68	13.96	2	73	17.59	2	95	25.12
Links	0	213	29.13	0	168	38.18	0	392	60.93
Connect	0	8.64	1.91	0	7.38	2.05	0	6.83	2.41
Spheres	0	8	4.04	0	9	4.63	0	10	4.95
Zones	0	8	2.02	0	10	2.90	0	9	3.48

The quantitative data were also compared with the students' perceptions of the quantity and types of their use of ICT collected in questionnaires administered in June 2000 and June 2001. Since the questionnaire data were recorded on a two-point scale (yes/no) it was difficult to establish strong correlations, but the baseline data showed significant positive correlations at all three key stages between students with high concept mapping scores and those who had home access to the Internet and their own personal email address. Significant positive associations were also found at all three key stages between high concept map scores in at least three categories (nodes, links, connectivity, spheres of thinking or zones of use) and experience of surfing the Internet. The importance of these correlations was confirmed by the fact that there was no pattern of significant associations between high concept map scores and those aspects of ICT ownership and use that are not directly related to the Internet (for example, games console ownership, mobile phone ownership, games playing, word processing and desk-top publishing). Further information about the concept mapping methods used in ImpaCT2 including the quantitative analysis can be found in one of the ImpaCT2 final reports (Somekh *et al.* 2002a) and in Mavers *et al.* (2002).

Emerging patterns of students' conceptions of ICT in their world

The concept maps provided the ImpaCT2 researchers with a large amount of information on students' conceptions of information and communication technologies, as well as how, and the extent to which, they conceptualised its role in their world. At the same time, it was important to recognise what these data did not reveal. The maps were representations of individual students' ideas at a particular moment in time, produced within a short period of 30 minutes. They could not be claimed to be inclusive of all their thinking about computers in the world, they were clearly not the same as the maps they might have drawn at another time, and they did not provide data on their levels of ICT skills, since cultural knowledge about ICT can be acquired through a wide range of media in addition to hands-on use. Their value, therefore, was twofold:

1   based on the assumption that variations in the reliability of data from individuals lose significance within the analysis of a large data set, they provided an accurate indication phenomenographically of the kinds of awareness of ICT across the whole cohort;

2   through semiotic analysis they provided insights into individual students' conceptions of computers in their world, and were much richer than the written texts produced by students in an accompanying written task they undertook in June 2000.

A phenomenographic approach

Phenomenographic analysis, using a combination of quantitative and qualitative methods, was used to identify patterns of students' awareness of computers in their world across the age cohorts. Follow-up interviews based on their maps, carried out after a lapse of nine months, indicated the ways in which each student experienced computers in their world, in terms of:

1   Their core focal awareness: the aspects of personal knowledge of computers that come into the student's mind first and with greatest apparent significance.
2   Their field awareness: the aspects of personal knowledge of computers that are of slightly secondary importance and prominence.
3   Their fringe awareness: the aspects of personal knowledge of computers, if any, that are more hazy and distant.

The analysis of the concept maps was extended to include quantitative analysis of each sub-category of the Spheres of Thinking (e.g. 'communication', 'information', 'games', 'advanced control') and Zones of Use (e.g. 'home', 'school', 'workplace', 'library') before comparisons were made with the interview data. Those SoT and ZoU which were represented by the most drawings were judged to be likely to be those which were the focus of the student's awareness when s/he produced the map; those which were represented by a lesser number of drawings were the field awarenesses and those represented by only a single drawing, or perhaps two where the total number of objects was large, were fringe awarenesses. This analysis quickly demonstrated that Marton's assumption (1994, p. 34) – that there will be four or five typical kinds of awareness of a phenomena among a group of individuals – was correct. Some had a core focal awareness of the technology itself, others of communications, others of computer control, others of games. There was some overlap between SoT and ZoU, since some students focused their awareness of computers in a range of locations of use. In that sense ZoU were, for some students, the focal awareness in their sphere of thinking.

Insights into individual students' conceptions of 'Computers in my world': a semiotic analysis

A detailed semiotic analysis of two of the maps is given in Mavers (2003). The following much briefer discussion of three maps is intended to illustrate the nature of the maps, the preliminary process of identifying and interpreting signs (Kress and Mavers 2005), and how the researchers' understanding was validated and deepened through the interviews.

Key Stage 2: Paul, boy aged 10

This concept map (see Figure 10.1) has 23 nodes and 132 links with a connectivity score of 5.7, indicating that many nodes are linked to several other nodes. The four

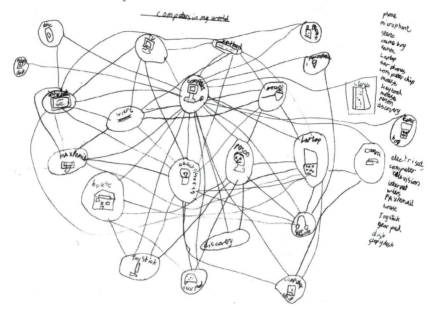

Figure 10.1 'Computers in My World' by Paul, aged 10

nodes which have the most links to other nodes are 'computer', 'electricity', 'person' and 'wiers'. Eight Spheres of Thinking are indicated by drawings: the computer (6), technical details about computers (3), games (3), music (3), communication (2), TV (1), information (1), images (1). There is one Zone of Use – home – and one node representing a person. This may be meant to represent Paul himself as it is linked to the computer, a mouse, a gear-pad, earphones and a joystick as well as to home. This person is also linked to 'discovery' indicating he sees computer use as about finding things out. The strong emphasis on technical details relating to computers was reinforced in the interview in which Paul recast the task as 'we were asked to draw a concept map on things which are electrical and things', and says that he started with 'electricity'. When drawing the map he said he then went first in drawing or linking to 'the computer because I have got three in my house and I like playing on this and things'. After providing details in the interview about the way that computers link with one another, discs, keyboards and the Internet, he began to broaden out his thinking to include 'games, downloading things, buying things, talking and sending emails and Internet chat rooms'.

The pattern of awareness that emerges from this concept map and interview is: Focal awareness of technical and electrical features of computers and how computer technologies are linked together, with field awareness of music, games and communications. Other SoTs are part of this boy's fringe awareness – for example, digital images.

Key Stage 3: Liz, girl aged 13

This concept map (see Figure 10.2) shows wide-ranging knowledge of computers in today's world, with eight SoT and nine ZoU including the Millennium Dome. The arrangement of the nodes on the page suggests that after the starting point of the computer itself in the top left-hand corner, the Internet is the focal awareness, linking to travel, home, school (indirectly), shops, workplaces and banks, as well as to the Millennium Dome via a branching link. From the number of objects in the map, there appears also to be a high level of awareness of the use of computers to control things such as services ('controls important things' is linked to 'fire brigade',

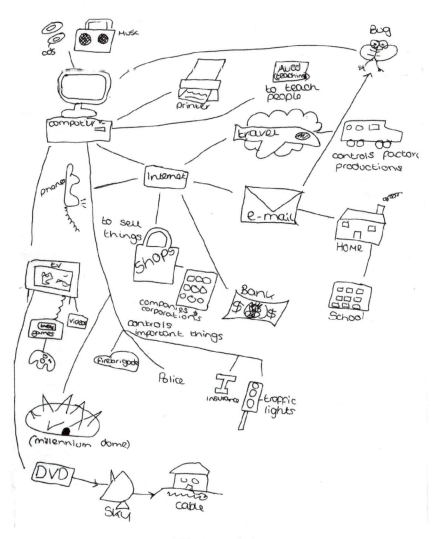

Figure 10.2 'Computers in My World' by Liz, aged 13

'police', 'insurance' and 'traffic lights'). The interview suggests that Liz's knowledge of the role of computers in today's world is extensive and that she is an experienced user. The computer and its printer attached were drawn first and next came the Internet 'because that's the main reason that I use the computer at home'. Phone lines, on-line shopping, banking and email came next, with the locations of home and school, computer games and other entertainment. The Internet is confirmed as the focal awareness but is defined to include communications: 'Is there any part of your map that's particularly important to you?' asked the interviewer. 'Probably the Internet, because I spend ages on the Internet and I'm always on it. I really like hotmail, MSN messenger and email. That's what I usually spend my time on.' There is a wide range of fringe awareness, which includes use of computers for control but without this having any greater prominence than many other things. The emphasis in drawing the map seems to have been on trying to think of 'loads of different ideas'. The 'bug' was included because 'there was a bug going round at the time, I think the "I love you" one that had everything going down'.

In summary, the core focal awareness is of the Internet, particularly for communications, and there is a wide range of field awarenesses which all seem to be of equal importance.

Key Stage 4: Heather, girl aged 15

There are 35 nodes in this map (see Figure 10.3), all represented by text labels in boxes. The focal awareness appears to be on communication (4) and there are an unusually large number of ZoUs (home, school, workplace, banking, shopping, hospital

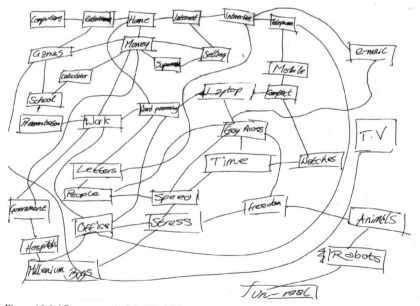

Figure 10.3 'Computers in My World' by Heather, aged 15

and government), suggesting focal awareness of the social impact of computers. Supporting evidence for the latter are several nodes representing abstract concepts, such as 'easy access', 'freedom', 'speed', 'stress', 'time' and 'unreal'. In the interview, the focal awareness on people is confirmed and the emphasis on communication is re-defined as relating mainly to commercial transactions. Her opening statement when asked to tell the interviewer about her map was: 'I think I sort of strayed on to the commercial use of computers because that is how I think it is going to affect us most.' The impact on people of social changes brought about by computers was of primary importance and she expresses strong concern about the growing dependence of people on computers:

> '... like speed, stress and time (are) all linked up and I think that the speed – I don't think it's helping everybody in everyday situations. I think we are just going to rely too heavily on computers ... I don't think we are using computers in the right way, I think because this is a very commercialised base with the Internet and the selling and the interaction between the people, I don't think enough time is being spent on the medical research like hospitals. I've written hospitals on this map and I haven't spread off it at all, because there isn't anything that I know about that actually comes from hospitals. It's just stuck in that one. Money for instance has six different sprigs and hospitals has only got two.'

She is also aware of the positive potential of computers, particularly through the easy access they provide: 'I think easy access is offering us good things like freedom and speed and communication with people and I think we need to build up on that in today's society.' Reflecting on one train of thought while producing the map she said: 'The computer is my main branch and then I moved on to entertainment because that's what I use computers mostly for, and moved on to home and games.'

In summary, this 15-year-old girl's focal awareness is on the social impact of computers in her world, particularly in relation to growing commercialism as a negative, and increased access and communication as positives. The implication is that people need to make important choices. The field awarenesses revealed in the interview are of computer use for entertainment in the home.

Implications

The ImpaCT2 concept mapping data strongly suggest that there is a mismatch between conventional national tests (which focus on pre-specified knowledge and concepts) and the wider range of knowledge which students are acquiring by carrying out new kinds of activities with ICT in the home. The concept maps give strong indications of children's rich conceptualisation of technology and its role in their world. Many are using the Internet at home for communications (email and chat), for entertainment (playing games and downloading music and images), and to access information; others who do not yet have regular access to ICT may still have a well-developed conception of what it offers drawn from cultural knowledge through a range of media and social interactions, and the work of Wartofsky (op. cit.) and Cole (op. cit.) described above suggests that, if this is the case, they are likely to acquire practical skills quickly. This certainly means that, at all key stages, classes currently include students with a very wide range of ICT skills and competences, so that for example those in Key Stage 2 who regularly use email at home are likely to find the QCA email unit dull, because it teaches skills step-by-step rather than permitting freedom of exploration. This suggests that there is an urgent need to develop more exploratory frameworks for teaching ICT which would allow students to begin by auditing and recording their own ICT skills prior to embarking on work which matches their needs – either further skills acquisition, preferably at their own pace, or a choice of projects from a range of options which allows them to use their skills to support subject learning, for example in literacy, numeracy, history, science or mathematics.

ICT provides a range of tools which are very different from those previously available to support students' learning. We know from the work of Vygotsky and Wertsch, cited earlier, that such radical changes in tools mediate human activity and radically change working methods and outcomes. Rather than being an unrealistic fantasy, megachange in schooling is more or less inevitable as a result. As yet ICT has been used in schools almost entirely to teach ICT skills rather than to support students' learning in subjects (Somekh *et al.* 2002a, p. 16), but now that more and more schools are acquiring portable laptops with wireless connectivity, students who have the necessary skills will be able to use ICT more and more as a normal part of their work across the whole curriculum. Reduction in the cost of lightweight laptops may soon lead to all students having constant access to ICT at school and at home. Perhaps that will be the time for a 'megachange' in schooling comparable to the megachanges that have already occurred in other areas of social interaction.

Notes

Introduction

1 I would like to thank the participants in this seminar series, in particular Charles Crook, Harry Daniels, Ian Derry, Kerry Facer, Martin Hughes, Matthew Pearson, David Middleton, Mike Sharples, Ros Sutherland and Sally Tweddle, to whom I owe the inspiration for much of my subsequent research.

3 Engaging with innovation

1 I would like to thank Cathy Lewin, Diane Mavers, Peter Scrimshaw, Andrew Haldane, Charmian Levin and John Robinson for their contribution to this research.

2 GridClub can be found at www.gridclub.com. It has continued to develop as a website since completion of the evaluation in 2003. It is important to note that at the time of conducting the evaluation the Think website used by GridClub allowed children to create and store much larger amounts of material than more recent 'upgrades'.

3 'Stickies' are simulated yellow self-adhesive notelets that children can send to another user.

4 The PELRS research was carried out with my colleague, Matthew Pearson, and I would like to thank him for his substantial contribution to the ideas contained here. I would also like to thank Lesley Saunders of the General Teaching Council for England for her great encouragement and support.

5 I would like to thank teachers and students who were partners in the research at the four PELRS case study schools: Sandilands Junior School, Seymour Road Primary School, Medlock Valley High School, all in Manchester, and Westhoughton High School Specialist Technology College, Bolton.

6 I would like to thank the following schools for their commitment and creativity in testing out and refining the PELRS strategies in Year 3: Broughton Junior School; Charles Kingsley's Church of England Primary School; Eckington School; Emley First School; George Spencer School and Technology College; Holme Valley Primary School; Kirby Hill Church of England Primary School; Kirkburton C of E First School; Kirmington C of E Primary School; Primrose Hill Primary School; St Bernadette's Catholic Primary School and St Nortbert's RC Primary School.

4 The human interface

1 This chapter was originally published in *Mindweave: Communicatons, Computers and Distance Education*, edited by Robin Mason and Tony Kaye, Oxford: Pergamon Press 1989.

6 New technology and learning

1 To combat 'new variant CJD' ('Mad Cow Disease') the UK government banned the sale of beef on the bone.
2 The Millennium Dome at Greenwich was intended to be a showcase for British Industry in 2000, but by 1998 its purposes and proposed contents were already the subject of major media criticism.
3 The numbers of modems that remained unused in cupboards became legendary.
4 Owen Lynch remained Chief Executive of Becta until his retirement in 2006.
5 All the quotes in this paragraph are taken from interviews with senior officials who were involved in setting up the TLTP.
6 The participating ITTEs were Chester College, Goldsmiths' College of London University, Liverpool Polytechnic, the University of Exeter and Worcester College of HE.
7 'Walled garden' was only later used to describe 'safe' access to the Internet within a limited-access site protected by security software. PALM teachers used 'the walled garden' to describe use of IT which was free within a secure curriculum framework set by the teacher.

9 Methodological issues

1 REPRESENTATION was funded by the European Union Educational Multimedia Task Force (MM1045) and co-ordinated by Kathy Kikis-Papadakis, FORTH, IACM, Greece. The partners were INRP, France; Orfeus, Denmark; MAC, Ireland; University of Crete, University of Amsterdam, University Open of Catalunya and University of Huddersfield, UK. Associate partners were IUFM de Creteil, France; and the University of Mons-Hainaut, Belgium.

10 Mapping learning potential

1 A shortened version of this paper, with some additional material by Diane Mavers, was published in *Assessment in Education* 10(3): 409–20, 2003.
2 The ImpaCT2 evaluation was directed by Colin Harrison, University of Nottingham and co-directed by Bridget Somekh, Manchester Metropolitan University and Peter Scrimshaw, the Open University. Other researchers in the team were Diane Mavers (MMU), Cathy Lewin (OU), Tony Fisher (Notts), Kaye Haw (Notts) and Eric Lunzer (Notts). It was funded by the DfES and managed by BECTA (British Educational and Communications Technology Agency).
3 REPRESENTATION, 1998–2000, funded by the European Union was a collaborative project between FORTH, Institute of Applied and Computational Mathematics, Greece; INRP, France; Orfeus, Denmark; MAC, Ireland; University of Crete; University of Amsterdam; University Open of Catalunya and University of Huddersfield.
4 Both of these words were used at different points in the introductory 'script'.

References

AEA (2004) *Guiding Principles for Evaluators*. Fairhaven, MA: American Evaluation Association. Available at http://www.eval.org/Publications/GuidingPrinciples.asp (accessed 10/8/06).

Alexander, R. (2000) *Culture and Pedagogy. International Comparisons in Primary Education*. Malden, MA and Oxford: Blackwell Publishing.

Andrews, R. (2000) 'Learning, literacy and ICT: what's the connection?', *English in Education*, 34(3): 3–18.

Angus, L., Snyder, I. and Sutherland-Smith, W. (2004) 'ICT and educational (dis)advantage: families, computers and contemporary social and educational inequalities', *British Journal of Sociology of Education*, 25(1): 3–18.

Arnot, M., David, M. and Weiner, G. (eds) (1999) *Closing the Gender Gap*. Cambridge and Malden, MA: Polity Press.

Audit Commission (1990) *Rationalising Primary School Provision*. London: HMSO.

Banks, F., Leach, J. and Moon, B. (1999) 'New understandings of teachers' pedagogic knowledge', in J. Leach and B. Moon (eds) *Learners and Pedagogy*. Milton Keynes: Open University Press.

Barbier, J.-C. and Simonin, B. (1997) 'European social programmes: can evaluation of implementation increase the appropriateness of findings?', *Evaluation*, 3(4): 391–407.

Barthes, R. (1983) *Barthes: Selected Writings*. Introduced by Susan Sontag. Glasgow: Fontana Paperbacks.

BBC (1997) *A Midsummer Night's Dream*. CD-ROM. London: BBC Worldwide.

Becker, H.J. (2000) 'Findings from the Teaching, Learning and Computing Survey: is Larry Cuban right?', *Education Policy Analysis Archives*, 8(51). Electronic-only journal. Available at http://epaa.asu.edu/epaa and at www.crito.uci.edu/tlc/html/findings.html (both accessed 16/10/06).

BECTA (1998) *Connecting Schools, Networking People: ICT Planning, Purchasing and Good Practice for the National Grid for Learning*. Coventry: BECTA.

Becta (2006) *Funding ICT in Schools*. Available at http://schools.becta.org.uk/index.php?section=lp&catcode=_le_fu_02&rid=10398 (accessed 16/10/06).

BERA (British Educational Research Association) (2004) *Revised Ethical Guidelines for Educational Research*. Available at http://www.bera.ac.uk/publications/pdfs/ETHICA1.PDF (accessed 10/8/06).

Bernstein, B. (1971) 'On the classification and framing of educational knowledge', in M.F.D. Young (ed.) *Knowledge and Control*. London: Collier-Macmillan.

Beywl, W. and Potter, P. (1998) 'RENOMO: a design tool for evaluations', *Evaluation*, 4(1): 53–71.

Bhola, H.S. (2000) 'A discourse on impact evaluation', *Evaluation*, 6(2): 161–78.

Bidwell, C.E. (2001) 'Analyzing schools as organizations: long-term permanence and short-term change', *Sociology of Education*, 74 (Extra issue: Current of thought: sociology of education at the dawn of the 21st century): 100–14.

Bigum, C. (2002) 'Design sensibilities, schools and the new computing and communication technologies', in I. Snyder (ed.) *Silicon Literacies: Communication, Innovation and Education in the Electronic Age*. London and New York: Routledge: 130–40.

Boucher, A., Davis, N., Dillon, P., Hobbs, P. and Tearle, P. (1997) *IT-assisted Teaching and Learning in UK Higher Education*. London: Higher Education Funding Council for England.

Bourdieu, P. (1977) *Outline of a Theory of Practice*. Cambridge and New York: Cambridge University Press.

Brown, J.S., Collins, A. and Duguid, P. (1989) 'Situated cognition and the culture of learning', *Educational Researcher*, 32(Jan–Feb): 32–42.

Bruner, J.S. (1966) *Towards a Theory of Instruction*. Cambridge, MA and London: The Belknap Press of Harvard University Press.

Bullock, A. (1975) *A Language for Life*. Report of the Committee of Inquiry appointed by the Secretary of State for Education and Science under the Chairmanship of Sir Alan Bullock. London: HMSO, Department of Education and Science.

Burbules, N.C. and Smith, R. (2005) '"What it makes sense to say": Wittgenstein, rule-following and the nature of education', *Educational Philosophy and Theory*, 37(3): 425–30.

Bush, T. (1995) *Theories of Educational Management*, 2nd edn. London: Paul Chapman.

Chaiklin, S. and Lave, J. (1996) *Understanding Practice: Perspectives on Activity and Context*. Cambridge, New York and Melbourne: Cambridge University Press.

Christiansen, E. (1997) 'Tamed by a rose: computers as tools in human activity', in B.A. Nardi (ed.) *Context and Consciousness*. Cambridge, MA and London: MIT Press.

Claxton, G. (2002) 'Education for the learning age: a sociocultural approach to learning to learn', in G. Wells and G. Claxton (eds) *Learning for Life in the 21st Century*. Oxford and Malden, MA: Blackwell Publishing.

Coburn, C.E. (2003) 'Rethinking scale: moving beyond numbers to deep and lasting change', *Educational Researcher*, 32(6): 3–12.

Coffield, F. (1998) 'A tale of three little pigs: building the learning society with straw', *Evaluation and Research in Education*, 12(1): 44–58.

Cole, M. (1996) *Cultural Psychology: A Once and Future Discipline*. Cambridge, MA and London: The Belknap Press of Harvard University Press.

Cole, M. (1999) 'Cultural psychology: some general principles and a concrete example', in Y. Engeström, M. Reijo and R.-L. Punamäki (eds) *Perspectives on Activity Theory*. Cambridge, New York and Melbourne: Cambridge University Press.

Cole, M. and Engeström, Y. (1993) A cultural-historical approach to distributed cognition', in G. Salomon (ed.) *Distributed Cognition: Psychological and Educational Considerations*. Cambridge and New York: Cambridge University Press.

Collis, B. (1998) 'WWW-based environments for collaborative group work', *Education and Information Technologies*, 3: 231–45.

Committee of Scottish University Principals (CSUP) (1992) *Teaching and Learning in an Expanding Higher Education System*. Edinburgh: SCFC.

Coopers and Lybrand, Institute of Education, Tavistock Institute (1996) *Evaluation of the TLTP*. Bristol: HEFCE External Relations.

Cousins, J.B. and Earl, L.M. (eds) (1995) *Participatory Evaluation in Education: Studies in Evaluation Use and Organizational Learning*. London and Bristol, PA: Falmer Press.

Cox, M., Webb, M., Abbott, B., Blakely, T., Beauchamp, T. and Watson, D. (2004) *An Investigation of the Research Evidence Relating to ICT Pedagogy*. London: BECTA.

Cronbach, L.J. (1982) *Designing Evaluations of Educational and Social Programs*. San Francisco, CA: Jossey-Bass.

Csikszentmihalyi, M. (1996) *Creativity: Flow and the Psychology of Discovery and Invention*. New York: Harper Perennial.

Cuban, L. (2001) *Oversold and Underused: Computers in Classrooms*. Boston, MA: Harvard University Press.

Cuban, L., Kirkpatrick, H. and Peck, C. (2001) 'High access and low use of technologies in high school classrooms: explaining an apparent paradox', *American Eductional Research Journal*, 38(4): 813–34.

Cullen, J., Kelleher, J. and Stern, E. (1993) 'Evaluation in DELTA', *Journal of Computer Assisted Learning*, 9: 115–26.

Cunningham, M., Kerr, K., McEune, R., Smith, P. and Harris, S. (2003) *Laptops for Teachers: An Evaluation of the First Year of the Initiative*. London: DfES.

Datta, L.-E. (2000) 'Seriously seeking fairness: strategies for crafting non-partisan evaluations in a partisan world', *American Journal of Evaluation*, 21(1): 1–14.

David, J.L. (1996) 'Developing and spreading accomplished teaching: policy lessons from a unique partnership', in C. Fisher, D.C. Dwyer and K. Yocam (eds) *Education and Technology: Reflections on Computing in Classrooms*. San Francisco, CA. Jossey-Bass and Apple Press: 237–50.

Davis, B. and Sumara, D. (2005) 'Complexity science and educational action research: towards a pragmatics of transformation', *Educational Action Research*, 13(3): 453–64.

Davis, N. (1997) 'Strategies for staff and institutional development for IT in education: an integrated approach', in B. Somekh and N. Davis (eds) *Using IT Effectively in Teaching and Learning: Studies in Pre-service and In-service Teacher Education*. London and New York: Routledge.

Davis, N. and Niederhauser, D.S. (2005) 'Socio-cultural analysis of two cases of distance learning in secondary education', *Education and Information Technologies*, 10(3): 249–62.

Davis, N., Desforges, C., Jessel, J., Somekh, B., Taylor, C. and Vaughan, G. (1997) 'Can quality in learning be enhanced through the use of IT?', in B. Somekh and N. Davis (eds) *Using IT Effectively in Teaching and Learning: Studies in Pre-service and In-service Teacher Education*. London and New York: Routledge.

Davis, N., Hawkes, M., Heineke, W. and Ween, V. (2000) 'Evaluating educational technology: an invited SITE panel'. Paper presented in the panel session of this name at the SITE conference in San Diego, CA, February.

DfEE (Department for Education and Employment) (1997) *Connecting the Learning Society*. London: DfEE.

DfES (Department for Education and Skills) (2003) *Excellence and Enjoyment: A Strategy for Primary Schools*. London: DfES.

Downes, T. (1996) 'The computer as a toy and a tool in the home: implications for schools and teachers', *Education and Information Technologies*, 1(3&4): 191–201.

Downes, T. (1999) 'Playing with computing technologies in the home', *Education and Information Technologies*, 4(1): 1–15.

Downes, T. (2002) 'Blending play, practice and performance: chidren's use of the computer at home', *Journal of Educational Enquiry*, 3(2): 21–34.

Doyle, W. (1979) Classroom tasks and student abilities', in P.L. Peterson and H.J. Walberg (eds) *Research on Teaching: Concepts, Findings and Implications*. Berkeley, CA: National Society for the Study of Education, McCutchan.

Dreyfus, S.E. (1981) 'Formal models vs human situational understanding'. Unpublished manuscript, US Air Force Office for Scientific Research under contract F49620-79-0063 with the University of California, Berkeley.

Ebbutt, D. (1996) 'Universities, work-based learning and issues about knowledge', *Research in Post-Compulsory Education*, 1(3): 357–72.

Ehrmann, S.C. (1997) *Flashlight Status Report*. Available at http://technologysource.org/article/flashlight_project__tools_for_monitoring_the_progress_of_our_hopes_and_fears_about_technology_in_edu/ (accessed 16/10/06)

Eisner, E.E. (1979) *The Educational Imagination*. London: Macmillan.

Elliott, J. (1993) 'Professional education and the idea of a practical educational science', in J. Elliott (ed.) *Reconstructing Teacher Education*. London and Washington, DC: Falmer Press.

Elliott, J. (2000) 'Towards a synoptic vision of educational change in advanced industrial societies', in H. Altrichter and J. Elliott (eds) *Images of Educational Change*. Milton Keynes: Open University Press.

Elliott, J. and Ebbutt, D. (1986) *Case Studies in Teaching for Understanding*. Cambridge: Cambridge Institute of Education.

Elsom-Cook, M. (ed.) (1990) *Guided Discovery Tutoring: A Framework for ICAI Research*. London: Paul Chapman.

Engeström, Y. (1991) '*Non Scolae sed Vitae Discimus*: toward overcoming the encapsulation of school learning', *Learning and Instruction*, 1: 243–59.

Engeström, Y. (1996) 'Developmental studies of work as a testbench of activity theory: the case of primary care medical practice', in S. Chaiklin and J. Lave (eds) *Understanding Practice: Perspectives on Activity and Context*. Cambridge, New York and Melbourne: Cambridge University Press.

Engeström, Y. (1999) 'Activity theory and individual and social transformation', in Y. Engeström, M. Reijo and R.-L. Punamäki (eds) *Perspectives on Activity Theory*. Cambridge, New York and Melbourne: Cambridge University Press: 19–38.

Engeström, Y. and Escalante, V. (1997) 'Mundane tool or object of affection? The rise and fall of the postal buddy', in B.A. Nardi (ed.) *Context and Consciousness*. Cambridge, MA and London: MIT Press.

Engeström, Y. and Middleton, D. (eds) (1996) *Cognition and Communication at Work*. Cambridge, New York and Melbourne, Cambridge University Press.

Engeström, Y., Miettinen, R. and Punamäki, R.-L. (eds) (1999) *Perspectives on Activity Theory. Learning in Doing: Social, Cognitive, and Computational Perspectives*. Cambridge, New York and Melbourne: Cambridge University Press.

Erstad, O. (2005) 'Expanding possibilities: project work using ICT', *Human Technology*, 1(2): 216–45.

Facer, K., Furlong, J., Furlong, R. and Sutherland, R. (2003) *ScreenPlay: Children and Computing in the Home*. London and New York: RoutledgeFalmer.

Fisher, C., Dwyer, D.C. and Yocam, K. (1996) *Education and Technology: Reflections on Computing in Classrooms*. San Francisco, CA: Jossey-Bass and Apple Press.

Fisher, T. (2006) 'Educational transformation: is it, like "beauty", in the eye of the beholder, or will we know it when we see it?' Paper presented at the working conference on Imagining the Future for ICT and Education, Alesund, Norway, IFIP.

Fitzgibbon, C.T. (2002) *Performance Monitoring and Evidence-Based Education: Measuring Added Value and Finding Out What Works*. London: David Fulton.

Ford, P. (1996) *Managing Change in Higher Education: A Learning Environment Architecture*. Milton Keynes: Open University Press.

Fothergill, R. (1987) (unpublished) Report of the Microelectronics Education Programme (MEP), Newcastle.

Foucault, M. (1972) *Power/Knowledge: Selected Interviews and Other Writings 1972–77*. Ed. C. Gordon, Bury St Edmunds: Harvester Press.

Freedman, E.S., Patrick, H., Somekh, B., McIntyre, D. and Wikeley, F. (2000) *Quality Conditions for Quality Research: Guidance for Good Practice in the Employment of Contract Researchers in Education*. Nottingham: British Educational Research Association.

French, S., Laurillard, D. and McDonach, R. (1991) *Report on the Computers in Teaching Initiative*. Oxford: CTISS.

Freud, S. (1986) *The Essentials of Psycho-Analysis*, selected with an introduction from Anna Freud. London: Penguin Books.

Fukuyama, F. (1992) *The End of History and The Last Man*. London, New York, Victoria, Ontario, Auckland: Penguin Books.

Fullan, M.G. (1982) *The Meaning of Educational Change*. Toronto: OISE Press, The Ontario Institute for Studies in Education and New York: Teachers College Press.

Fullan, M.G. with Suzanne Stiegelbauer (1991) *The New Meaning of Educational Change*. New York: Teachers College Press and London: Cassell.

Furlong, J., Sutherland, R., Furlong, R. and Facer, K. (2000) *Screen Play: An Exploratory Study of Children's Techno-Popular Culture*. Final Report to the ESRC.

Galton, M.J., Hargreaves, L., Comber, C. and Wall, D. (1999) *Inside the Primary Classroom: 20 Years On*. London: Routledge.

Gamoran, A. (2001) 'American schooling and educational inequality: a forecast for the 21st century', *Sociology of Education*, 74 (Extra issue: Current of thought: sociology of education at the dawn of the 21st century): 135–53.

Geertz, C. (1973) *The Interpretation of Cultures*. New York: Basic Books. Reprinted 1993, London: Fontana Press.

Giddens, A. (1984) *The Constitution of Society*. Cambridge: Polity Press.

Goffman, E. (1959) *The Presentation of Self in Everyday Life*. London: Penguin.

Graves, D.H. (1983) *Writing: Teachers and Children at Work*. London: Heinemann Education.

Greene, J.C. (1999) 'The inequality of performance measurements', *Evaluation*, 5(2): 160–72.

Greene, J.C. and Caracelli, V.J. (eds) (1997) 'Advances in mixed-method evaluation: the challenges and benefits of integrating diverse paradigms', *New Directions for Program Evaluation*, 74, San Francisco, CA: Jossey-Bass.

GTC (2006) PELRS Summary of Research Findings. The Pedagogies with E-Learning Resources Project. London: General Teaching Council for England.

Hall, G.E., Loucks, S.F., Rutherford, W.L. and Newlove, B.W. (1975) 'Levels of use of the innovation: a framework for analyzing innovation adoption', *Journal of Teacher Education*, 26: 52–6.

Hall, I. and Higgins, S. (2005) 'Primary school students' perceptions of interactive whiteboards', *Journal of Computer Assisted Learning*, 21: 102–17.

Hall, J., McPake, J. and Somekh, B. (1997) *Scottish Superhighways Evaluation*. Final Report. Edinburgh: Scottish Council for Research in Education.

Hall, R.H. (1996) *Organizations: Structures, Processes and Outcomes*, 6th edn. Englewood Cliffs, NJ: Prentice Hall.

Hall, R.H. and Harding, D. (2000) 'Driving departmental change through evaluation: some outcomes and problems', *Association for Learning Technology Journal*, 8(1): 19–29.

Hargreaves, D. (1996) 'Teaching as a research-based profession: possibilities and prospects', Teacher Training Agency Annual Lecture, London: Teacher Training Agency.

Harris, S. (2002) 'Innovative pedagogical practices using ICT in schools in England', *Journal of Computer Assisted Learning*, 18: 449–58.

Harrison, C., Youngman, M., Bailey, M., Fisher, T., Phillips, R. and Restorick, J. (1997) *Multimedia Portables for Teachers Pilot: Evaluation Report*. Nottingham: University of Nottingham.

Harrison, C., Fisher, T., Haw, K., Lewin, C., Lunzer, E., Mavers, D., Scrimshaw, P. and Somekh, B. (2002) *ImpaCT2: The Impact of Information and Communication Technologies on Pupils' Learning and Attainment*. Coventry: DfES. Available on www.becta.org.uk/research/reports/ImpaCT2.

Hennessy, S., Deaney, R. and Ruthven, K. (2005) 'Emerging teacher strategies for mediating "Technology-integrated instructional conversations": a socio-cultural perspective', *The Curriculum Journal*, 16(3): 265–92.

Heppell, S. (1993) 'Teacher education, learning and the information generation: the progression and evolution of educational computing against a background of change', *Journal of Information Technology for Teacher Education*, 2(2): 229–38.

Higgins, S. (2001) 'ICT and teaching for understanding', *Evaluation and Research in Education*, 15(3): 164–71.

Higgins, S., Falzon, C., Hall, I., Moseley, D., Smith, F., Smith, H. and Wall, K. (2005) *Embedding ICT in the Literacy and Numeracy Strategies: Final Report*. Newcastle: University of Newcastle School of Education, Centre for Learning and Teaching.

Hillage, J., Pearson, B., Anderson, A. and Tamkin, P. (1998) *Excellence in Research on Schools*. London: Department for Education and Employment.

Hinostroza, J.E., Guzman, A. and Isaacs, S. (2002) 'Innovative uses of ICT in Chilean schools', *Journal of Computer Assisted Learning*, 18: 459–69.

Hirst, P.H. (1974) *Knowledge and the Curriculum*. London: Routledge and Kegan Paul.

Hope, A. (2005) 'Panopticism, play and the resistance of surveillance: case studies of the observation of student Internet use in UK schools', *British Journal of Sociology of Education*, 26(3): 359–73.

House, E.R. (1974) *The Politics of Educational Innovation*. Berkeley, CA: McCutchan Publishing.

House, E.R. (1980) *Evaluating with Validity*. Beverly Hills, CA and London: Sage.

House, E.R. (1993) *Professional Evaluation: Social Impact and Political Consequences*. Newbury Park, CA and London: Sage.

House, E.R. (2000) 'The limits of cost–benefit evaluation', *Evaluation*, 6(1): 79–86.

House, E.R, Haug, C. and Norris, N. (1996) 'Producing evaluations in a large bureaucracy', *Evaluation*, 2(2):135–50.

Hoyle, E. (1969) 'How does the curriculum change?', *Journal of Curriculum Studies*, 1(2): 132–41; reprinted in T. Hooper (ed.) *The Curriculum: Context, Design and Development*, Edinburgh: Oliver and Boyd.

Hoyle, E. (1989) 'Organizations as social inventions: rethinking assumptions about change', in T. Bush (ed.) *Managing Education: Theory and Practice*. Milton Keynes and Philadelphia, PA: Open University Press: 66–80.

Hutchins, E. and Klausen, T. (1996) 'Distributed cognition in an airline cockpit', in Y. Engeström and D. Middleton (eds) *Cognition and Communication at Work*. Cambridge, New York and Melbourne: Cambridge University Press.

IES (2002) *Computers for Teachers. An Evaluation of Phase 2: Survey of Recipients*. London: Institute for Employment Studies for the Department for Education and Skills.

Illich, I.D. (1971) *Deschooling Society*. London: Pelican.

Ilomaki, L., Lakkala, M. and Legtinen, E. (2004) 'A case study of ICT adoption within a teacher community at a Finnish lower secondary school', *Education, Communication and Information*, 4(1): 53–69.

Jackson, P.W. (1968) *Life in Classrooms*. New York: Holt, Rinehart and Winston.

James, A. and Prout, A. (eds) (1997) *Constructing and Reconstructing Childhood*. London: Falmer Press.

John, P. and Sutherland, R. (2005) 'Affordance, opportunity and the pedagogical implications of ICT', *Education Review*, 57(4): 405–13.

Johnson, P. (2004) 'Making social science useful', *British Journal of Sociology*, 55(1): 23–30.

Kemmis, S. (1987) 'Schools, computing and educational reform', in C. Bigum, S. Bonser, P. Evans, S. Groundwater-Smith and S. Kemmis (eds) *Coming to Terms with Computers in Schools*, Report to the Commonwealth Schools Commission. Geelong, VIC: Deakin Institute for Studies in Education: 289–306.

Kennewell, S. and Morgan, A. (2003) 'Student teachers' experience and attitudes towards using interactive whiteboards in the teaching and learning of young children', in J. Wright, A. McDougall, J. Murnane and J. Lowe (eds) *Young Children and Learning Technologies*. Sydney: Australian Computer Society: 71–76.

Kerawalla, L. and Crook, C. (2002) 'Children's computer use at home and at school: context and continuity', *British Educational Research Journal*, 28(6): 751–71.

Kimbell, R. (2000) 'Creativity in crisis', *Journal of Design and Technology Education*, 5(3): 206–11.

Klemp, G.O. (1977) *Three Factors of Success in the World of Work: Implications for Curriculum in Higher Education*. Boston, MA: McBer and Co.

Kompf, M. (2005) 'Information and communications technology (ICT) and the seduction of knowledge, teaching, and learning: what lies ahead for education', *Curriculum Inquiry*, 35(2): 213–33.

Koppi, A.J., Lublin, J.R. and Chaloupka, M.J. (1998) 'Effective teaching and learning in a high-tech environment', *Innovation in Education and Training International*, 34(4): 245–51.

Kozma, R.B. (1991) 'Learning with media', *Review of Educational Research*, 61(2): 179–211.

Kress, G. (1985) *Linguistic Processes in Sociocultural Practice*. Geelong, VIC: Deakin University Press and (1989) Milton Keynes: Open University Press.

Kress, G. and Mavers, D. (2005) 'Social semiotics and multimodal texts', in B. Somekh and C. Lewin (eds) *Research Methods in the Social Sciences*. Thousand Oaks, CA and London: Sage: 172–9.

Kress, G. and van Leeuwen, T. (1996) *Reading Images: The Grammar of Visual Design*. London: Routledge.

Kress, G., Jewitt, C., Ogborn, J. and Tsatsarelis, C. (2001) *Multimodal Teaching and Learning: The Rhetorics of the Science Classroom*. London: Continuum.

Krumsvik, R.J. (2006) *ICT in the School: ICT-initiated School Development in a Lower Secondary School*, Bergen: University of Bergen, Department of Education and Health, Faculty of Psychology.

Langemeyer, I. and Nissen, M. (2005) 'Activity theory', in B. Somekh and C. Lewin (eds) *Research Methods in the Social Sciences*. London and Thousand Oaks, CA, Sage: 188–96.

Lankshear, C. (2003) 'The challenge of digital epistemologies', *Education, Communication and Information*, 3(2): 167–86.

Lankshear, C. and Bigum, C. (1999) 'Literacies and new technologies in school settings', *Curriculum Studies*, 7(3): 445–65.

Lankshear, C., Peters, M. and Knobel, M. (2000) 'Information, knowledge and learning: some issues facing epistemology and education in a digital age', *Journal of Philosophy of Education*, 34(1): 17–39 and 203–8.

Lauder, H., Brown, P. and Halsey, A.H. (2004) 'Sociology and political arithmetic: some principles of a new policy science', *British Journal of Sociology*, 55(1): 3–22.

Laurillard, D. (1993) *Rethinking University Teaching*. London and New York: Routledge.

Lave, J. (1996) 'The practice of learning', in S. Chaiklin and J. Lave (eds) *Understanding Practice: Perspectives on Activity and Context*. Cambridge, New York and Melbourne: Cambridge University Press.

Lave, J. and Wenger, E. (1991) *Situated Learning: Legitimate Peripheral Participation*. Cambridge, New York and Melbourne: Cambridge University Press.

Law, N., Kankaanranta, M. and Chow, A. (2005) 'Technology-supported educational innovations in Finland and Hong Kong: a tale of two systems', *Human Technology*, 1(2): 176–201.

Lewin, C. (2004) 'Access and use of technologies in the home in the UK: implications for the curriculum', *The Curriculum Journal*, 15(2): 139–54.

Lewin, C., Mavers, D. and Somekh, B. (2003) 'Broadening access to the curriculum through using technology to link home and school: a critical analysis of reforms intended to improve students' educational attainment', *The Curriculum Journal*, 14(1): 23–53.

Lewin, K. (1951) *Field Theory in Social Science: Selected Theoretical Papers*. New York: Harper Row.

Lings, P. and Desforges, C. (1999) 'On subject differences in applying knowledge to learn', *Research Papers in Education*, 14(2): 199–221.

Living Books (1994) *Tortoise and the Hare*. CD-ROM. Hartlepool, Cleveland, UK.

Livingston, K. and Condie, R. (2004) *Final Report of the Evaluation of Phase Two of the SCHOLAR Programme*. Glasgow: The University of Strathclyde, Quality in Education Centre.

Livingstone, S. and Bovill, M. (1999) *Young People, New Media: Summary*. London: London School of Economics and Political Science.

Loveless, A. (2003) 'Creating spaces in the primary curriculum: ICT in creative subjects', *The Curriculum Journal*, 14(1): 5–21.

Lyotard, J.-F. (1979) *The Postmodern Condition: A Report on Knowledge*. Minneapolis, MN: Minnesota University Press and Manchester: Manchester University Press.

MacDonald, B. (1974) 'Evaluation and control of education', in Ford SAFARI Project, *Innovation, Evaluation, Research and the Problem of Control*. Norwich: CARE, University of East Anglia.

MacDonald, B. (1992) 'Microworlds and real worlds: an agenda for evaluation', Invited address at the European Conference about Information Technology in Education: a Critical Insight, Barcelona, November.

MacDonald, B. (2000) 'How education became nobody's business', in H. Altrichter and J. Elliott (eds) *Images of Educational Change*. Milton Keynes: Open University Press.

MacDonald, B. and Jenkins, D. (1979) *Understanding Computer Assisted Learning. The Final Report of the Educational Evaluation of the National Development Programme in Computer Assisted Learning*. Norwich: CARE, University of East Anglia.

MacDonald, B., Kemmis, S. and Jenkins, D. (1976) 'The educational potential of computer assisted learning: qualitative evidence about student learning'. Paper prepared by UNCAL, the independent evaluation of the National Development Programme in Computer Assisted Learning. CARE, University of East Anglia, Norwich.

MacDonald, B., Beattie, C., Schostak, J. and Somekh, B. (1988) 'Summary of findings from each of three investigations', DTI Micros in Schools Support 1981–84, an Independent Evaluation. Norwich: CARE, University of East Anglia.

Mackenzie, D. and Wajcman, J. (1985) *The Social Shaping of Technology*. Milton Keynes: Open University Press.

Marton, F., Hounsell, D. and Entwistle, N. (1997) *The Experience of Learning: Implications for Teaching and Studying in Higher Education*. Edinburgh: Scottish Academic Press.

Marton, F. (1994) 'Phenomenography', in T. Husen and T.N. Postlethwaite (eds) *The International Encyclopedia of Education*. Oxford: Pergamon, 8: 4424–9.

Marton, F. and Booth, S. (1997) *Learning and Awareness*. Mahwah, NJ: Lawrence Erlbaum Associates.

Mavers, D. (2003) 'Communicating meanings through image: composition, spatial arrangement and links in student mind maps', in G. Kress and C. Jewett (eds) *Multimodal Literacy*. New York: Peter Lang.

Mavers, D., Somekh, B. and Restorick, J. (2002) 'Interpreting the externalised images of pupils' conceptions of ICT: methods for the analysis of concept maps', *Computers and Education*, 38: 187–207.

Mavers, D., Somekh, B., Scrimshaw, P., Harrison, C., Fisher, T., Haw, K. and Lewin, C. (2000) 'Pupil attainment and the new technologies: some methodological design issues in the ImpacT2 Project'. Paper presented at the British Educational Research Association Conference, Cardiff.

McCormick, R. (2004) 'ICT and pupil assessment', *The Curriculum Journal*, 15(2): 115–37.

McCormick, R. and Scrimshaw, P. (2001) 'Information and communications technology, knowlege and pedagogy', *Education, Communication and Information*, 1(1): 37–57.

McEldowney, J. (1997) 'Policy evaluation and the concepts of deadweight and additionality', *Evaluation*, 3(2): 175–88.

McFarlane, A. (2001) 'Perspectives on the relationships between ICT and assessment', *Journal of Computer Assisted Learning*, 17: 227–34.

McLuhan, M. (1964) *Understanding Media*. London and New York: Routledge and Kegan Paul.

McNay, I. (1995) 'From the collegial academy to corporate enterprise: the changing cultures of university' in T. Schuller (ed.) *The Changing University*. Milton Keynes: Open University Press.

Mead, G.H. (1934) *The Works of George Herbert Mead, Vol. 1: Mind, Self and Society*. Chicago, IL: University of Chicago Press.

Mercer, N. (1995) *The Guided Construction of Knowledge*. Clevedon: Multilingual Matters.

Mercer, N., Phillips, T. and Somekh, B. (1991) 'Research note: spoken language and new technology', *Journal of Computer Assisted Learning*, 7(3): 195–202.

Milken Exchange for Education Technology (1998) *Technology in American Schools: Seven Dimensions for Gauging Progress: A Policy-maker's Guide*. Available at: www.milkenexchange.org.

Miller, D. (2004) 'Enhancing mathematics teaching: using interactive whiteboards with compass, ruler and protractor', *Mathematics in School*, 33(4): 13–16.

Mills, C.W. (1959) *The Sociological Imagination*. London and New York: Oxford University Press.

Moran, E. (1999) *Les sept savoir necessaires a l'education du futur*. Paris: UNESCO.

Morgan, G. (1986) *Images of Organization*. Beverly Hills, CA and London: Sage.

Mort, P.R. (1964) 'Studies in educational innovation from the Institute of Administrative Research: an overview', in M.B. Miles (ed.) *Innovation in Education*. New York: Teachers College Press.

NAACE (1999) *All Our Futures; Creativity, Culture and Education*. London: DfEE, National Advisory Committee on Creative and Cultural Education.

Nardi, B.A. (ed.) (1997) *Context and Consciousness: Activity Theory and Human–Computer Interaction*. Cambridge, MA and London: MIT Press.

National Gallery (1997) *The National Gallery. Complete Illustrated Catalogue*. CD-ROM. London: National Gallery.

Natriello, G. (2001) 'Bridging the second digital divide: what can sociologists of education contribute?' *Sociology of Education*, 74(July): 260–5.

NCET (1994a) *Integrated Learning Systems: A Report of the Pilot Evaluation of ILS in the UK*. Coventry: National Council for Educational Technology.

NCET (1994b) *IT Works*. Coventry: National Council for Educational Technology.

NCET (1996) *Integrated Learning Systems: A Report of Phase 2 of the Pilot Evaluation of ILS in the UK*. Coventry: National Council for Educational Technology.

NCIHE (National Committee of Inquiry into Higher Education) (1997) *Higher Education in the Learning Society*. Report of the Dearing Committee. London: DfEE.

NCSR (2006) *Evaluation of Curriculum Online*. Coventry, National Centre for Social Research for Becta.

Noffke, S.E. (1995) 'Action research and democratic schooling: problematics and potentials', in S.E. Noffke and R.B. Stevenson (eds) *Educational Action Research: Becoming Practically Critical*. New York: Teachers College, Columbia University.

Norris, N., Davies, R. and Beattie, C. (1990) 'Evaluating new technology: the case of the Interactive Video in Schools (IVIS) programme', *British Journal of Educational Technology*, 21(2): 84–94.

Novak, J.D. and Gowin, D.B. (1984) *Learning How to Learn*. New York: Cambridge University Press.

November, A. (2001) *Empowering Students with Technology*. Glenview, IL: Skylight Professional Development. See also www.anovember.com/alan.html (accessed 16/10/06).

Page, R.N. (1999) 'The uncertain value of school knowledge: biology at Westridge High', *Teachers College Record*, 100(3): 554–601.

PALM (1990/1) Teachers' Voices series (35 titles) PALM Project. Norwich: CARE, University of East Anglia.

Papert, S. (1980) *Mindstorms: Children, Computers, and Powerful Ideas*. London: Harvester Press.

Papert, S. (1993) *The Children's Machine: Rethinking School in the Age of the Computer*. New York and London: Harvester Wheatsheaf.

Parsons, T. (1951) *The Social System*. Glencoe, IL, The Free Press.

Patton, M.Q. (1986) *Utilization – Focused Evaluation*. Newbury Park, CA and London: Sage Publications.

Pea, R.D. (1993) 'Practices of distributed intelligence and designs for education', in G. Salomon (ed.) *Distributed Cognitions: Psychological and Educational Considerations*. Cambridge and New York: Cambridge University Press: 47–87.

Pearson, M. (2005) 'Splitting clips and telling tales: students interactions with digital video', *Education and Information Technologies*, 10(3): 189–206.

Pearson, M. and Somekh, B. (2003) 'Concept-mapping as a research tool: a study of primary children's representations of information and communication technologies (ICT)', *Education and Information Technologies*, 8(1): 5–22.

Pearson, M. and Somekh, B. (2006) 'Learning Transformation with technology: a question of socio-cultural contexts?', *Qualitative Studies in Education*, 19(4): 519–39.

Pelgrum, W.J. and Law, N. (2003) *ICT in Education Around the World: Trends, Problems and Prospects*. Paris: UNESCO.

Perkins, D.N. (1993) 'Person-plus: a distributed view of thinking and learning', in G. Salomon (ed.) *Distributed Cognitions: Psychological and Educational Considerations*. Cambridge, New York and Melbourne: Cambridge University Press.

Peters, R.S. (1966) *Ethics and Education*. London: Allen & Unwin.

Polanyi, M. (1958) *Personal Knowledge: Towards a Post-critical Philosophy*. London: Routledge and Kegan Paul.

Prawat, R.S. (1991) 'The value of ideas: the immersion approach to the development of thinking', *Educational Researcher*, 20(2): 3–10.

Punie, Y. and Cabrera, M. with Bogdanowicz, M., Zinnbauer, D. and Navajas, E. (2006) *The Future of ICT and Learning in the Knowledge Society*. Report on a Joint DG JRC-DG EAC Workshop held in Seville 20–21 October 2005, Brussels: European Commission, Directorate General, Joint Research Centre.

Quinney, D. and Harding, R. (1996) *Calculus Connections: A Multimedia Adventure*. CD-ROM. New York: John Wiley.

Raikes, N. and Harding, R. (2003) 'The horseless carriage: replacing conventional measures', *Assessment in Education*, 10(3): 267–77.

Ridgway, J. and McCusker, S. (2003) 'Using computers to assess new educational goals', *Assessment in Education*, 10(3): 309–28.

Rogers, E.M. (2003) *Diffusion of Innovations*, 5th edn. London and New York: Simon and Schuster International.

Roschelle, J., Sharples, M. and Chan, T.W. (2005) 'Introduction to the special issue on wireless and mobile technologies in education', *Journal of Computer Assisted Learning*, 29: 159–61.

Roszak, T. (1986) *The Cult of Information: The Folklore of Computers and The True Art of Thinking*. London: Paladin Grafton Books.

Ruthven, K. (2002) 'Instrumenting mathematical activity: reflections on key studies of the educational use of computer algebra systems', *International Journal of Computers for Mathematical Learning*, 7: 275–91.

Ruthven, K., Hennessy, S.K. and Deaney, R. (2005) 'Incorporating internet resources into classroom practice: pedagogical perspectives and strategies of secondary-school subject teachers', *Computers & Education*, 44(1): 1–34.

Saljo, R. (1999) 'Learning as the use of tools: a sociocultural perspective on the human–technology link', in K. Littleton and P. Light (eds) *Learning with Computers*. London: Routledge.

Salomon, G. (1992) 'Computer's first decade: Golem, Camelot, or the promised land?' Invited Address to Division C, AERA Conference, San Francisco, April.

Salomon, G. (1993a) 'No distribution without individuals' cognition: a dynamic interactional view', in G. Salomon (ed.) *Distributed Cognitions: Psychological and Educational Considerations*. Cambridge, New York and Melbourne: Cambridge University Press: 111–38.

Salomon, G. (ed.) (1993b) *Distributed Cognitions: Psychological and Educational Considerations*. Cambridge, New York and Melbourne: Cambridge University Press.

Sanders, J.R. (1994) *The Program Evaluation Standards: How to Assess Evaluations of Educational Programs*, 2nd edn. Thousand Oaks, CA, New Delhi and London: Sage Publications.

Sanger, J., Wilson, J., Davies, B. and Whitakker, R. (1997) *Young Children, Videos and Computer Games*. London and Washington, DC: Falmer Press.

Sandholtz, J. and Ringstaff, C. (1996) Teacher Change in Technology-rich Classrooms', in C. Fisher, Dwyer, D.C. and Yocam, K. (eds) *Education and Technology: Reflections on computing in classrooms*. San Francisco, Jossey-Bass and Apple Press.

Sandholtz, J., Ringstaff, C. and Dwyer, D. (1997) *Teaching with Technology*. New York: Teachers College Press.

Scardamalia, M. and Bereiter, C. (1996) 'Engaging students in a knowledge society', *Educational Leadership*, November: 6–10.

Schön, D.A. (1971) *Beyond the Stable State*. London: Penguin.

Schostak, J. (2000) 'Developing under developing circumstances: the personal and social development of students and the process of schooling', in H. Altichter and J. Elliott (eds) *Images of Educational Change*. Milton Keynes: Open University Press.

Scrimshaw, P. (1997) *Preparing for the Information Age: Synoptic Report of the Education Departments' Superhighways Initiative*. London: DfEE.

Scrimshaw, P. (1998) 'Teacher specialisation, extended professionalism and the new technologies'. Paper presented at the conference of the British Educational Research Association, Queens University, Belfast, September.

Scrimshaw, P. (2002) *The NOW Study: Technology in Education – Futures in Practice*. Brussels: European Schoolnet.

Selinger, M. (2004) 'Cultural and pedagogical implications of a global e-learning programme', *Cambridge Journal of Education*, 34(2): 223–39.

Selwyn, N. (2002) *Telling Tales on Technology: Qualitative Studies of Technology and Education*. Aldershot: Ashgate Publishing.

Sharples, M. (1998) 'Nine hours to live in Eden', *Times Higher Education Supplement*, 2 October: 16–17.

Sharples, M. (2003) 'Disruptive devices: mobile technology for conversational learning'. *International Journal of Continuing Engineering Education and Lifelong Learning*, 12(5/6): 504–20.

Shulman, L. (1987) 'Knowledge and teaching: foundations of the new reform', *Harvard Education Review*, 57: 1–22.

Smeyers, P. and Marshall, J.D. (1995) *Wittgenstein: Philosophy, Postmodernism, Pedagogy*. Westport, CT: Bergin and Garvey.

Snyder, I. (2001) '"Hybrid vigour": reconciling the verbal and the visual in electronic communication', in A. Loveless and V. Ellis (eds) *ICT, Pedagogy and the Curriculum*. London and New York: RoutledgeFalmer.

SOED (1933) *Shorter Oxford English Dictionary*, reprinted with corrections, 1972. Oxford: Oxford University Press.

Somekh, B. (1985) 'An enquiry into the use of quinkeys for word-processing in secondary English teaching', MA dissertation, University of East Anglia.

Somekh, B. (1993) *Project INTENT, 1990–92: Final Report*. Coventry: National Council for Educational Technology.

Somekh, B. (1994a) 'Reflections on first encounters with human resource managers', in *Congress Papers of World Congress 3 on Action Learning, Action Research and Process Management*. University of Bath, July: pp. 216–19.

Somekh, B. (1994b) 'Making ready for change: acquiring enabling skills', in D. Bridges (ed.) *Transferable Skills in Higher Education*. Norwich: ERTEC, University of East Anglia.

Somekh, B. (1995) 'The contribution of action research to development in social endeavours: a position paper on action research methodology', *British Educational Research Journal*, 21(3): 339–55.

Somekh, B. (1996) 'Designing software to maximise learning: what can we learn from the literature?', *Association for Learning Technology Journal*, 4(3): 4–16.

Somekh, B. (1997) 'Classroom investigations: exploring and evaluating how IT can support', in B. Somekh and N. Davis (eds) *Using IT effectively in Teaching and Learning: Studies in Pre-service and In-service Teacher Education*. London and New York: Routledge.

Somekh, B. (2001) 'The great courseware gamble: the trials and tribulations of a government-funded courseware development project', in D. Murphy, R. Walker and G. Webb (eds) *Online Learning and Teaching with Technology*. London and Sterling, VA: Kogan Page and Stylus Publishing.

Somekh, B. (2006a) 'Constructing inter-cultural knowledge and understanding through collaborative action research', *Teachers and Teaching: Theory and Practice* (Special issue: The 'Dark Side of The Moon': a critical look at teacher knowledge construction in collaborative settings) 12(1).

Somekh, B. (2006b) *Action Research: A Methodology for Change and Development*. Maidenhead and New York: Open University Press.

Somekh, B. and Davies, R. (1991) 'Towards a pedagogy for information technology', *The Curriculum Journal*, 2(2): 153–70.

Somekh, B. and Groundwater-Smith, S. (1988) 'Take a balloon and a piece of string', in D. Smith (ed.) *New Technologies and Professional Communications in Education*. London: National Council for Educational Technology: 125–45.

Somekh, B. and Saunders, L. (2007) 'Developing knowledge through intervention: meaning and definition of "quality" in research into change', *Research Papers in Education*, 2(2): 183–97.

Somekh, B. and Thaler, M. (1997) 'Contradictions of management theory, organisational cultures and the self', *Educational Action Research*, 5(1): 141–60. Reprinted in S. Hollingsworth (ed.) *An Action Research Reader*. London: Falmer Press.

Somekh, B., Hall, J. and Brown, C. (1996a) *ACOT in Scotland: A Preparatory Study for a Future Evaluation*. Final Report. Edinburgh: Scottish Council for Research in Education.

Somekh, B., Tinklin, T., Edwards, L. and Mackay, R. (1996b) *The Evaluation of the National Record of Achievement*. Edinburgh: Scottish Council for Research in Education: 26.

Somekh, B., Whitty, G. and Coveney, R. (1997) 'IT and the politics of institutional change', in B. Somekh and N. Davis (eds) *Using IT Effectively in Teaching and Learning: Studies in Pre-service and In-service Teacher Education*. London and New York: Routledge.

Somekh, B., McPake, J. and Hall, J. (1999) 'Serving multiple stakeholders: issues arising from a major national evaluation study', *Education and Information Technologies*, 4(3): 263–80.

Somekh, B., Blackmore, M., Blythe, K., Byrne Hill, G., Clemson, D., Coveney, R., Davis, N., Jessel, J., Taylor, C. and Vaughan, G. (1992) 'A research approach to I.T. development in initial teacher education', *Journal of Information Technology in Teacher Education*, 1(1): 83–100.

Somekh, B., Lewin, C., Mavers, D., Fisher, T., Harrison, C., Haw, K., Lunzer, E., McFarlane, A. and Scrimshaw. P. (2002a) *ImpaCT2 Final Report Part 3: Learning with ICT: Pupils' and Teachers' Perspectives*. London: DfES. Available at http://partners.becta.org.uk/index. php?section=rh&rid=11217 (accessed 17/10/06).

Somekh, B., Woodrow, D., Barnes, S., Triggs, P., Sutherland, R., Passey, D., Holt, H., Harrison, C., Fisher, T., Flett, A. and Joyes, G. (2002b) *NGfL Pathfinders: Final Report on the Roll-Out of the NGfL Programme in Ten Pathfinder LEAs*. London: DfES.

Somekh, B., Mavers, D. and Lewin, C. (2002c) *Using ICT to Enhance Home–School Links: An Evaluation of Current Practice in England*. London: DfES.

Somekh, B., Underwood, J., Convery, A., Dillon, G., Lewin, C., Mavers, D., Saxon, D., Sing, S., Twining, P. and Woodrow, D. (2006) *Final Report of the ICT Test Bed Project*. British Educational Communications and Technology Agency. Available at http://www.evaluation.icttestbed.org.uk/

Somekh, B., Haldane, M., Jones, K., Lewin, C., Steadman, S., Scrimshaw, P., Bird, K., Cummings, J., Downing, B., Harber-Stuart, T., Jarvis, J., Mavers, D. and Woodrow, D. (2007) *Evaluation of the Primary Schools Whiteboard Expansion Project*. London: Report to the Department for Education and Skills.

Somekh, B., Haldane, M., Jones, K., Lewin, C., Steadman, S., Scrimshaw, P., Bird, K., Cummings, J., Downing, B., Harber-Stuart, T., Jarvis, J., Mavers, D. and Woodrow, D. (in preparation) *Evaluation of the Primary Schools Whiteboard Expansion Project*. Report to the Department for Education and Skills. Manchester: Manchester Metropolitan University.

Stake, R. (1998) 'When policy is merely promotion, by what ethics lives an evaluator?', *Studies in Educational Evaluation*, 24(2): 203–12.

Stenhouse, L. (1975) *An Introduction to Curriculum Research and Development*. London: Heinemann Educational.

Stevenson, D. (1997) 'Information and communications technology in UK schools: an independent inquiry'. London: Independent Inquiry set up by Tony Blair to report to the Labour Party.

Strauss, A. and Corbin, J. (1990) *Basics of Qualitative Research: Grounded Theory Procedures and Techniques*. Newbury Park, CA and London: Sage.

Sumara, D.J. and Davis, B. (1997) 'Enactivist theory and community learning: toward a complexified understanding of action research', *Educational Action Research*, 5(3): 403–22.

Sutherland, R. (2004) 'Designs for learning: ICT and knowledge in the classroom', *Computers & Education*, 43(1): 5–16.

Sutherland, R., Facer, K., Furlong, R. and Furlong, J. (2001) 'A new environment for education? The computer in the home', *Computers and Education*, 38 (Special issue containing papers from the CAL2001 conference).

Turkle, S. (1984) *The Second Self: Computers and the Human Spirit*. London, Toronto and New York: Granada.

Turkle, S. (1995) *Life on the Screen: Identity in the Age of the Internet*. London and New York: Phoenix.

Underwood, J. and Underwood, G. (1990) *Computers and Learning: Helping Children Acquire Thinking Skills*. Oxford: Basil Blackwell.

Underwood, J., Cavendish, S., Dowling, S., Fogelman, K. and Lawson, T. (1994) *Integrated Learning Systems in UK Schools*. Coventry: NCET.

Underwood, J., Ault, A., Banyard, P., Bird, K., Dillon, G., Hayes, M., Selwood, I., Somekh, B. and Twining, P. (2005) *The Impact of Broadband in Schools*. Nottingham: Nottingham Trent University, Becta.

Venezky, R.L. (2004) 'Technology in the classroom: steps toward a new vision', *Education, Communication and Information*, 4(1): 3–21.

Voogt, J. and Pelgrum, W.J. (2005) 'ICT and curriculum change', *Human Technology*, 1(2): 157–75.

Vygotsky, L. (1978) *Mind in Society: The Development of Higher Psychological Processes*. Cambridge, MA: Harvard University Press.

Vygotsky, L. (1986) *Thought and Language* (original Russian edition 1934). Cambridge, MA and London: MIT Press.

Waller, W. (1932) *The Sociology of Teaching*. New York: John Wiley.

Wartofsky, M. (1979) *Models: Representation and Scientific Understanding*. Dordrecht: Reidel.

Watson, D. (2001) 'Pedagogy before technology: re-thinking the relationship between ICT and teaching', *Education and Information Technologies*, 6(4): 251–66.

Watson, D., Cox, M.J. and Johnson, D.C. (1993) *Impact: The Report of an Evaluation of the Impact of Information Technology on Children's Achievements in Primary and Secondary Schools*. London: King's College.

Webb, M. and Cox, M. (2004) 'A review of pedagogy related to information and communications technology', *Technology, Pedagogy and Education*, 13(3): 235–86.

Wegerif, R. and Dawes, L. (2004) *Thinking and Learning with ICT: Raising Achievement in Primary Classrooms*. London and New York: RoutledgeFalmer.

Wenger, E. (1998) *Communities of Practice: Learning, Meaning and Identity*. Cambridge, New York and Melbourne: Cambridge University Press.

Wertsch, J.V. (1998) *Mind as Action*. New York and Oxford: Oxford University Press.

Whyte, W.F. (1991) *Participatory Action Research*. Newbury Park, CA and London: Sage.

Wildavsky, A. (1993) *Speaking Truth to Power: The Art and Craft of Policy Analysis*. New Brunswick and London: Transaction Publishers.

Wood, D. (1998) *The UK ILS Evaluations: Final Report*. Coventry: British Educational Communications and Technology Agency.

Wood, D. (2002) *The Think Report: Technology in Education – Futures for Policy*. Nottingham (djw@psychology.nottingham.ac.uk), European Schoolnet.

Wood, D. (2003) *Think Again: Hindsight, Insight and Foresight on ICT in Schools*, Brussels: European Schools Network (EUN), Brussels.

Worthen, B.R. and Schmitz, C.C. (1997) 'Conceptual challenges confronting cluster evaluation', *Evaluation*, 3(3): 300–19.

Young, M.F.D. (1998) *The Curriculum of the Future: From the 'New Sociology of Education' to a Critical Theory of Learning*. London and Philadelphia, PA: Falmer Press.

Index

eBooks

eBooks – at www.eBookstore.tandf.co.uk

A library at your fingertips!

eBooks are electronic versions of printed books. You can store them on your PC/laptop or browse them online.

They have advantages for anyone needing rapid access to a wide variety of published, copyright information.

eBooks can help your research by enabling you to bookmark chapters, annotate text and use instant searches to find specific words or phrases. Several eBook files would fit on even a small laptop or PDA.

NEW: Save money by eSubscribing: cheap, online access to any eBook for as long as you need it.

Annual subscription packages

We now offer special low-cost bulk subscriptions to packages of eBooks in certain subject areas. These are available to libraries or to individuals.

For more information please contact webmaster.ebooks@tandf.co.uk

We're continually developing the eBook concept, so keep up to date by visiting the website.

www.eBookstore.tandf.co.uk